THIS
BUSINESS
OF LIVING

THIS BUSINESS OF LIVING

DIARIES
1935-1950

CESARE PAVESE

WITH A NEW INTRODUCTION BY JOHN TAYLOR

TRANSACTION PUBLISHERS
NEW BRUNSWICK (U.S.A.) AND LONDON (U.K.)

New material this edition copyright © 2009 by Transaction Publishers, New Brunswick, New Jersey. Originally published in 1961 by Peter Owen Ltd., London.

This book is printed on acid-free paper that meets the American National Standard for Permanence of Paper for Printed Library Materials.

Library of Congress Catalog Number: 2009002450
ISBN: 978-1-4128-1019-7
Printed in the United States of America

Library of Congress Cataloging-in-Publication Data

Pavese, Cesare.
    [Mestiere di vivere. English]
    This business of living : diaries, 1935-1950 / Cesare Pavese.
        p. cm.
    ISBN 978-1-4128-1019-7 (acid-free paper)
        1. Pavese, Cesare–Diaries. 2. Authors, Italian–20th century–Diaries.
I. Title.

PQ4835.A846Z46 2009
858'.91209–dc22
    [B]
                                                                2009002450

Come d' un stizzo verde, che arso sia
   dall' un de' capi, che dall' altro geme
   e cigola per vento che va via:

sì della scheggia rotta usciva insieme
   parole e sangue ...

As a green brand that burns at one end
   and at the other oozes sap and hisses
   with the wind escaping:

so from that broken splint, words and
   blood came forth together ...

—Dante, *Inferno*, XIII, 40-44

Contents

Introduction to the Transaction Edition   ix

This Business of Living   7

INTRODUCTION TO THE TRANSACTION EDITION

"Non scriverò piú." With these solemn words, which mean "I won't write anymore," the Italian novelist, short story writer and poet Cesare Pavese (1908-1950) concluded his diary, and killed himself nine days later by taking an overdose of sleeping pills in a Turin hotel room. Not long beforehand, he had published his novel *The Moon and the Bonfires* (1950), won one of the highest Italian literary distinctions (the Strega Prize for Fiction), but he had also faced the end of his relationship with the American actress, Constance Dowling.

Of what is a writer's suicide emblematic? Of writing's inability to save a life? Ardent lovers of literature may even find it hard to believe that a talent like Pavese's could not somehow have kept on producing, plunging anew into the toils of composition as a way of resolving perfunctorily (or at least of putting off) the comparatively minor problems of unrequited love and daily living. But of course I am waxing ironic. It is arresting and, I daresay, grimly informative that Pavese's extraordinarily lucid and pessimistic diary is entitled *Il mestiere di vivere* (1952), a book translated twice into English respectively as *The Burning Brand* and *This Business of Living*, and all too significantly emphasizing the "métier" or "trade" of living—as in, say, "Mastering the Trade of Living." Both versions have long been out of print, and this is why this revival of *This Business of Living* is so welcome.

Discovered among the writer's papers after his death, *Il mestiere di vivere* is one of the most intellectually fascinating and excruciatingly honest writer's diaries in modern European literature. It offers penetrating insights, not only into Pavese's personality, but also into his high craft and literary acumen. Pages bristle with his sharp critical thinking about his own poetry and fiction, about the books that he was reading or translating, or about literature in general. But the poet and writer set even more ambitious goals for this diary, and wondered to what extent it, too, was a literary work comparable to his poetry:

> The interest of this journal would be the unforeseen profusion of ideas, the periods of inspiration that, of themselves, automatically, indicate the main trends of your inner life. From time to time you try to understand what you are thinking, and only as an afterthought do you go on to link your present ideas with those of days gone by. The originality of these pages is that you leave the construction to work itself out, and set your own spirit in front of you, objectively. There is something metaphysical in your confidence that this psychological sequence of your thoughts will shape itself into a well-constructed work. (22 February 1940)

If Pavese failed at the trade of living, he successfully—to mimic his own penchant for implacable ironies—analyzed the failure in *This Business of Living*, which he began keeping in 1935 and maintained frequently thereafter, with many entries recorded for every year until 18 August 1950. This is why the challenge put forward by the title must be kept in mind when reading his creative work, and notably his gripping, life-filled short stories, as well as four of the important novels—*The Beach* (1942), *The House on the Hill* (1949), *Among Women Only* (1949), *The Devil in the Hills* (1949)—that were brought together a few years ago, by New York Review Books, as *The Selected Works of Cesare Pavese*, in a translation by R. W. Flint. As the diary amply reveals, few authors have worked so long with such a heightened awareness of the perilous gap between living and writing—and this tension can be felt in the fiction. Few writers have so bravely stood astride the chasm, as it were, observing how it widens inexorably, ever awaiting—while continuing to write—the fated moment when they must fall.

Yet if Pavese's fiction is personal in this essential sense, its deep-running autobiographical orientation is not immediately visible on the surface. Whereas his lifelong struggle with the prospect of self-afflicted death is exhibited straightforwardly in his diary, it is transposed imaginatively in haunting stories like "Wedding Trip" or "Suicides" (to mention just those two), or in a novel like *Among Women Only*. As early as 10 April 1936, he noted in *This*

Business of Living: "I know that I am forever condemned to think of suicide when faced with no matter what difficulty or grief.... My basic principle is suicide, never committed, never to be committed, but the thought of it caresses my sensibility." Fourteen days later, he was musing on whether "an optimistic suicide will come back to the world again." On 23 March 1938, he declared that "no one ever lacks a good reason for suicide," adding that "you will never have the courage to kill yourself." (For the preceding quotation, the Italian original is, interestingly, in the plural form.) Such avowals and self-tauntings are countless. The unity of his oeuvre is thus that of a coin: two sides superficially different in the images that they put forward to the world, yet intimately connected, even perhaps ultimately identical.

From the onset of his diary writing, Pavese alludes to the troubled relationship between living and writing by means of a subtitle, *Secretum professionale*, which covers four months during the first two years (1935-1936) that he records. Evoked as well in stories like "Land of Exile" and "Gaol Birds," this same period was marked by his arrest and ten-month imprisonment in Brancaleone (Calabri) because of his editorials in the anti-fascist magazine *La Cultura*. But surely the subtitle also recalls Petrarch's highly self-conscious *Secretum* (composed in Latin around 1347), an imaginary confessional dialogue with his intellectual mentor, Saint Augustine. Their dialogue revolves around Petrarch's poetic, spiritual, and amatory qualms.

While analyzing in his diary (on 1 January 1940) what he calls "stylized situations" (one of several critical concepts that he forged), Pavese actually criticizes Petrarch for "confusing life and art"; he sides with Dante, Stendhal, and Baudelaire because they departed from real life by constructing self-contained "mental situations" governed by internal laws. This distinction being made (and whatever surprise one feels upon finding Stendhal thus cited), Pavese's own conflict between life and art remains arduous to grasp in all its complexity. He himself admitted as much; his first diary entry in fact focuses on this question. His experiences quite evidently fuel his fiction, yet he aims, stylistically, to transform them—and in no simplistic manner. (It was Stendhal, after all, who proposed that a novel, as it was borne down a road, held up a mirror to reality.)

To return to this parallel with Petrarch, a pre-eminent European autobiographer, it is furthermore hard not to notice that, like the author of the *Canzoniere* and *Secretum*, Pavese is a perpetual doubter who constantly delves—in both his diary and fiction—into Christian questions like guilt, charity, selflessness, and necessary solitude; and secondly, that he likewise aspires to the most sensual aspects of love all the while developing an authorial vision whereby literature is the medium *par excellence* through which life is approached or, alternately, kept at bay. Paradoxically, for sensibilities such as Pavese's (or Petrarch's), only writing can near one to life, or to the beloved other. The life one is living daily actually remains—in one's conscience, in one's consciousness—at a strange, and estranging, remove. This fundamental existential aloneness and the inner life that results from it are analyzed time and again by Pavese in his diary. To cite a telling maxim: "What matters to an artist is not experience, but inward experience." (17 September 1938). Hence, once again, the intimate relationship between the diary and the creative oeuvre.

Although Petrarch's ornate rhetoric in his Italian love poetry (his Latin prose is something else again) could not be more distant from Pavese's deceptively realist prose, the two writers equally idealize yet at the same time harshly scrutinize women. Bordering on misogyny (as he himself admitted in his diary), Pavese fatally linked love to morbidity. His grim final poetry collection, found on his desk after he had committed suicide, is significantly entitled *Verrà la morte e avrà i tuoi occhi* (1951), literally "Death will Come and [She will] Have Your Eyes. "Death," a feminine noun in Italian, is here associated with Dowling, who had recently left him. The poems are composed in short lines and there is little emphasis on storytelling. In one tale collected in A. E. Murch's *Cesare Pavese: Stories* (The Ecco Press), the first-person narrator envisions self-destructive desires as occurring one step earlier. He coolly concedes that every time he is in love he thinks of killing himself. It seems that Pavese was driven by a perpetually adolescent romanticism with respect to women, as well as, in contrast, by an amorous philosophy so inflexibly pessimistic that any enduring partnership was excluded in advance. This theme, too, is amply present in the diary. On 18 November 1945, for instance: "I am your lover, and therefore your enemy." And the theme of "adolescence," in all its aspects, is another frequent concern of the diarist, even and especially on 16 August 1950: "Why die? I have never been so much alive as now, never so young." (Pavese's term for "young" here is, once again, "adolescente.")

Interestingly, scenes in Pavese's novels more often than not involve, not a single man and a single woman interacting, but rather a group of characters. Prolonged conversations between these characters build up tension and authenticity; the author's written words, which presumably record once-spoken words, are ontologically closer to what actually happened (i.e., was uttered) than are descriptions. As they bring to the fore the difficulties of lasting friendship, the forces of sexual attraction, the impasses of love, many fictional passages are conspicuously theatrical in narrative structure. Plots shift decisively during parties, dances, or outings. A prime example is the *ménage à trois* artfully studied in *The Beach*, a novel otherwise portraying a small crowd of friends who have gathered at the same summer resort. Not surprisingly, the dichotomy of the individual and the group runs through the diary as well, such as in this stunning remark of 5 June 1940, at the beginning of the Second World War: "The reality of war suggests this simple thought: it is not sad to die when so many of your friends are dying. War gives one a sense of being one of a group. Welcome! Come on in!"

It should already be obvious that the social dimension of Pavese's novel-writing deftly masks a much more somber awareness of an individual's abject aloneness. A clue to this subtle double-layering can once again be found in his diary, when Pavese advises caustically, on 9 February 1938, that any person convinced of a human being's utter solitude should "lose himself in innumerable social entanglements, for they have little attraction for him." He also contended, on 31 December 1937, that writers "spoke" their characters; that it was essentially the same thing if a novelist employed one character or several. "My lot is to hug shadows," he confessed in a letter dated 6 July 1950, referring not only to Dowling but also—I would posit—to his habit of sectioning himself off into characters. As lively and full-rounded as these characters seem to us, they were hopelessly phantom-like for Pavese.

Though resembling early-twentieth-century American realism in certain ways, Pavese's stories and novels are thus more deeply structured around a series of fascinating oppositions. He once noted that he lived "amid contradictions," which he began to list as "voluptuous-tragic, craven-heroic, sensual-idealistic..." (3 January 1938). In his fiction, such antinomies add fathomless ambiguity to relatively simple plot lines; they also enable him to experiment with himself, even in novels ostensibly offering social panoramas. He imaginatively crossed distances that he could not cross in real life. He even uses a woman first-person narrator in *Among Women Only*, an engrossing novel exploring solitude and the quest for affection even as it satirizes the affluent milieus of postwar Turin, Pavese's hometown.

Some stories similarly test hypotheses about how he might have behaved in this or that amorous situation. In one of his most absorbing tales, "The Family," the fictional Corradino runs into an old girlfriend at a dance, starts going out with her again, only to learn that he is the likely father of her illegitimate son—not coincidentally named "Dino" and aged six-and-a-half. Having himself suffered from the early deaths of his father (when he was six) and mother (when he was twenty-two), Pavese seems to toy here with what founding a family—even under such circumstances—might be like. In *Among Women Only*, Momina, Morelli, and the narrator Clelia likewise debate the advantages of "accepting life" and "having children." Pavese's characters and alter egos often assay the potential happiness of lifestyles that he never possessed.

In "The Family," moreover, Corradino longs "for something...to change his life without robbing him of...his old habits." He would like "to become a different man without being conscious of it." These secret aspirations for change—effortless changes, immobile escapes—intensify Pavese's stories because the changes never come about. On the surface, his tales thereby recount "long illusions," as he himself puts it in *The House on the Hill*, a novel set during the final stages of the Second World War and charting the attempts of a Turin teacher, linked to the Italian underground movement, to hide out in the surrounding hills, the very territory of his lost childhood. During his seclusion, his recollected boyhood tellingly becomes his surrogate "companion, colleague, son." Yet beneath his acts lurks the bleak truth that no recovery of the past is possible, that no evolution in a human heart can take place. Pavese's diary (which, incidentally, comments very little on the Second World War) discloses how relentlessly such dire axioms ate away at him. In European literature, Marcel Proust is by no means the only writer to probe the existential and philosophical consequences of the urge or necessity to remember.

Expectedly, Pavese elucidated, both for himself and more generally as a critic, the "static essentials" of a novel, as they are incarnated in a hero who remains the same from the beginning to the end. In "Evocation," an oddly rambling prose text departing from the classical short-story form that Pavese normally practiced, the narrator accordingly despairs because "nothing happens." Sitting in an empty corner of a tavern, he tries to "fill the silence with the sound of a distant tram." Eventually a stranger sits down nearby, rests his elbow on the table and his jaw on his fist. The narrator becomes fascinated with the man's knuckles—just one of countless instances, throughout Pavese's oeuvre, where a minuscule detail is magnified obsessively, radiantly. In his poems, similarly, a nameless woman's "husky voice" recurrently crystallizes longing and resentment. Scholars have since determined that this lady with the "voce rauca" was the fiancée who broke off with Pavese shortly before his return from prison. Whatever the autobiographical inspiration underlying them, such details are "caressed," as Vladimir Nabokov counseled his disciples, and for reasons that transcend mere craftsmanship.

Of course, Pavese surely learned much from the inherent empiricism of English-language writing—a salient quality of our literature, yet one which also harbors potential philosophical limitations. As an Americanist (who wrote a thesis on Walt Whitman), he had already translated Sinclair Lewis's *Our Mr. Wrenn*, Herman Melville's *Moby Dick*, Sherwood Anderson's *Dark Laughter*, John Dos Passos's *42nd Parallel*, as well as James Joyce's *Portrait of the Artist as a Young Man*, by the time his first poetry collection, *Lavorare stanca* (*Hard Labor* or *Work's Tiring*), devoted to village life and to his exile from it, was published in 1936. By 1943, when the second, revised and much expanded, edition of this pioneering collection came out, he had produced versions of Daniel Defoe's *Moll Flanders*, Charles Dickens's *David Copperfield*, Gertrude Stein's *Three Lives*, William Faulkner's *The Hamlet*, and Melville's *Benito Cereno*. But what he learned from Anglo-American literature is perhaps not exactly what we Anglo-American readers might think. Once again, the diary includes several revealing passages on this subject; the most original is surely this observation, of 28 April 1949:

> The Americans are not realists. I discovered this while watching an American film remade from an old French film. What had been real atmosphere, a genuine setting, was now a shabby backcloth. Their vaunted realism 1920-1940 was a particular kind of romanticism about "living reality." The fanciful idea that everything is realism (Dos Passos). The point of view is not tragic, but "voluntaristic." Tragedy is a clash with reality; "voluntarism" is to make a comfort of it, a way to escape from true reality.

In a few sentences, Pavese overturns what is normally assumed with respect to modern American fiction.

Although Pavese was raised and schooled in Turin, a large town in full sight of the nearby Alps, he spent childhood summers and once an entire year in his father's native village of Santo Stefano Belbo, located in the Langhe hills outside of the city. In his diary, he makes this comment about the various influences on his sensibility:

> Your classical knowledge stems from the Georgics, D'Annunzio, and the hill of Pino. To that background you added America because its language is rustic-universal...and because it's the place where town and country meet. Yours is a rustic-classicism that could easily become prehistoric ethnology. (3 June 1943)

So-called realistic details in Pavese thus conceal a still more intricate motivation. The opposition between town and country-side, as experienced during his childhood, directly relates to his conscientious use of "images." This opposition arises thematically in the plots of several stories and novels, but also and especially in probing reflections in the diary about how images spontaneously engage his mind while he is writing. As early as 11 October 1935, he worries, for example, whether his "images" are perhaps nothing more than an "ingenious elaboration" of a single "fundamental image" associated with his *paese*, his homeland, the Piedmont region. Ever scrupulous about the authenticity of his inspiration (in its autobiographical aspects) and about the accuracy of his perceptions (as he scrutinized the particulars of the outside world), he sought to measure the extent to which he was naturally, that is unconsciously, a "regional writer." The earnestness and obsessiveness of his self-interrogation of course reveals how unnatural a regionalist he actually was. It is because he felt, as an adult, incurably separated from his at once beloved and tragic childhood memories, attached to village life and the death of his father, that he could use them so profoundly in his writing. This is why *The House on the Hill* (to cite just that novel) is cryptically, essentially, autobiographical.

His remarkable details, moreover, function like bridges leading away from the self, enabling the Italian writer to cross over into the pure, emotionless, objective world of matter. Such bridge-crossings perhaps brought temporary relief. The reader certainly takes pleasure whenever Pavese abruptly focuses on, say, "the toes of Cate's little shoes." But probably the pleasure (for Pavese) of these lovingly rendered close-ups, of these desperate leaps toward the "thing-in-itself," was short-lived. He confessed in his diary, on 24 November 1935, that his "contemplation of things" was ultimately always "inquieta"—"anxious," "troubled," "uneasy," "restless."

"Inquieta" indeed. One senses that Pavese was soon gazing, no longer at the thing, but inwards. In his diary, he declares that people in a story have a given character and that things happen in accordance with "pre-determined laws." But the point of the story, he insists, must lie neither in these characters nor in those laws. For all his apparent realism, it is to his credit that such "points" are rarely easy to deduce or define. But they certainly stir up a pervasive "un-quietness" extending well beyond the narratives themselves, and one imagines Pavese—his own analysis of Dante, Stendhal, and Baudelaire notwithstanding—ultimately holding up a mirror to himself, self-splintered into a host of surrogate characters, each struggling to recover an impossible wholeness and to master that redoubtable "trade of living."

*   *   *

This exciting reissue of Pavese's diary also follows upon the rediscovery of his poetry in the United States, thanks to Geoffrey Brock's vivid renderings in *Disaffections: Complete Poems 1930-1950* (Copper Canyon). As with his fiction, Pavese surprised the first readers of his poetry with his sharp "American" eye for detail. Even taking into account the reservations that I have expressed above about his realism, Pavese's stylistic directness nonetheless dissociated him from contemporaneous "Hermetic" poets like Giuseppe Ungaretti, Eugenio Montale, or Salvatore Quasimodo, all noted for their highly personal symbolism. Pavese, moreover, had an intimate knowledge of the countryside, of its villagers and farm laborers, as well as of those who had migrated to large cities in search of work. (And Turin exemplified the postwar socio-economic transformation of Italy.) This being said, he was never a committed writer, despite his membership in the Communist Party after the Second World War and his passing interest in Marxism. He possessed something much more precious than a political theory: a natural sensitivity to the plight and dignity of common people, be they bums, priests, grape-pickers, gas-station attendants, office workers, or anonymous girls picked up on the street (though to women, the author could—as he admitted—be as misogynous as he was affectionate). Some of Pavese's most memorable poems depict peasant girls who become prostitutes in Turin. In "The Country Whore," he describes one such woman awakening, details her memory of being sexually abused during childhood, then adds:

> It often returns, in the slow rise from sleep,
> that undone aroma of far-off flowers,
> of barns and of sun. No man can know
> the subtle caress of that sour memory.

As I have mentioned, although Pavese was raised in Turin, he spent childhood summers and one entire year in his father's village of Santo Stefano Belbo. Both the style and subject matter used by some American writers—surely Anderson and Lewis, not to forget Edgar Lee Masters, whose *Spoon River Anthology* is discussed in the diary—helped the aspiring Italian poet understand more profoundly the universal significance (and lasting enigmas) of this double childhood linked to a cosmopolitan city as well as to lower Piedmont. Certainly American writers' interest in manual labor, small towns, and the new urban working classes provided an encouraging literary paradigm for Pavese, who sought the aesthetic means to deal with what he had eyewitnessed among his family members and their acquaintances. One of his first poetic experiments, "South Seas" (which is, moreover, attributed a key role in Pavese's first diary entry and also subsequently), notably relates the life of a cousin who leaves the poverty of his village behind and, for two decades, sails the world, seeking his fortune. He finally returns and opens a gas station—which fails. For southern Europeans, self-imposed economic exile was frequent; and not all homecomings were glorious.

In two important memoirs, "The Poet's Craft" and "On Certain Poems That Have Not Yet Been Written," as well as in the opening *Secretum professionale* section of his diary, Pavese recalls his struggle to find a poetic language that could reflect an Italy that was evolving rapidly, indeed brutally. This language would also have to express his personal pain associated with the countryside, notably his father's early death. So convincing is the autobiographical atmosphere of Pavese's poems that it is impossible to read those (implicitly) set in Santo Stefano Belbo without thinking of their real-life models: friends and neighbors of the poet's father. Could Pavese have sensed that his father, too, was somehow temporarily revived in such poems? Masters and Whitman were especially decisive in Pavese's quest to resuscitate the archetypal figures of this doomed rural past, even if he ultimately rejected free verse along with classical Italian poetic forms. One day, as he recounts in "The Poet's Craft," he spontaneously discovered (or rather, re-discovered) the thirteen-syllable, four-feet anapestic lines that would become his hallmark: "I found myself muttering a certain jumble of words (which turned into a pair of lines from 'South Seas') in a pronounced cadence that I had used for emphasis ever since I was a child, when I would murmur over and over the phrases that obsessed me most in the novels I was reading."

This particular meter, which is rather strange for ears trained in the *endecasillabo* and the *settenario*, is respected quite rigorously in *Work's Tiring* (as Brock prefers to call *Lavorare stanca*, as opposed to William Arrowsmith's 1976 version, *Hard Labor*). Pavese occasionally adds or deletes a metrical foot, but he otherwise creates a unified metrical impression. In the introduction to his French translation (*Travailler fatigue / La Mort viendra et elle aura tes yeux*, 1969), Gilles de Van praises the originality of this "regular rhythm, without syncopation, without abrupt surprises, without [lyrical] research, without [undue] refinement."

Brock's highly crafted translation much improves on Arrowsmith's rendering. Brock's volume also comprises poems contemporaneous to *Work's Tiring* but not included in the two editions of that book, as well as the posthumously published, dark-toned, and still very popular sequence, *Death Will Come and Will Have Your Eyes*. In all cases, Brock finely renders Pavese's "tight-lipped rhythm," as he aptly puts it. Intensity, even sometimes despair, characterize Pavese's verse, though brief moments of hope are recorded. In "Two Cigarettes," for example, a woman asks the narrator for a match to light her cigarette, then engages a conversation with him. Pavese concludes:

> Two butts, now, on the asphalt. We look at the sky:
> that window up there, she says pointing, is ours—
> but the heater's not working. At night, lost steamers
> have little to steer by, maybe only the stars.
> We cross the street, arm in arm, playfully warming each other.

Yet such amorous optimism is rare. Pavese's ephemeral love affairs are delineated in stark lines because the poet was already tormented, at the onset of the relationship, by the inevitability of loss. An early poem, "Words for a Girlfriend" already formulates this fundamental pessimism: "I am alone, and I'll be alone always." In a diary entry dated 18 June 1946, he remarks: "It is ridiculous to look for altruism in a passion composed wholly of pride and voluptuousness." The next day he adds: "I begin to write poetry when the game is lost, but a poem has never been known to change things."

Though solitude is Pavese's most salient theme, his poetry also sometimes resembles the "neighborly" short story that we associate with, say, *Winesburg, Ohio.* In *Work's Tiring*, the poems are long (averaging twenty-five to thirty lines), center on a character or two, evoke action directly, or use action as a mirror of a character's thoughts. The Italian poet invented this specific literary genre, which he called a *poesia-racconto*, a "poem-story." Despite their length, however, the poems contain no excess lyricism, bathos, or extensive description. As for dialogue, a quoted remark or two suffices to conjure up an entire personality. In "Betrayal," which is typical of Pavese's simultaneous yearning for and cynicism toward women, the narrator takes a "new woman" for a rowboat ride. She responds to "the boisterous Po, its bright sun, its echoes / of quick waves and sand-diggers" with this terse comment:

> "So enchanting," she said
> without moving her body or taking her eyes off the sky.

Pavese excels at bringing out the density of such moments, in which nothing really happens. Yet also impressive are several poems in which he announces a tragedy ("Last night, there was a boy / who fell off this roof, breaking his back"), then immediately focuses on the so-called insignificant events taking place nearby:

> The wind riffles the cool leaves of the trees.
> The red clouds above are warm and move slowly.
> A stray dog appears in the alley below, sniffing
> the body on the cobblestones, and a raw wail
> rises up among chimneys: someone's unhappy.

Here and elsewhere, he develops the notion that the saddest dramas occur almost imperceptibly, a philosophy reinforcing his theme of solitude. Yet beyond this poetic exposition of an idea, it is more characteristic of Pavese to aim for a scrupulous rendering of reality—the ideas being illustrated, not explained. After all, from a strictly phenomenological viewpoint, cool leaves, slowly moving red clouds, and a stray dog indeed vie for our attention as insistently as a boy's corpse. One can compare this poem—"Affairs"—to Auden's "Musée des Beaux Arts," in which a similar philosophy is brought to the fore, yet more explicitly.

Few lines in Pavese's poetry are memorable, but an overall impression remains indelible in the reader's mind. Perhaps this is because many "poem-stories" are in fact "poem-portraits." In

"Dina Thinking," Pavese goes so far as to adopt the voice of a prostitute who, while swimming naked in a stream, reflects on her life in the first-person personal. For a poet who evokes incurable solitude so often, Pavese was a master empathizer. With admirable subtlety, he reveals the intricacies of another person's thought patterns, even as he is describing the character from the outside, in the third person. In "Deola Thinking," for instance, he portrays a prostitute who has left a brothel for good and now "only works evenings, making slow conquests / to music, in her usual bar." Each morning she spends time in a café, drinking milk, eating brioches, and smoking serenely. "This morning she's nearly a lady," remarks Pavese, whose objective descriptions gradually merge with the woman's thoughts:

> The girls at the house are still sleeping. The air stinks,
> the madam goes out for a walk, it's crazy to stay there.
> To work the bars in the evening you have to look good;
> at that house, by thirty, you've lost what little looks you had left.

Brock's translations of these Edward Hopper-like scenes bristle with intelligent decisions. Even the hesitating quibbler (who notices a singular "street" in the English for an Italian plural, and a few other minor departures from the original) perceives how much attention Brock has paid to the way that Italians and English-language readers respectively form mental pictures with words. He often brilliantly translates at this conceptual level. And he has been very careful with the music of these poems—they are a delight to read. On the whole, this version is outstanding and deserves a wide readership. In his introduction, he alludes to American poets (like Philip Levine) who have acknowledged their debt to Pavese. Thanks to Brock, there will be others. And their appreciation of both the fiction and poetry will be greatly enhanced by *This Business of Living*.

John Taylor

Note: A shorter form of this introduction appeared in John Taylor's *Into the Heart of European Poetry* (Transaction Publishers, 2008).

1935

INNERMOST THOUGHTS ON MY WORK[1]

(October – December, 1935, and February, 1936, at Brancaleone)

The fact that some of my latest poems carry conviction in no way minimizes the importance of the truth that I compose them with ever-increasing diffidence and reluctance. With me, the joy of creation is sometimes extraordinarily keen, yet even that no longer matters much. Both these things can be explained by the facility I have acquired in handling metrical forms, which robs me of the thrill of hewing out a finished work from a mass of raw material, or by my concern with the practical aspects of life, which adds a passionate exaltation to my meditation on certain poems.

There is this to consider, too. More and more, the effort seems to me pointless, not worth while, and what is produced is either a harping on the same string or the fruit of prolonged searchings for new things to say, and consequently for new modes of expression. What gives poetry its intensity, from its very inception, is in reality a preoccupation with hitherto unperceived spiritual values, suddenly revealed as possibilities. I find my ultimate defense against this mad craze for novelty at all costs in my unshaken conviction that the apparent monotony and austerity of the style at my com-

[1] Ideally, Pavese's essay "On Writing Poetry," contained in his collection of poems *Lavorare Stanca* (1934) should be read as an introduction. Ed.

7

mand may still make it the best medium for conveying my spiritual experiences. But such examples as I can find in history—if in the realm of spiritual creativeness it is permissible to dwell upon precedents of any sort—are all against me.

There was, however, a time when I had very vividly in mind a store of material—passionate and supremely simple, the substance of my own experience—to be clarified and interpreted in writing poetry. Every attempt I made was subtly, but inevitably, linked with that fundamental purpose, so that, no matter how fantastic the nucleus of each new poem, I never felt I was losing my way. I sensed that I was composing a whole that always transcended the fragment (of the moment).

The day came when my vital stock had been entirely used up in my works and I seemed to be spending my time merely in retouching or polishing. So true is this, that—as I realized more clearly after studying the work I had already done—I no longer troubled to seek for deeper poetic discoveries, as though it were merely a question of applying a skillful technique to a state of mind. Instead, I was making a poetic farce of my poetic vocation. In other words, I was reverting to an error that earlier I had recognized and avoided, (which is how I first learned to write with assurance and creative freshness), the error of writing poetry, even though indirectly, about myself as a poet. My reaction to this sense of involution is that henceforth it will be vain for me to seek a new starting point within myself. From the time when I wrote *Mari del Sud,* in which I first began to express myself precisely and completely, I have gradually created a spiritual personality that I can never, wittingly, set aside, on pain of nullifying or calling into question all my future hypothetical inspiration as a writer. In response, therefore, to my present feeling of impotence, I bow to the necessity for cross-examining my own mind, using only those methods which it has found congenial and effective in the past, and considering each individual discovery in relation to its potential importance. Granted that poetry is brought to light by striving after it, not by talking about it.

So far, I have confined myself, as if by caprice, to poetry in verse. Why do I never attempt a different genre? There is only one answer, inadequate though it may be. It is not out of caprice, but from cultural considerations, sentiment, and now habit, that I cannot get out of that vein, and the crazy idea of changing the form to renovate the substance would seem to me shabby and amateurish.

9th October

Every poet has known anguish, wonderment, joy. The admiration we feel for a passage of great poetry is never inspired by its amazing cleverness, but by the fresh discovery it contains. If we thrill with delight on finding an adjective successfully linked with a noun never seen with it before, it is not its elegance that moves us, the flash of genius or the poet's technical skill, but amazement at the new realities it has brought to light.

It is worth pondering over the potent effect of images such as cranes, a serpent or cicadas; a garden, a whore or the wind; an ox, or a dog. Primarily, they are made for works of sweeping construction, because they typify the casual glance given to external things while carefully narrating affairs of human importance. They are like a sigh of relief, like looking out of a window. With their air of decorative detail, like many-colored chips from a solid trunk, they attest to the unconscious austerity of their creator. They require a natural incapacity for rustic sentiment. Clearly and frankly they make use of nature as a means to an end, as something subordinate to the main issue, entertaining but incidental. This, be it understood, is the traditional view. My own conception of images as the basic substance of a theme runs counter to that idea. Why? Because the poetry we write is short; because we seize upon and hammer into some significance a particular state of mind, which in itself is the beginning and the end. So it is not for us to embellish the rhythm of our abbreviated discourse with naturalistic flourishes. That would be pure affectation. We can either concern ourselves with some other subject and ignore nature with all its fertile imagery, or confine ourselves to conveying the naturalistic state of mind, in which case the glance through the window becomes the substance of the whole construction. But with other kinds of writing, we have only to think of any vast modern work—I have novels in mind—and amid the usual medley of homespun interpolations due to our irrepressible romanticism we find clearcut instances of this play of natural imagery.

Supreme among ancients and moderns for his ability to combine the diverting image and the image-story is Shakespeare, whose work is constructed on an immense scale and yet is essentially a glance through the window. He evokes a flash of scintillating imagery from some dull clod of humanity and at the same time constructs the scene, indeed the whole play, as an inspired interpretation of his state of mind. The explanation lies in his superlative technique as a dramatist, embracing every aspect of humanity—and to a lesser degree of nature.

He has snatches of lyrics at his finger tips and builds them into a solid structure. He, alone in all the world, can tell a story and sing a song simultaneously.

Even assuming that I have hit upon the new technique I am trying to clarify for myself, it goes without saying that, here and there, it may contain traits borrowed in embryo from other techniques. This hinders me from seeing clearly the essential characteristics of my own style. (Contradicting Baudelaire, with all due respect, it may be said that not everything in poetry is predictable. When composing, one sometimes chooses a form not for any deliberate reason but by instinct, creating without knowing precisely how.) It is true that instead of weaving my plot development objectively, I tend to work in accordance with the calculated, yet fanciful, law of imagination. But to know how far calculation may go, what importance to attach to a fanciful law, where the image ends and logic begins, these are tricky little problems.

This evening, walking below red cliffs drenched in moonlight, I was thinking what a great poem it would make to portray the god incarnate in this place, with all the imaginative allusions appropriate to such a theme. Suddenly I was surprised by the realization that there is no such god. I know it, I am convinced of it, and therefore, though someone else might be able to write that poem, I could not. I went on to reflect how allusive, how *all-pervading*,[1] every future subject must be to me, in the same way that a belief in the god incarnate in these red rocks would have to be real and *all-pervading*[1] to a poet who used this theme.

Why cannot I write about these red, moonlit cliffs? Because they reflect nothing of myself. The place gives me a vague uneasiness, nothing more, and that should never be sufficient justification for a poem. If these rocks were in Piedmont, though, I could very well absorb them into a flight of fancy and give them meaning. Which comes to the same thing as saying that the fundamental basis of poetry may be a subconscious awareness of the importance of those bonds of sympathy, those biological vagaries, that are already alive, in embryo, in the poet's imagination before the poem is begun.

Certainly it ought to be possible, even for me, to create a poem on a subject whose background is not Piedmont. It ought to be, but hardly ever has been, so far. Which means that I have not yet progressed beyond the simple re-elaboration of the images materially represented by my innate links with my environment. In other words, there is a blind spot in my work as a poet, a material limitation that I do not want, but cannot succeed in eliminating. But is it then really an objective residuum or something indispensable in my blood?

11th October

Could all my images be nothing more than an ingenious elaboration of a fundamental image: as my native land, so am I? But then the poet's imagination would be impersonal, indistinguishable from the terms of comparison, regional and social, of Piedmont. The essence of his message would be that he and his country, regarded as mutually complementary, are beautiful. Is this all? Is this the fateful Quarto?[2]

[1] Pavese stresses this term in English in the original text. Ed.
[2] The point from which Garibaldi set out on his expedition to Sicily. Pavese is quoting, ironically, a line from Carducci. Ed.

Or, rather, is it not simply that between Piedmont and myself there runs a current of sympathetic impulses, some conscious, some unconscious, which I shape and dramatize as best I can: in image-stories? A relationship that begins with an affinity between one's blood and the climate, the very air, of home, and ends in that wearisome spiritual drift that disturbs me and other Piedmontese? Do I express spiritual things by speaking of material things, and vice versa? And this labor of substitution, allusion, imagination, how far can it be valued as an indication of that "allusive and all-pervading essence" of ours?

To counter any suspicion that my work may be merely a Piedmontese Revival, there are good reasons for believing it may broaden and deepen Piedmontese values. My justification for saying so? This. My writing is not dialectic. (How fiercely instinct and reason made me fight to avoid dialectism!) It refuses to be superficial—I paid for that by experience! It draws its sustenance from the strongest roots, national and traditional; it strives to keep its eyes on world trends in literature, and has been particularly aware of literary experiments and achievements in North America, where at one time I thought I had discovered an analogous development. Perhaps the fact that American culture no longer interests me in the least, means that I have outgrown this Piedmontese point of view. I think it does; at any rate the viewpoint I have had hitherto.

15th October

Yet we must have a new starting point. When the mind has grown used to a certain mechanical method of creation, an equally strong force is needed to get it out of that rut, so that, instead of those monotonous, self-propagating fruits of the spirit, it can produce something with a strange new flavor, sprung from a graft never tried before. Not that some external impetus can take the place of mental effort, but that one must completely transform the subject and the means, and so come face to face with new problems. Given a fresh starting point, the mind will, of course, regain its usual zest, but without some such springboard I cannot rise above my lazy habit of reducing everything to the pattern of an image-story. I need some outside intervention to change the direction of my instinctive lines of thought and so prepare them for fresh discoveries.

If I have truly lived these four years of poetry, so much the better: that cannot but help me towards greater incontestability and a better sense of expression. The first few times, it will seem to me that I have reverted to my own earliest days. It will even seem to me that I have nothing to say. But I must not forget how much at a loss I felt before *Mari del Sud,* and how, as I went along, I grasped an understanding of my world that I created. Not before. That does not mean, though, that my difficulties, today, have not grown worse. In *Lavorare Stanca* there was all my experience from the day when I opened my eyes, and such was my joy at bringing my first gold to light that I felt no tedium. Then, everything in me was yet to be discovered. Now that I have exhausted that vein, I am too worn-out, too circumscribed, to be still strong enough to throw myself with high hopes into making a new excavation. The terrain is all sounded and measured, and I know what constitutes my originality. Furthermore, in my innumerable pre-poetic attempts, the very things I dropped and crushed were the methods of narration used in prose and the novel. I know only too well the obstacles of this path. I have even shorn from it the stimulating joy of an initial contact. Yet this is the path I must pursue.

16th October

Now that I have, as I intended, expressed the parallel I am glad to know exists between myself and Piedmont, what will be the new atmosphere of my poetry? The new set of values, abstract yet empiric, that will enable me to gather up and unify the various scattered fragments? And perhaps make the accumulation into a book?

This atmosphere, this revaluation, ought to be such as

to justify me in history. Now, what historical developments do I actually believe in? Revolutions, perhaps? But, leaving aside the fact that never has any good poetry been inspired by a revolution in action, any enthusiasm I feel about them is no more than skin deep. Naturally, it would not be a question of describing the tumults, the speeches, the bloodshed and triumphs of a revolution, but of living in its moral atmosphere and from that standpoint surveying and judging life. Have I experienced this spiritual regeneration? No, and so far in life my tendency has been to advocate enjoying things as they are, rather than to agitate for reforms. Hence my incapacity for becoming a revolutionary, even with the motive of studying life from a new angle, however much it may please me to toy with the idea. I can only hope that I may come across other historical values, not violently revolutionary, and exercise my imagination on those as best I can.

Which is very reasonable. From what one hears, the only trends that exist nowadays are towards violent revolution. But everything in history is revolution; even a reformation that comes about gradually and peacefully. Then away with all this carefully worked-up oratory, these speakers who urge reform by means of active violence (by other people, naturally!). Away with that childish need for noise and being one of a crowd! I must content myself with a tiny little discovery expressed in a single poem, and show my moral rejuvenation by my humble submission to the destiny imposed on me by my very nature. Which is most reasonable. Unless it is just laziness or cowardice.

17th October

This morning I took up again, and finished, the poem about the hare. I had lost heart with it, simply because a hare hardly seemed a worth-while subject, and I feel a certain self-satisfaction at having persisted in my effort. It really seems to me that my technique has become automatic, so that, without deliberately thinking about it, my ideas now come out in the form of images, as if in obedience to that fanciful law I mentioned on the 10th. And I am very much afraid that this means it is time to change the tune, or at least the instrument. Otherwise I shall find myself sketching out a critical study of a poem even before I write it. And it becomes a burlesque affair, like the bed of Procrustes.

So my formula for the future is discovered: if once I tormented my mind to create a blending of my lyrical forms (praised for their passionate ardor) and my style of letter-writing (praiseworthy for its logical, imaginative restraint), and the result was *Mari del Sud,* with all the works that followed it; now I must find the secret of fusing the fantastic, trenchant vein of *Lavorare stanca* with that of the *pornoteca:*[1] slapstick, realistically declaimed to its public. And beyond all doubt, that will mean prose.

For one thing (among many) seems to me intolerable to an artist: to lose the feeling of starting something fresh.

19th October

On rereading the 16th October, I think that precisely because I have already expressed the parallel between myself and Piedmont, this element must nevermore be lacking in my future poetry. For I imagine that nothing I have sought out can be lost, and that progress consists of an ever-increasing pulverization of experiences, casting new upon the old.

21st October

> "... *sicut nunc foemina quaeque*
> *cum peperit, dulci repletur lacte ..."*

27th October

> "*in gremium matris terrai praecipitavit."*

28th October

Poetry begins when a simpleton says of the sea: "It looks like oil!" This is not exactly the best possible description

[1] Cf. Pavése's essay on *Il mestiere di poeta,* in the Appendix to *Lavorare Stanca.* Ed.

of a flat calm, but he is pleased at discovering the similarity, tickled by the idea of a mysterious connection, and feels he must tell the world what he has noticed. But it would be equally foolish to stop at that. Having started the poem, one must finish it, work up the idea with a wealth of associations and skillfully arrive at an assessment of its value. There you have a typical poem, based on an idea. But usually the writing stems from sentiment—the exact description of a flat calm— that occasionally foams with the discovery of relationships. The typical poem may possibly be remote from reality, consisting up to now (just as we can even live on microbes) of mere odds and ends of similarities (sentiment); constructive thought (logic); and associations caught at random (poetry). A more arbitrary combination would probably be foolish and unbearable.

1st November

It is interesting, this idea that sentiment in art may be purely a fragmentary likeness, such as a precise description of a flat calm, a description, that is, in plain terms without any mention of imaginary associations and without the intrusion of logic.

But if it is conceivable to describe something without evoking images (which the very nature of language denies), can there possibly be any description without logical thought? If one remarks that a tree is green, is not that an expression of opinion? Or if it seems ridiculous to associate such a banal thought with logic, where does banality end and logical thought begin? The second paragraph I leave to a better philosopher. It seems to me generally correct that sentiment is describing something appropriately. To utilize the emotions to discover connecting links is, in fact, already a matter of elaborating these experiences rationally.

And how is it that the nature of language denies the possibility of not using images? That *verde* is derived from *vis,* and alludes to the power of vegetation, is a fine point of contact and beyond question; but equally beyond question is the actual simplicity of this word and its immediate application to a single idea. The fact that *arrivare,* to arrive, once meant *approdare,* to disembark, and that originally it evoked a nautical imagery to say that winter was arriving, does not detract from the absolute objectivity of the same observation, made now. So my parenthesis was stupid, and we can go and eat nuts.

9th November

This search for a new starting point is linked with a craze for construction. I have already said there can be no poetic value in a collection of lyrics masquerading as a poem, and yet I am always wondering how to arrange my little poems in such a way as to be able to add to their number and make their significance complete. Again it seems to me that all I have done is to depict states of mind. Again, I have fallen short of the standard I should have reached in summing up the world around me.

It is certain that the studied arrangement of the poems in a *canzone* depends on nothing more than the pleasure of ornamentation and reflection. That is, taking for example the poems of *Fleurs du Mal,* they may be arranged this way or that, and the effect can be charming, illuminating, even critical, but nothing more. Given the poems as already composed, *but the fact that Baudelaire composed them in that way, one by one, yet convincing and closely linked in their total effect, like a tale, could that not stem from the moral, well-judged, exhaustive conception of them as a whole?* Perhaps a page of the *Divina Commedia* would lose its intrinsic value as a comment upon the whole if it were cut away from the poem or transposed?

But, postponing to a better time the analysis of the unity of the *Commedia,* is it possible to evaluate as part of a whole a poem conceived as an individual work, under the swift wing beat of inspiration? Did Baudelaire not conceive a poem as complete in itself? Did he think it out as a link in a chain with the others? It does not seem likely to me.

There is another point. Granted that a poem is not clear to the author, in its deepest significance, until it is completely finished, how is it possible for him to construct the book except by reflecting upon the poems already written? The *canzone* is therefore always an afterthought. Yet the objection still remains that long poetical works *have* been conceived as a whole—leaving aside the *Commedia,*—certainly the plays of Shakespeare. It must be said: the unity of these works comes precisely from the realistic persistence of the character, from the naturalistic evolution of the action, which, taking place in a keenly acute consciousness, loses its material nature and acquires a spiritual significance, becomes a state of mind.

10th November

Why am I forever insisting that the subject in my poems must be treated exhaustively, ethically, critically? I, who cannot feel it is right for one man to judge another? This pretension of mine is nothing more than a vulgar desire to "have my say." Which is far from dispensing justice. Do I live justly? Does justice mean anything to me in human affairs? Then why claim to pass judgment on matters of poetry?

If there is any human figure in my poetry, it is that of a truant running back, full of joy, to his own village, where to him everything is picturesque and full of color; a man who likes to work as little as he can; finding great pleasure in the simplest things; always expansive, good-natured, set in his views; incapable of deep suffering; happy to follow nature and enjoy a woman, but also glad to be free and on his own; ready every morning to start life afresh. As in *Mari del Sud.*

12th November

The above may be a generalization. I would have to make an inventory of the poems in the book that do not fit in that framework. It is obvious that they cannot be classified by differences in what happens, because everything happens to my protagonist, but by differences of feeling, for example:

endurance in suffering, dread of solitude, dissatisfaction with nature, prudence and malice. Of these attributes, the only one so far that I find exceptionally well expressed is impatience with sexual loneliness. (*Maternità and Paternità.*)

But I have a presentiment that the new way will not be in the manner I have already pursued far and wide, nor in the various "refusals" conjured up in my mind by opposition, but by making use of some indirect method that, while conserving the personality already acquired, will imperceptibly displace those interests and that experience. This happened at the time of *Una stagione*, when, by interesting myself in the carnal life I had till then despised, I conquered a new world of forms (a leap from *Mari del Sud* to *Dio caprone*). But the search for a new personality is sterile. What is fruitful is the human interest the old personality can have in new activities.

16th November

The most pressing aesthetic problem, mine and of my era, is, of course, this question of the unity of a work of poetry: whether one should content oneself with the rule-of-thumb limitations accepted in the past, or explain those limitations as a transfiguration of matter into poetic spirit, or seek for some new co-ordinating principle of the substance of poetry. Those present-day pulverizers of poetry, *poets of precision,* have been aware of this problem and have refused to recognize the three points just mentioned. We must return to the poetry of situation. Accepting the *situations* of the past, just as they are, or presenting a new spiritual method of resolving facts or actions into situations?

The new manner that I thought I had created—the image-narrative—now seems to me of no more value than any other hellenistic rhetorical medium. A simple discovery, in other words, of a sort of repetition or *in medias res,* which has on occasion a great effect, but does not suffice to form an adequate perspective.

17th November

Being at a distance from it, I begin to discover qualities that condition art in Piedmont, and particularly in Turin. City of fantasy, through her aristocratic culture composed of elements new and old; city of decorum, through the complete absence of any jarring note, material or spiritual; city of passion, in her kindly indulgence towards idleness; city of irony, through her own good taste for life; a model city, with her calm rich in underlying tumult. A city virgin in art, like a girl who has already seen others making love but, for her own part, has tolerated only caresses so far, yet is now ready, if she finds the right man, to take the step. The city, in fine, where I am spiritually reborn when I reach it from anywhere outside: my lover, not my mother nor my sister. And many others feel this same relationship with her. How can she fail to exert a cultural influence? And I form a part of a group. The conditions are all present.

24th November

It seems to me I am discovering my new vein. It would concern itself with a *restless contemplation* of things, even the things of Piedmont. I perceive that first I worked in *dreamy contemplation* (*Mari del Sud, Paesaggio a Tina, Ritratto d'autore*), and that, not only after the 15th of May[1] but even in works I wrote before this year (*Lavorare stanca, Ulisse, Avventure, Esterno*) there intruded a tremor, a sadness, a note of pain, at first unconscious or sternly repressed. It goes without saying that, since the period May-August, this has become the rule. This new quest of mine fuses together overtones that are more apprehensive, more spiritual, and a renewed, passionate materialism sure in its promise. Can these be my *whispers of heavenly death?* Anyway, to have a clear idea of the transition, compare the *Paesaggio* about the gun with the *Luna*

[1] The date when Pavese was sentenced to prison for anti-communist activities. Ed.

d'Agosto: what, in the first, was an entirely descriptive spiritualization of a scene, in the second is in reality the creation of a natural mystery concerning human anguish.

5th December

There must be some significance in the fact, when evolving my literary style, I had no help at all from any facility I may have in dealing with sexual matters, *Mari del Sud, Antenati, Fumatori di carta,* all ignore that vein. If it entered into the argument at all, it was as something known and despised. (Remember *Donne Perdute, Blues dei Blues, Maestrine.*) A fresh preoccupation with the subject began in *Canzone di Strada* and *Tradimento,* in the form of vivid descriptions of sensory experiences. Then it burst forth like new material projected into the world in *Una Stagione,* in which the argument was solely concerned with the importance and *all-pervadingness* of sex, interpreting every sensation as the equivalent of a sex reaction ("the March wind pressing against one's clothing"). One way of avoiding the quagmire of actual, facile, matter-of-fact description is a mischievous humbling of sexual sensations. But how is it that this teasing sexual exhilaration can exist side by side with disquieting abstract thought? At first sight it seems that they would counteract each other.

6th December

To those old-fashioned types who are not quite sure that God exists, but who, even while they scoff, are aware of Him every now and then under their skin, it seems a fine thing to blaspheme. A man has an attack of asthma and starts to swear furiously, with the precise intention of offending that hypothetical God. He thinks that if, after all, God does exist, every oath is a hammer blow on the nails of the cross, an insult hurled at Him. Then God will avenge himself—His normal procedure—and rage like the devil, inflict further evils, send the man to hell. But, even though He turns the world upside down, no-one can take away the insult He has received, the hammering He has suffered. *No one!* That is a fine consolation. And it certainly shows that, after all, this God did not think of everything! Just consider! He is Lord of All, the Supreme Autocrat, the Absolute. Man is as dung, a mere nothing, and yet man has this power of irritating Him, provoking Him to anger, spoiling an instant of His beatific existence! This is truly "the best testimony we can give of human dignity." Why ever didn't Baudelaire write a poem on the subject?

7th December

There is a good deal to be learned from the statement that the secret of much great art lies in the handicaps, in the form of rules, imposed on it by contemporary taste. These rules of art, by setting a definite ideal for the artist to achieve, prevent him from working aimlessly. The value paintings have for us never lies in their observance of rules, of course, but, leaving aside their differences in quality and purpose, in the composition that grew under the artist's hands while he was seeking to give what the rule or "taste" demands. Genius, however, inflamed to white heat by this game of wits, this attempt to achieve certain results said to be of value, transcends the abstract, conventional limitations of those "tastes" and in this state of ecstasy creates new forms. Without knowing it! And that is logical if you reflect that the secret of an artistic creation eludes its creator until the very moment when the solution strikes him, whereupon he transfers his interest to some other point. That, in my view, is the function of "intelligence" in art; the conscious application of it solely to those contemporary standards that apply to the artist and his period; standards that may then be fused by the white heat of genius into an eruption of poetry.

The artist labors with his brain under restrictions that will be valueless in the eyes of posterity, but by so doing his brain may create new intellectual realities in advance of

22

criticism. For example: the craze for the "conceit" among the Elizabethans and the Shakespearean result—the image-narrative. The preference for the concrete example in the scientific and classical world and the consequent cosmic vision of Lucretius.

15th December

As for me, the composition of a poem comes about in a way I should never have believed if experience had not shown me it is so. I find myself turning over in my mind an inchoate but significant idea; I murmur the thought to myself; I embody it in an open rhythm, always the same. Different words and different connecting links will color the new condensed, harmonious form and give it individuality. Now most of the work is finished. All that remains is to revise those two, three or four verses, which are usually already in a definite though rudimentary form; twist and torment them, question them, work out their various possible developments until I hit on the right one. The poem must be evolved entirely from the nucleus I spoke of, and each additional verse will define the idea even more precisely by excluding false impressions, until, finally, every potentiality inherent in my initial idea has been examined, separated, and developed to the best of my ability. As I go along, new rhythmic nuclei form under my pen, identifiable in the various individual "images" of the presentation. So, growing listless as my interest wanes, I come to the final verse which is nearly always long and restful, surveying the theme again from the beginning, mentioning all the kernels of thought in turn and bringing them to a conclusion. What must Stendhal's crystallization be? I have before me a complex, rhythmic theme, full of color, movement, new ideas, amplifications, in which the different moments of discovery and transition—the nuclei, in short—merge and throw fresh light on one another, ceaselessly kept in motion by the rhythmic pulse that beats through the whole. I smoke on it and try to think of something else, but I smile, stimulated by my secret.

16th December

It may be by chance, or not, that while expounding my method I have left on one side the image-narrative. I speak of a suggestive situation: of nuclei, the blood pulse, complex rhythms. And I say that each nucleus is an image in the narrative.

Whence it is clearly seen that the image-narrative was nothing else but an attempt to give a technical interpretation of my poetry; probably itself a metaphor; generally not at all a definite program. That the various images that "merge and throw fresh light on one another" may be the *progressus* of each poem is a matter of fact, and leaves unexplored the question of whether poetry may be a narration of images, or whether it is not, rather, a play of images actuated by a primitive nucleus of ethical and rhythmic importance. Would it not be better to make some research into the basic meaning (ethical and rhythmical) of these poems? It is a fact that, more often than not, a page of mine leaps from one image to the next, grows intoxicated by the persistent rhythm, plays with each idea and then reaches a conclusion (not necessarily at the actual end of the work) in a sentence, a *dictum* that throws light on the whole. But what if the nerve centers of the composition were sayings and not myths? If, for example, in the last *Paesaggio* the point did not lie in the horses and the fugitive from home, but in the concluding line?

I add that one of the most purely imaginative of my poems—*Grappa a settembre*—does actually end with the maxim *that unifies all the images:* "so the women will not be the only ones to enjoy the morning."

Can it be that, till now, I have been subtly in error?

18th December

But, then, if the point of my poems lies in their summing-up, whether clearly expressed or left in doubt, many things I was still seeking, theoretically, I have already attained.

24

This, among other things, must be true beyond all doubt, if it is true that I have already composed poems that are actually definitive. For instance, here is an ethical evaluation of the things of this world; the grave importance of reasoning; the nemesis awaiting mere sensuality. Here, in what I feared might be simply a literary jest, is expressed the universality of the inner world. Here, in a word, is everything! Today is indeed a red-letter day!

20th December

Life without smoking is like the smoke without the roast.

Either police or criminals.

29th December

Of the two things, writing poetry and studying, it is the second that gives me greater and more constant comfort. However, I do not forget that my pleasure in studying is always with a view to writing poetry. But, fundamentally, writing poetry is an ever-open wound whence the health-giving life blood drains away.

1936

16th February

Chance made me begin and end *Lavorare stanca* with poems about Turin—more precisely on Turin as a place one is leaving, then as the place to which one will return. One could call the book San Stefano Belbo spreading into and conquering Turin. This is one of many interpretations of the poem. The countryside becomes the city, nature becomes human life, the boy becomes a man. As I see it, "from San Stefano to Turin" is a myth composed of every conceivable significance of this book.

It is equally curious that the poems composed after the last *Paesaggio* all speak of some other subject, not Turin. Chance seems to want to teach me to transform my own misfortune into a drastic change in my poetry.

To replace Turin, my favorite subject, will mean constructing another world, based, as always, on a very definite period of suffering and silence. Because anything written during these months of feverish idleness will never be anything more than a "curiosity," so silence it shall be. During these months, many former values lapse, many ingrained habits are destroyed, and—a strange twist of fate—nothing comes to take their place. I must learn to take this futile collapse, this wearisome uselessness, as a blessed gift—such as only poets can receive—like a curtain before the play begins again. A period of self-questioning. I return to a state of childlike immaturity, with all its crudities and fits of despair. I again become the man who has *not* yet written *Lavorare stanca,* and spend hours biting my nails, despairing of mankind, despising light and nature, shaken by childish but agonizing fits of terror, as I did in my twenties. What world lies beyond that stormy sea I do not know, but every ocean has a distant shore, and I shall reach it. To have to endure all this a second time makes me sick of life.

What is certain is that the poems written now—*Parole, Altri tempi, Poetica, Mito, Semplicità, Un ricordo, Paternità, L'instinto, Tolleranza, U steddazzu*—are akin in spirit to *Dio caprone, Balletto, Pensieri di Dina, Gelosia, Creazione, Dopo, Agonia* and others I have forgotten: this will be a little book of *Epaves,* not the work of the future.

What is to come will emerge only after long suffering, long silence. There must a period of feeling lost, bewildered, downcast, until I discover new values, a new world. The only advantage I shall have over my early twenties will be the skill I have acquired, my intuitive perception. The disadvantages, the months of suffering that must come first, the utter exhaustion. The new work will begin only when my suffering is over. All I can do, at the moment, is to fix my mind on aesthetic problems and try to find answers that will end my agony.

17th February

It is good to go back to Homer. What is the unity of his poems? Each book has its own unity of sentiment, of attitude, whereby it is read harmoniously, as well as physically, as a whole. *Odyssey*, Book VIII: the pleasure of poetry, dancing, rivalry; song, the light-hearted golden myth; a vindication of the nobility of life, in an oasis of pleasure and idyllic tears. *Odyssey*, Book X: adventure, the succession of obstacles, human weeping, the growing callousness. *Iliad*, Book III: the beautiful woman, the war over her, and enervating love. And so on. Did Homer, or the man we call Homer, think of these definitions? I believe not, but it is a revealing thing that the book wherein all Greece comes to life is composed in this way, or, which comes to the same thing, that it can be so interpreted.

But let us be careful. The great fascination of the two poems lies in the *material* unity of their characters, which time after time flares up in a blaze of poetic fire. Which means that even from the first example of great poetry, written intentionally as such, we have this double play: a natural unfolding of events (which could be doubled or halved without adversely affecting the issue), and successive, fundamental, poetic beams of light. The *story* and the *poetry*. The union of the two elements is merely a matter of *aptitude*, of *skill*.

This opens up the problem of whether it may not be possible to recreate the miracle in separate poems; for the very reason that the mind, in all its manifestations, strives towards *unity*. To compose with inspiration, but with an underlying skill that merges the various fragments together to form a poem.

The simplest way would seem to be to keep one and the same protagonist element in the successive poems. And this does not do, because then it would be better to make the work a single narrative poem, which is obviously absurd.

What remains is to seek out, in a group of poems, the subtle, and almost always hidden, affinities between the *subject* (the *material* unity) and the clarification (spiritual unity).

Seeking them out means putting them to ourselves as if composing them, and the methods are: accustoming oneself to regard nature (the world of subjects) as a well-defined whole, yielding judiciously to the echoes and appeals from the preceding poems; in short, searching for the subjects in cold blood, calculating their position, and at the same time surrendering oneself intuitively and at white heat to the rhythmic surge of the past. To say to oneself, when composing a poem: I am discovering another little piece of the world that I already know in part; assisting oneself in this search by recalling what is already known; investigating, in short, how far one's own past is good and just. Never aspiring to take a leap into the unknown, or being suddenly reborn one morning. Using up the cigarette butts of the night before and convincing oneself that time, now and later, is only a fixation. But, above all, never doing as the serpent does, never shedding one's skin: for what really belongs to a man, in life, except what he has already lived? But keeping a balanced view, because what has a man to live for, except what he is not yet living?

Another interesting point in Homer lies in the appellatives and the lines that recur; everything, in short, that constitutes in each case a lyric nerve center of incontestable value, and that, each time, is repeated identically, or nearly so, without taking the trouble to recall the original inspiration. (And it is no excuse for this to point out the truth that he is using poetic language, consecrated jargon, phrases that, by use, have become mere expressions, canonical crystallizations of a sentiment. It may be so, in fact, it is: but on me they have a different effect, and I have every right to discuss them as though they were Homer's deliberate choice. His intention does not count; what counts is what I see in them, I, the reader.)

I believe, therefore, that this represents a very important method of technique, whereby the individual books obtain a part of their unity. I do not know whether every reader has noticed that each book is characterized by a special group of appellations and recurring lines that apply to it alone. It would seem that the materialism of certain actions, certain figures, certain repetitions, is in this way given the semblance of poetry—even if only mnemonic or conventionalized—to disguise the inevitable paucity of invention. That, in short, the first Greek may have felt the opposition between narration and poetry, and forced himself—naively, as it seems to our taste— to sublimate it in this way. It goes without saying, that when changing from one book to another he also changed—but not invariably, of course—the tone of the repetitions, according to the individual colorization, or, if we like, the basic conception, of each book.

In conclusion, one way of obtaining unity is the recurrence of certain lyrical formulae that recreate vocabulary, transforming an appellation or a phrase into a mere word. Of all the ways of inventing language (the work of the poet), this is the most convincing and, when one thinks of it, the only real one. And it explains why, in all that part of the work where similar formulae recur, there circulates an air of unity: it is the same man—the inventor—who is speaking.

23rd February

The more I think of it the more remarkable it seems to me, the way Homer achieved unity between books. At one stage, when everything would seem to presuppose a bent towards uniformity, he reveals instead a zest for weaving a brightly colored piece of tapestry, complete in itself—the study of a differentiated unity. He is, in reality, a writer of stories conditioned in different ways (by love, heroic passion, war, idylls, homecoming, the world of pleasure, social delights, revenge, anger and so on). In this he is like his peers, Dante and Shakespeare: powerful, fabulous creators who delight in detail keenly perceived and embroidered; who breathe in the whole of life with their regular, daily, perfect respiration. Above all, these are not the men for the unexpected, irritating exclamation that breaks out at any experience, takes it as having a hidden meaning, works it up into a sensation; but clear-sighted observers meticulously describing what they see; calm, imperturbable instigators of variety, subtly skilled in exploiting experience, cutting it into facets and shapes as if in sport, ending by taking its place. Men of the utmost astuteness, with nothing in the least naive about them.

Understood in this way, these creative geniuses seem well equipped for that task requiring majestic and most subtle skill, an astuteness essential if the gulf between narrative and poetry is to be satisfactorily bridged. They are marvelous at compromise, the wholly social and prudent art of experience. Instead of deriving grandeur from the violence of feeling, they draw it from the art of knowing how to live. This biographical basis is the only thing that lyric-writers and creators have in common. But while, for the lyric-writers, everything is exhausted in this violence, for the others, the *masters,* knowing how to live is an art that simply helps in fashioning the human material, set free to be itself, purified, *complete,* made available for all men. Thus these great ones merge invisibly into their work, while the lyric-writers distort themselves in theirs.

28th February

There is a parallel between this past year of my life and a certain aspect of poetry. My keenest sufferings were not when I was keyed up to great excitement, but during those furtive moments that lay between. In the same way, the unity, the coherence of a poem, does not depend on the climax but on the subtle inter-reaction of all the creative touches. Which means that unity owes less to plot construction than to an apt handling of slight, almost illusory indications appearing again and again in different guise.

How did she hurt me? Was it the day when she raised her arm to wave at someone across the street? The day when no one came to open the door to me, and then she appeared with her hair all ruffled? The day when she was whispering with him on the embankment? The thousands of times she made me hurry here and there?

But this has nothing to do with aesthetics; this is grief. I wanted to count my memories of happy moments, and all I can remember is the pangs I suffered.

Never mind, they serve the same purpose. My love story wi h her is not made up of dramatic scenes but of moments filled with the subtlest perceptions. So should a poem be. But it is agony.

15th March

Today my imprisonment ends.

*   *   *

10th April

When a man is in such a state as I am, there is nothing left for him to do but examine his conscience.

I have no grounds for discarding my own firm conviction that whatever happens to a man is conditioned by his whole past. In short, it is deserved. Evidently, I must have been an utter fool to find myself at this point.

First, *moral irresponsibility*. Have I really ever asked myself what I ought to do according to conscience? I have always followed sentimental, hedonistic impulses. Of that there is no question. Even my period as a woman-hater (1930-1934) was in essence self-indulgent. I wanted to avoid becoming involved and the pose pleased me. How spineless that attitude was soon became apparent. And even where my work is concerned, have I ever been anything but a hedonist? I enjoyed working feverishly by fits and starts, under the spur of ambition, but I was afraid, too; afraid of getting tied up. I have never really worked and in fact I have no skill in any occupation.

Another fault is quite apparent. I have never been a single-minded, easygoing sort of fellow who enjoys his pleasures without a second thought. I haven't the nerve. I have always flattered myself with the illusion that I am a man of moral sensibility because I spend delicious moments—that's the right term—inventing conscientious scruples without pluck enough to solve them by action. I have no wish to resurrect the complacency that at one time I felt at this moral coward-ice from aesthetic motives—hoping it meant my career would be that of a genius—but still I have not yet passed that stage.

Having reached such utter abjectness, morally, the thought occurs to me that there should be material abjectness, too. How fitting it would be if, for example, my shoes were in holes!

Only so can I explain my actual suicidal urge in life. I know that I am forever condemned to think of suicide when faced with no matter what difficulty or grief. It terrifies me. My basic principle is suicide, never committed, never to be committed, but the thought of it caresses my sensibility.

The terrible thing is that whatever remains to me, now, is not enough to put me right, because I have already found myself in this identical state, in the past, but have never found in it any help towards moral well-being. Nor shall I be reso-lute enough to take that step this time. That much is clear.

Yet, unless infatuation deceives me, and I do not think it does, I have found the way of salvation. In spite of all my instability, a certain lady managed to make me conform to discipline, to self-sacrifice, simply by giving herself to me. By so doing, she raised me to an intuition of new tasks, made them take shape before my eyes. Because, left to myself, as I know from experience, I am *convinced* I shall not succeed. Made one flesh and one destiny with her, I should have succeeded. Of that I am equally certain. Even because of my cowardice, she would have become a spur in my flank.

Instead, what has she done! Perhaps she does not know it, or, if she does, it means nothing to her. And that is fair enough, for she is herself, with her own past that marks out her future.

But this is what she has done. I have had a love affair, during which I have been judged and pronounced unworthy to continue. In the face of this cataclysm, I feel not only the pangs of a lover, agonizing though they are; not only the break-up of our association, serious as it is; but in my mind the whole thing becomes confused with a sensation of being hammered by life, a feeling I have not known since 1934. Away with aesthetics and poses! Away with genius! Away with the lot! Have I ever in my life done anything that was not the action of a crack-brained fool?

A fool in the banal, incurable sense of the word. A man who has no idea how to live, who has not developed morally, a futile dolt, propping himself up with thoughts of suicide, but not committing it.

20th April

Let us see whether, even from this, we can dig out a lesson in technique.

There is the usual one, elementary but not yet fully grasped. It is supremely voluptuous to abandon oneself to sincerity, losing all sense of self in the contemplation of the absolute; but—and here's the point—it is voluptuous, and therefore to be avoided. That, of all things, should be clear to me from now on: all the rubs I have endured had their origin in my voluptuous abandonment to the absolute, the unknown, the inconsistent. I do not yet understand what the tragedy of existence may be—I am not yet fully convinced—but this point is so clear. I must overcome this luxurious indulgence and stop regarding states of soul as an end in themselves.

For a poet, that is difficult. Or possibly very easy. A poet delights in submerging himself in a state of mind and enjoying it—that is his way of escape from tragedy. But a poet should never forget that, for him, a state of mind is less than nothing. All that counts is the poetry he will write. This effort of purposeful restraint is his taste of tragedy.

The need for living tragically and not voluptuously is proved by how much I have suffered so far, and suffered uselessly. It has opened my eyes to read again the poems I wrote in '27. I am utterly downcast to find in that sloppy, Neapolitan naiveté the same thoughts, even the same words, as I have written in this past month. Nine years have passed, and is my response to life just as childish? And this virility that seemed my special characteristic, hard won through years of work, is that so meaningless?

Such inadequacy is a fault that bears less heavily upon poetry than on any other art. Indeed, poetry has taught me to master myself, pull myself together, see things clearly; poetry has made something of me, in the most practical sense of the term. The fault lies in daydreaming, a very different thing and the enemy of all good art. My need is to avoid responsibilities, to *feel* things without paying for them.

There is not only a similarity but an actual parallel between a life given over to voluptuousness and the writing of little isolated poems, one every so often, with nothing to link them together. It becomes a habit to live by fits and starts, without development and without principles.

The lesson is this: to build in art, or build in life, banish sensuousness from art, as from life; exist tragically. (That does not forbid you, of course, to get randy now and then, or scribble a silly little sonnet or novelette. Indeed, you need to. Only remember that you don't have to upset heaven and earth just to write a novel or arrange a party.)

To add an explanatory postscript, it is human for me to let off steam and think that no one has ever treated me so badly. Not as far as sex is concerned—sex is a pain in the ass—but for the other reason that this time I was intending to "pay," to respond, to fetter and limit myself, in short to turn sensual delight into tragedy. Fortunately what happened was the opposite: so we shall see whether my virility can recover. That's all right, but still it was a very dirty trick. And, thinking it over again between ourselves, deliberately excluding every voluptuous day dream and passion, who can say whether or not the torment I suffered was primarily due to the fact that I resented the injustice of it, the malice behind the action? And isn't this, too, a lesson in the technique of poetry?

22nd April

The truth is that nothing of the world has ever yet penetrated my spirit, or brought home to me the fact of the dismal, everlasting skeleton that lies under my flesh. I have enjoyed colors, perfumes, caressing gestures, and found them satisfying, inspiring, recuperative. I have joked as one does with friends, and been happy alone.

My words have not really expressed thoughts, only sensations. My portraits were pictures, not dramatic presentations. I would decide on a subject—a figure, for example— and ponder over it until what I produced was a transfiguration to my own satisfaction. I simplified the world into a banal gallery depicting acts of power or pleasure. In these pages there is the spectacle of life, not life itself. I must begin all over again.

24th April

The frenzy for self-destruction has to be felt. I am not talking of a suicide. People like ourselves—in love with life, enjoying the unexpected and the pleasures of human intercourse—cannot get as far as suicide except through some imprudence. And then suicide seems like one of those mythical acts of heroism, those affirmations, in fables, of the dignity of Man in the face of Destiny, that make interesting statues but have nothing to do with us.

The self-destroyer is a different type, more despairing but more practical. He has a compulsion to discover every fault, every baseness in his own nature; then he views these tendencies so leniently that they become mere nothings. He looks for more, enjoys them, finds them intoxicating. He is more sure of himself than any conqueror of the past, and he knows that the thread connecting him with tomorrow, with the potentialities of life, with a prodigious future, is a stronger cable—when it comes to the ultimate strain—than any faith or integrity.

The self-destroyer is, above all, a comedian and his own patron. He never misses an opportunity to listen to himself and prove himself. He is an optimist, hoping for everything from life. He cannot endure solitude. But he lives in constant peril that one day, all unawares, he will be seized with a craze for creating something or setting everything in proper order. Then he suffers unceasingly and may even kill himself.

Consider this point carefully: nowadays, suicide is just a way of disappearing. It is carried out timidly, quietly, and falls flat. It is no longer an action, only a submission.

Who knows whether an optimistic suicide will come back to the world again?

To express an inward tragedy in an art form, and so purge himself of it, is something that can be achieved only by an artist who, even while living through his tragedy, was already putting forth sensitive feelers and weaving his delicate threads of construction; who in short, was already incubating his creative ideas. There can be no such thing as living through the storm in a state of frenzy and then liberating pent-up emotions in a work of art as an alternative to suicide. How true that is can be seen from the fact that artists who really have killed themselves because of some tragedy that happened to them are usually trivial songsters, lovers of sensation, who never, in their lyrical effusions, even hint at the deep cancer that is gnawing them. From which one learns that the only way to escape from the abyss is to look at it, measure it, sound its depths and go down into it.

To suffer an injustice gives one a bracing shock—like a winter morning. It restores to the highest pitch our exhilaration and joy of living, gives us back a sense of our importance in relation to things, flatters us, while to suffer from mere mischance is humiliating. I have experienced it, and wish the injustice, the ingratitude, had been even greater. That's living, and to learn it at the age of twenty-eight is hardly precocious.

Speaking of humility. Only very rarely does one suffer a real out-and-out injustice. Our own actions are so tortuous. In general, it always turns out that we are a little at fault ourselves, and then—good-bye to the feeling of a winter's morning.

A little at fault? It's all our fault and there's no getting away from it. Always.

The knife thrust may be dealt you heedlessly or in jest by someone who lacks perception, but that does not lessen your sufferings. Rather it makes them more excruciating, by leading you to brood over the casualness of the blow and your own responsibility for not having foreseen it. I imagine it would be a comfort to know that the one who wounded you was stricken with remorse, that she *attached some importance to the matter?* Such comfort cannot come from anything except one's need not to be alone, the desire to tighten the bonds between one's true self and other people. Furthermore, if her remorse was for having hurt, not me in particular, but only a man considered as a fellow creature, would I wish for such remorse? Then the essential thing is that I myself, not the man in me, should be given recognition, compassion and love.

And does it not open the field to another, long-lasting torture, remembering that she who wounded me is *not* unthinking, heedless or flippant? Remembering that she is usually serious-minded, understanding and highly strung? and that it is only as far as I am concerned that she takes things lightly?

Not only does she *not* regret having hurt me, as an individual, but she feels pleased about it, precisely because I am the one involved. That would be nothing more than a method of humanizing the situation, and I am opposed to doing so. Better and better.

25th April

Today, nothing.

26th April

There is, too, the type of man who, the more he is cast down and should be thinking only of getting on his feet again, thinks of flying and finds exaltation in that thought.

That, primarily, arises from a love of contrasts and the habit of self-contemplation. Only a man whose vice is considering himself as another person—a most important person—can, while suffering or preoccupied, grow exhilarated, instead, at the thought of pleasure and freedom.

A man who has lived with an ideal for twelve years—especially a secret ideal, inevitably finds his character affected by it. Of all the monstrous things in the world, the habit of following an ideal is the ugliest. One can recover from anything else, but not from that. It may be possible to change the direction of the ideal, but nothing more.

How fortunate it is that of all spiritual habits—passion, distortion, complacency, serenity and so on—the only one that endures is calm. It will return.

One must go very gently when communicating psychological discoveries about potent forms of depravity to someone whom one does not know to be that sort of person, for the first victim of such a course will be the well-meaning discoverer. The old story of Perillos and the bull.

The man who lets a woman know her potential influence, will be the first she will make a cuckold. That is mathematically certain. That's it exactly, *mathematically*.

When a woman wants to make a fool of a man, what better way can she find than to take him out of his own environment, dress him up in ridiculous clothes, expose him to unfamiliar circumstances, and every now and then find other things to do herself, things that the man does not know how to do? Not only does she make a fool of him in the eyes of the world, but, and this is important to a woman, the most rational animal in existence, she convinces herself that it suits him to be a fool, and so her conscience is clear. With aptitude and experience she (incredibly) gets to the stage of being able to prearrange facts and events to her liking, without compromising her own principles of ethical behavior.

27th April

He says: "She told me, one day, how she would have treated me. We were at that uneasy stage when nothing had happened, but was likely to. I made her talk about her past, so eager was I to know all I could about her, to amplify my daydreams.

"She was talking of a nice young man who made a pass at her in a train. She described him as common and persistent, and without much trouble she infatuated him. With words and actions. (She went on a trip with me, too.) Then she broke off, giving him a false name.

"And the young man had written asking her to marry him."

28th April

"I notice you like to have things clear, sir, a credit to your good taste, I'm sure. But you should remember, sir, that once things are clear, they are soon digested and then appetite returns. Much better to chew something solid, trying to find a succulent morsel in it somewhere. That way, you make hope last longer."

Why worry? I'm back as I was in '29, writing idle poetry, troubled because I cannot work, alone and unhappy in the midst of life, wandering aimlessly, infuriated by all I see going on around me. What is missing? My seven vanished years?

Bah! Has youth ever counted for anything, in the sort of work I do? And if those seven years were not lost, if they had turned out well, if, that is, I had composed lasting poetry, worked with satisfaction, married and settled down, enjoyed watching the spectacle of the general public—if that's how things had gone, should I be any better off? Would it have been worth the trouble? Should I be any happier, sitting here now at this table?

And, if you reply that I should be happy to be tied down, to have responsibilities, isn't that a pointless thing to say, since a man can have responsibilities all the time, if he wants them?

Then am I only sorry about her? The woman who made a fool of me? But, if nothing else has changed, what more does she stand for than a commonplace, sentimental delusion?

Young man, stop brooding over losing her as if it were a great disaster. It is no such thing. We are as we were before; we have burned up seven years and enjoyed some happy times. We must begin again, but without whining, and remember that there is no reason why we should not do the same again with another seven years. But who told you life was to be enjoyed? My boy, we still have childish illusions.

But, if it is true that this sort of thing happens to all men, how is it that old men do not seem overwhelmed, driven crazy, broken by life; that, on the contrary, they all look so tranquil?

The only understandable thing is why dead men rot, with all that poison inside them.

1st May

That poetry is born of privation is confirmed by the fact that Greek poetry about the heroes came about when their descendants were driven out of the countries where those heroes lay entombed. (Cf. *Psyche,* I, p. 43.)

5th May

Sin is not one action rather than another, but a whole maladjusted way of life. What is a sin for one, is not for another. The same things—hatred, making a fool of someone, ill-treating them, humbling oneself or being arrogant— are sins for some men, not for others.

To have sinned means that you are convinced that, *in some mysterious way,* what you have done will bring misfortune on you in the future; that it has broken some *mysterious* law of harmony, and is a link in a chain of past and future discords. Living is like working out a long addition sum, and if you make a mistake in the first two totals you will never find the right answer. It means involving oneself in a complicated chain of circumstances.

9th May

Even the comfort that comes from self-abasement, is it a form of voluptuousness or a valid principle?

40

That is to say, do we humble ourselves in order to gain some reaction from the experience, making it a pretext for a gratuitous self-regard (without any moral obligations), or to hew out a new vein of ethical behavior, to seek out, in short, a conscientious level of duties?

That there can be a sort of pleasure in self-humiliation, is a fact. To decide whether one is enjoying it voluptuously or tragically seems impossible.

Fundamentally, since I have found nothing against voluptuousness except that it ruins the man who indulges in it (makes him "suffer uselessly"), that would be sufficient to clarify the question of whether self-humiliation makes one suffer, uselessly or to a lesser degree. And in my own case, how can I get out of my normal habit of testing the legitimacy of whatever state I am in by *whether it is productive or sterile, creatively?* Since, certainly, that standard is false or, at least, inadequate, granted that not everyone can work creatively. For all men, the question of whether suffering is useful or useless must be determined in relation to their whole existence. And if the man concerned happens also to be a creator, that has no bearing at all on his conscience. We are talking now of essentials that get right down to his very roots, deeper than his occupation, class or nationality. But if one takes away this and takes away that, what is left to make one the slave of duties? So I must not exclude my own state as a creator and burrow in the cellar to try and find the cornerstone, but must simply reflect that, besides being a creator, I am also a man, a man who is unemployed, with no political faith, immature and a good many other things that escape me. A fine job it would be to examine the effect of self-humiliation on all those states and find the highest common divisor! And not only in the present, but in all my past. Because, remember, sin is not one action rather than another, but a whole existence maladjusted.

Then is my self-humiliation a sin?

An idea. Just as I could argue about aesthetics only when I had a cluster of my own poems in front of me, and dissected the problems they contained (seen, too, that everything needed to be started afresh), so, now, I shall have to put before me a number of my own ethical actions, think about them and decide which I can do again, and which not; determine their recurring motives, if any (without doubt there are some), and all the rest. The difficulty is to isolate these actions, work on them as I do on every single poem. But, after all, that will be nothing new. It's a little piece of work I have often done already.

16th May

That the public plays a necessary part in the production of a work, is beyond question. Many works are born, nevertheless, without that manifest circle, anxious, unsettled, argumentative, which makes great art.

But their public was not lacking. Simply, the author imagined it, *created* it (which means he defined, chose and loved it). In general, the ancients, up to the period of romanticism, had their circle materially defined; the moderns are distinguished by the absence of such a circle. The ancients revealed their greatness by their instinctive understanding of their true public, other than pedants; the moderns reveal theirs, above all, in the choice and creation of readers they know how to make for themselves.

Note, though, that it is false to think that a writer can make this creation of his own public progressive. That is how, if ever, a material public is created, the concern of the editor or publisher. But the author's *true* public must have been envisaged, complete, from his first work.

6th September

I have discovered a type of man who regards moral responsibilities with deadly seriousness. He instantly takes the view that a moral principle should be upheld even in the face of prison, death, or torture on the wheel, and, terrified by such an obligation, he does not dare to define and obey his own moral principle. Such a man is, in fact, self-indulgent, and has no principles. (Cf. 20th April.)

42

13th September

Among the signs that warn me that my youth is over, the greatest is my realization that literature no longer really interests me. I mean that I no longer open books with that eager, anxious hope of discovering spiritual things which, in spite of everything, I once felt. I do read, and wish I could read still more, but now I do not welcome with enthusiasm, as once I did, the varied experiences to be found in books, or fuse them into a bright, pre-poetic mental tumult. The same thing happens to me when I stroll through Turin: I no longer feel aware of the city as a romantic, symbolic goad to creative effort. "That's been done already" is my reaction, every time.

After taking accurately into account the various knocks I have had, all my periods of fury and lassitude and lying fallow, it remains clear that I no longer feel life as a discovery (and consequently poetry that much less), but rather as a cold material for speculation and analysis, as a matter for duties. This is what my life consists of now: politics, practical affairs, all those things one can enjoy from books, but books cannot inspire love, as does the hope of creation.

Now, even from boyhood, I was methodical about ethical matters: once I had found my place as an insatiable seeker I made it my life and brought it to fruition in creation. Now that I have laid aside in earnest this will to create, I perceive that it does not even suffice me to be alive.

It is a grave dilemma: have I been wasting my time till now by concentrating on poetry, or is my present state a prelude to the creation of something deeper, more vital, than before?

14th September

I agree with Berg[1] that racialism and the natural goodness of man are political myths to be judged by what they achieve, but it is dishonest to excuse the recognized philosophical weakness of racialism by the fact that, *now*, we have

[1] Bergson? Ed.

43

also recognized the philosophical weakness of natural goodness. For a myth, to be historically sound, must be believed
in its time; must be the last word of the critics of that period.
Such was natural goodness in the 1700's; racialism is not so
in the 1900's.

15th September

　　If I try to balance up my poetical work, I do not find
in it all these advantages. Leaving aside the glory or discredit
—I examine myself as if I had published nothing—I find
that the world has now lost for me its air of enchantment,
since many things that pleased and satisfied me are now
extinguished in the printed page that reduced them to ashes.
That realization, by showing me the entirely imaginary nature
of my transports and outbursts, my loves and attachments,
has rendered them null and void. I explain: it is not out of
ambition that I am tormented by my love of novelty; it is
very clear to me that those discoveries had no more than a
pre-poetic significance and therefore, once they were trans-
muted into poetry, they had fufilled their function.

　　That was why I maintained that poetic genius ought
to be extremely fertile and last as long as life. Its spirit should
never cease making discoveries to be expressed in poetry, for,
if it stops it reveals, by the mere fact of doing so, that those
few things it has produced did not stem from a temperament
born to discover, but were mere sentimental fancies mistaken
for pre-poetic discoveries.

　　I do not yet know whether I am a poet or a senti-
mentalist, but one thing is certain. These months of anguish
are the decisive test. If, as I hope, even the greatest seekers
after truth have passed through months like this, then the joy
of achievement is dearly bought. Life avenges itself in no
uncertain manner if anyone usurps its functions. The agony
of composition—that famous torment—is nothing, compared
to the mental anguish of having finished composing and not
knowing what to do next.

　　Lévy-Bruhl's book, *Mythologie Primitive*, allows one

to suppose that the primitive mentality thinks of reality as a continuous interchange of qualities and essences, like an everlasting ebb and flow in which a man may become a banana or a bow or a wolf and vice versa (but the bow could not become a wolf, for example). Then poetry (images) is born as a simple description of this reality (the god is not *like* the shark, but *is* the shark), and as a matter of anthropocentric interest.

In short, the images (and that is what concerns me!) would not be a play of expression, but positive description. In its origins, of course. As for anthropocentricism, I never doubted it.

2nd October

Finally, something positive. My hatred of noisy crowds, my disgust at spiteful actions, the remorse I feel for my conventional hesitation and timidity in the past, all show that I do not lack self-respect and a sense of discretion, qualities that have a certain dignity. Even my searching after poetic truth means the same thing.

Today, however, I much regret that, until now, I have always ignored formal rules of deportment and have not acquired my own style of social behavior but have acted at random, being casual or off-hand, according to my mood and so committing endless faux pas.

Why do women in general have better manners than men? Because they depend for everything upon the formal effect they produce, while men act and think. I must become more ladylike.

13th October

Balzac exposed the great city of Paris as a hotbed of mystery, and his appeal is always to our curiosity. His muse is an urge for finding out. He is never comic or tragic, he is curious. He involves himself in a maze of intricate detail with the air of a man who scents a mystery, promises to unearth it for you, and goes on to reveal the whole mechanism of it, piece by piece, with eager, pungent, triumphant gusto. See how he makes his approach to new characters, listing all that is odd about them, defining, commenting, bringing out their inconsistencies, assuring you of marvels to come. His assessments, observations, tirades, the words he uses, are not psychological truths, but suspicions, tricks of a prosecuting counsel, punches aimed at the mystery that, by God, he *must* solve. When there comes a pause in the mystery hunt, early in the book or in the middle (never at the end, for by then all the mystery is explained), Balzac holds forth about the baffling perplexities of his plot with lyrical enthusiasm, revealing his deep understanding of human relationships and the workings of men's minds. Then he is wonderful. Look at the opening pages of *Ferragus* or the beginning of the second part of *Splendeurs et misères des courtisanes*. He is sublime. He foreshadows Baudelaire.

28th December

One should be able to see what is real from a prison cell, where a man has nothing left to do but think. His company would be only the dregs of society. His occupation, looking at a wall, hearing a voice, breathing the air of heaven. Any man (since any man may find himself in such a place and there is always someone there, even if he is someone else), can get down to the basic substratum of life and examine it in real earnest. Living consists simply of adding various embellishments to this eternal reality.

So one discovers that almost everything one does in life is a pastime, a diversion. The prisoner therefore makes up his mind that, if he ever gets out, he will live like a recluse, savoring his favorite pastime and obtaining the utmost satisfaction he can from it—*a resolve all prisoners make*.

The point is that reality is a prison, where, in just the same way, one vegetates and always will. All the rest—thought, action—is just a pastime, mental or physical. What counts then, is to come to grips with reality. The rest can go.

If you are alone, as once you were, you cannot even indulge in the pastime of thoughts and words, but must be like a tree, doing nothing but living. Here (I repeat) is the drama: avoid thinking aloud; stop regarding life as a pastime; mourn all the rest in silence; and find exaltation in raging against reality. Inward segregation is always possible for any man.

1937

8th January

Mistakes are always initial.

13th January

I vecchi e i giovani[1] is a mistake as a novel because, crammed with antecedent events and social or political explanations that should have made of it a moral poem with ideas about the structure of life and dramatic development, it is, instead, broken up into figures whose inner law is solitude, and makes each one of them end up—with the logic of solitude—in madness, apathy, suicide or unheroic death. They are all warped by some eccentricity, some inner habit of thought, that tends to express itself in monologue or in little peculiarities.

The story lacks a rhythm of alternating prose passages and dialogue; and there is no *semblance* of solitude except for each character considered separately; the epic quality of the world of lonely people is missing. Furthermore, each individual character is built up from the outside, composed of antecedents, analyses and outlets in which there is no harmony; one feels that the author sacrifices, with calculated logic, many things in order to justify the *moments* when the lonely one reaches a climax and expresses himself, sometimes very effectively.

[1] A novel by Pirandello, published in 1913. Ed.

The proof that it was essentially composed in cold blood lies in the style, lucid, as polished as glass, even though now and then it has colorful, passionate outbursts. And those, too, are calculated, carefully reasoned.

17th January

The more a man becomes involved in an emotion, the more do chance events, impersonal in themselves, turn out to his disadvantage. The very fact that they are impersonal leads him into false conclusions, so tense and eager is he. An ambitious man will suffer because some celebrity failed to recognize and speak to him; wishing to enliven his conversation with an evangelical type of man, he will hint at his own conscientious scruples, scruples that make him look a fool in the opinion of a sturdy individualist who unluckily overhears them. Envy, ambition's reverse side, lies at the root of every pang he suffers. He finds it intolerable that a thing can happen impersonally, by chance, without human intervention.

Any fervor, no matter what, brings with it the tendency to feel there is a predetermined law in life, a law which punishes those who abuse or ignore that particular fervor. A state of passion—even the intoxication of absolute self-determination—can so change the very structure and spirit of one's universe that any set-back seems to imply a breakdown of the vital balance of that all-pervading passion. Then, depending on his temperament, a man feels either that he has gone too far in his zeal or fallen short. Usually he feels he has been *deliberately* punished by the law of that passion, and of the universe. Which is as much as to say that every form of zeal or passion brings with it a superstitious conviction of having to face a day of reckoning. Even the zeal of a disbeliever.

28th January

Any misfortune is either due to error, not bad luck, or it arises out of our own culpable inadequacy. And since an error is our own fault, we should not blame anyone but ourselves for any misfortune. So now you can cheer up.

18th June

      1. A rabble—a priest—speeches (Afternoon).

      2. Flight—the street—the sound of a whistle (Dusk).

      3. Investigation—the priest at prayer.

      4. The woman and the priest (In the dead of night).

      5. (Morning) Investiture—Return.

3rd August

A woman, unless she is an idiot, sooner or later meets a piece of human wreckage and tries to rescue him. She sometimes succeeds. But a woman, unless she is an idiot, sooner or later finds a sane, healthy man and makes a wreck of him. She always succeeds.

27th September

The reason why women have always been "bitter as death," sinks of iniquity, faithless jades, Delilahs, is, fundamentally, simply this. A man, unless he is a eunuch, can always achieve ejaculation with any woman. But women hardly ever experience this joyous liberation, and then not with just any man, often not with the man they love, simply because they love him. If once they know it, they dream of nothing else, and because of their (legitimate) longing for this moment of ecstasy they are ready to commit any wickedness. They are *driven* to it. It is the fundamental tragedy of life, and a man who ejaculates too soon had better never have been born. It is a failing that makes suicide worth while.

30th September

The only women worth the trouble of marrying are those a man cannot trust enough to marry.

But this is the most terrible thing: the art of living consists in not letting our loved ones know the pleasure it gives us to be with them, otherwise they leave us.

31st October

One stops being a child when one realizes that telling one's trouble does not make it better.

6th November

The worst thing a suicidal type of man can do is not killing himself, but thinking of it and not doing it. Nothing is more abject than the state of moral disintegration that inspires the idea—the habitual idea—of suicide. Responsibility, conscience, strength of mind, all drift aimlessly about in that dead sea, submerged or brought to the surface again by any chance current.

The real failure is not the man who does not succeed in great things—who ever has?—but in little things, making a home, keeping a friend, keeping a woman happy, earning his living like anyone else. He is the most miserable failure.

9th November

The repetition in my new poems is not for reasons of harmony but of construction. Notice how the key phrases in them are always in the present, and the others converge towards it even when they are in the past. I mean that in these poems I happened to seize upon an actual reality, not narrative but evocative, *in which something takes place in the imagery,* takes place *now,* in so far as the image is at this moment being elaborated by the thought, is seen to be in action, thrusting its roots down into reality.

The word or phrase that is repeated is nothing else but the mainspring of this image, constructed from top to bottom like a scaffolding, the pivot enabling the imagination to revolve on itself and sustain itself like a gyroscope which exists only *in the present,* while it is in action, and then falls and becomes just a bit of iron.

13th November

With petty, self-important men, there always comes a moment when you can make them pay for their greatness by

50

saying to them: "You are an important man, so I will not venture to trust my life to you."

When a man mourns for someone who has played him false, it is not for love of her, but for his own humiliation at not having deserved her trust.

16th November

Surely all his destiny is revealed when a child of three, while being dressed, wonders anxiously how he will manage to dress himself when he is grown up, he who does not know how?

To *possess* something or someone, we must not surrender ourselves to it completely or lose our heads; in short, we must remain superior to it. But it is a law of life that we can enjoy only what we can give ourselves up to completely. Those who invented the love of God were pretty shrewd; there is nothing else we can possess and enjoy at the same time.

17th November

Every woman longs for a man friend to confide in, to fill the empty hours when the one she loves is away; she insists that this friend does not affect her love for the absent one; she takes offense if he makes any demand that might interfere with her love; but if that friend grows cautious and keeps his words and glances under control, with the sole object of saving himself further suffering, then the woman— any woman—immediately does her best to increase her hold upon him so that she can watch him suffer. And she does not even realize she is doing it.

Remember, writing poetry is like making love: one will never know whether one's own pleasure is shared.

It is amazing that the woman you love may tell you her days are empty and unbearable, but yet she has no wish to know what yours are like.

The recompense for having suffered so is that then one dies like a dog.

Great poets are rare, like great lovers. Flights of fancy, frenzy, dreams, are not enough; one needs something better: good, hard balls. Otherwise called an Olympian gaze.

20th November

All that I could concede to "pure poetry" results from the ecstatic unification of all poetry in the instant of contemplation. Oratory fails, lacking a framework of intricate thought. The whole will resolve itself in a blaze of light fired by those various thoughts, those interwoven sensations. The *image-story* was just this. Only, it was *one* story made out of one single verb (he killed, smoked, drank, rejoiced, etc.). The problem is how to get out of the simple statement and write complete sentences.

Will it be so in the actual novel? Substitute for the concatenation of facts an inner prospect? Revert to the idea of presenting thought in motion?

The most ordinary and banal method of *narrating thought* is to set up a figure that builds itself up as it goes along, with its own past and future. The little old man in *Semplicità*. The god-man in *Mito*. The prostitute in *Puttana contadina*. The scheme of these poems is a compromise between the position of the characters and the fanciful logic of the material from which they are made. I do not record only their essence, nor do I record only my own flights of imagination. It is always doubtful whether they think for themselves or whether I think for them. I am interested in their experiences as well as in my own fanciful logic. But let us be clear: my logic is a means, a method of bringing their experiences into being. The "discovery of points of contact, making that the very plot of my story" would thus seem to be an illusion.

Let us be clear: in the back of my mind I do not tolerate that the plot shall be the discovery of contacts. Even in ecstasies the means is not the end. In practice, no one can tell his own style: style is, by definition, something that one employs for a purpose.

When style becomes an end in itself, it will become something objective, a situation, and one does not see why it should have more dignity than any other matter in the world of narrative.

Of the cousin in *Mari del Sud,* I said he was doing one thing and another, while of the country prostitute I say that in the morning there returns to her, invoked by her surroundings (scents, sunlight, limbs, bed) a longing for her childhood, and it is on this postulation that the deeply significant finale depends.

Of the hermit in *Primo Paesaggio,* too, I said that he was doing one thing and another, but the innovation, compared to *Mari del Sud,* was that the things he did had objective imaginative connections. It is only with the "I" of *Gente Spaesata* that I begin to say that the character thinks in terms of an imaginative complex, and this train of thought is the subject of the story.

So the *image-story* is born of the "I" character (cf. especially the "I" who is the little boy in *Mari,* and who, in his little way, is already a person of whom less is said about what he does than about what he thinks). This is the point: the "I" concealed in *Dio caprone,* the "I" of *Mania di solitudine* and the "I" of *Pensieri di Dina* all confirm it: the "I" who relates his own thought has created the method for the ensuing poems in the third person, in which the subject is no longer what the character does, but what he thinks. My poetry from then on speaks of the character's complex thought processes within himself. And the fact that the bare thought, starting with the hermit, should have thenceforth blossomed out into sensations has no specific importance.

I was wrong in *Mestiere del poeta,* in stating that with the hermit I made his thought process the subject of the story: with the hermit I for the first time enjoyed dealing with sensations and their connecting links, but the subject was still the events.

So, once this moment of evolution is glimpsed, it is clear why it seemed to me I had to speak of a compromise. If the image story is born empirically out of the situation of an "I" narrating his actions in the form of thoughts (images), objective poems in the third person are a simple transposition into the third person of the time-honored introspective technique. No matter how shrewd or surprising the evocation of the various imaginative complexes (the *image-story*) may be, it becomes clear that the subject is not *the logical or imaginative thought process of a particular mind,* but *what that mind thinks and feels.* Not the style, but the content. A conclusion so banal that it seems stupid.

Let us be extremely clear: to get a true account of a train of thought I should have to evoke the inner consciousness of someone who meditates on his ways of thinking. And that does not seem a great subject.

The truth of the saying: "Renounce the world, and the world will give you more than you know what to do with," lies in this. Having renounced everything, the tiniest things left to you assume gigantic importance. It is, in short, a way of getting the utmost savor out of trifles you would normally overlook.

There is this, too. For other people, the value of the things they deny us is indicated largely by our eagerness to possess them. We only have to look in another direction and the owners of those things immediately feel they are not worth keeping, so they throw them after us.

So much for worldly wisdom. If the phrase is intended to refer to some mystical teaching, so much the worse for mysticism. What if God puts a value on His creations according to whether we desire them more or less? A God with an inferiority complex? Who would ever have thought it?

21st November

If it is true that one gets used to suffering, how is it that as the years go by one always suffers more?

No, they are not mad, those people who amuse themselves, enjoy life, travel, make love, fight—they are not mad. We should like to do the same ourselves.

If hammering away at things always brings success, why not in this, too?

To think that that body has thoughts, reawakening, repose, relaxation, a daily routine! If I were that man I should really have all that, in the next room or under my eyes. The day would end with her. This, this is what I have lost, and no human power can give it back to me. And all that has been thrown away, without love. It is not a crime, not a sin, not even misbehavior: just one of those little things one does, with no more compunction than killing a fly.

Look on the bright side! There *is* a moral law.

23rd November

The only joy in the world is to begin. It is good to be alive because living is beginning, always, every moment. When this sensation is lacking—as when one is in prison, or ill, or stupid, or when living has become a habit—one might as well be dead.

That is why, when a painful situation is repeated identically, or *seems* identical, the horror is overwhelming.

This is not, however, the principle of a *bon viveur*. For experience at any cost, like senseless traveling at all costs, is more a matter of habit than any ordinary way of life accepted as a duty and lived with intelligence and enjoyment. I am convinced that habit plays a larger part in casual love affairs than in a good marriage. In an affair, one always keeps certain mental reservations as a form of self-defense, hence there is no such thing as a good, completely satisfying love affair. To find it good, one must surrender oneself to it unreservedly: in short, marriage. Even marriages made in heaven.

A man who does not feel this sensation of always starting afresh that animates normal married life is, in reality, a fool. Whatever he may say, he would find nothing fresh in a new love affair.

It is the same lesson as always: plunge headlong into whatever you do, and learn to bear the pain. It is better to suffer from having dared to try, than from shirking the ordeal. As children know: it is their nature to do so, and to hang back is a disgrace. In the end, as you see, you pay a higher price.

25th November

Moral law serves to keep us from injuring ourselves, not to give protection to others. Only *charity* can tell us what harm we do to others by carrying out our duty. That is seen not only in matters of love, but in the whole of life. What a great ideal it would be to ask every man, unceasingly, tirelessly, what is troubling him, penalizing or torturing him, and comfort him, embrace him, kindle him afresh.

But every man means all men, all the time, and that one cannot do. It is impossible, for the very reason that there would always be at least one man who would not have that comfort, that embrace—oneself. For one thing is certain: to see a man made happy, even through our own effort, is not enough to give us peace. (Consider, for example, unsatisfied women.)

This may seem a mixture of the sacred and profane, but is not. Life begins in the body.

I write . . . have pity. And then?

Never again take anything seriously that does not depend on you alone. Like love, friendship and glory.

And those things that do depend on you alone, does it much matter whether you take them seriously or not? Who is to know anything about it? For, if you are alone, there is no who: even "I" becomes meaningless. Better and better.

26th November

Why do we forget the dead? Because they are no longer any use to us. Just as we forget, or push into the background, someone who is ill or bowed down with grief, because, physically or mentally, they have nothing to give us. No one will ever devote himself to you except for what he will get out of it.

And you? I believe I did once feel wholehearted, disinterested devotion. Then I should not weep at losing the object of my devotion, for if I do I am no longer disinterested.

Yet, seeing the suffering it entails, the sacrifice is

against nature. Or greater than I can bear. I cannot help grieving. But to grieve is to yield to the way of the world, and recognize that I was seeking some personal advantage. But is there anyone who can renounce something he could have? Such charity is simply idealizing impotence.

That's enough of virtuous indignation. If I had had the fangs and the cunning, I should have captured the prey.

But that does not make the cross of having been deceived, of failure, of being myself, any less painful to bear. After all, the most famous person crucified was a god: not deceived, not vanquished. And yet, with all his omnipotence, he cried: "Eli." But then he went on to resurrection and triumph, as he knew he would, beforehand. On those terms, who would not be willing to be crucified?

So many men have died in despair. And those suffered more than Christ.

But the real, tremendous truth is this: suffering serves no purpose whatever.

All men have a cancer that gnaws them, a daily discharge, a recurring evil: their own dissatisfaction; the point of conflict between their real, skeletal being and the infinite complexity of life. And all men realize it, sooner or later, by slow perception or a sudden flash of insight. Almost all men, it seems, can retrace, in their childhood, the signs foreshadowing their adult agony. To investigate this hotbed of retrospective discoveries, alarming as they prove to be, is to see the sufferings of the grown man predicted by the irreparable acts and words of his infancy. *I Fioretti* of the Devil. Contemplate this horror always: what has been, will be.

28th November

In love, all that counts is having a woman in one's home, in one's bed. All the rest is a pack of nonsense, pernicious nonsense.

The most commonplace kind of love is fed by what one does not know about the loved one. But what can surpass a love based on what one does know?

The truth is that I always arrive at a point three or four years after my contemporaries: hence my habit of clinging desperately, if wrongly, to the verities I have discovered for myself.

A proof of *vanitas vanitatum:* we are each so interested in ourselves, yet it is only by chance that we are ourselves and not someone else. I could have been born a woman and become a maidservant, and then, what problems?

Is it not a mere illusion, too, how important we think we are when any attention is centered on us, whether we are a servant girl or any member of the whole human race? *A person of vast interest.*

Is it not tragic, the fact that everyone with a religious faith is a little ridiculous? If there were only one faith, that could not happen. The great, the fearful irony of life is that at any moment we could be fools. That is a thing all men dread: one would rather be a louse than an imbecile. The old story. The reason is that every imbecile is also a louse, and not vice versa. A prudent louse is conceivable, but could there be a prudent imbecile? For a moment, possibly, but the whole year long? The life of an imbecile is always made up of lousy tricks, because his stupidity leads him into situations he cannot escape from, except by violating the rules of the social game.

I know an idiot who refused to learn the rules of the game when he was young, lost as he was in fantasies. Now the fantasies are vanishing and the game is shattering him.

Problem: woman, is she the prize of the strong or the prop of the weak, depending on how the men want her?

The irony of life: woman gives herself as a prize to the weak and as a prop to the strong. And no man ever has what he should have.

29th November

Shouldn't it surprise me, on some morning of mist and sunshine to think that whatever I have had was a gift, a great gift? That out of the nothingness of my ancestors, that hostile nothingness, I emerged and grew all by myself, with all my bad and good qualities, and, by dint of hard work and toughness, overcoming all sorts of hazards, I became what I am today, a living, vigorous man? And then to meet that one woman, she herself another miracle brought out of nothingness by the workings of chance! The joy I have known with her, and the pain, what was it but a gift, a great gift?

30th November

Every critic is really a woman at the critical age, spiteful and repressed.

A man has committed murder. Ignore for a moment his dread that someone may come, his anxiety as to how he will face the world, his terror at the thought of the whole world up in arms against him. Leave out of it his worry about getting away and going on as if nothing has happened. Take it that he is certain to escape. Does there not still remain an abyss of horror: the realization that his victim, whether loved or hated, *no longer exists,* can never more be something to love or hate? The agony of having to start life over again, for with the death of our victim, we, too, have died! The unforeseen sinking of our own vitality, for, if this was in truth a crime of passion, our life was once identified with that of our victim!

I can never think of death without shuddering at this idea of mine. Death will necessarily come, from ordinary causes. It is inevitable, and one's whole life is a preparation for it, an event as natural as the fall of raindrops. I cannot resign myself to that thought. Why not seek death of one's own free will, asserting one's right to choose, giving it some significance? Instead of passively letting it happen? Why not?

Here's the reason. One always puts off the decision, feeling (or hoping) that one more day, one more hour of life, might also prove an opportunity of asserting our freedom of choice, which we should lose by seeking death. In short, because one thinks—and I speak for myself—that there is plenty of time. So the day of natural death comes, and we have missed the great opportunity of performing, *for a specific reason,* the most important act in life.

A love thought: I love you so much that I could wish I had been born your brother, or had brought you into the world myself.

1st December

I should be perfectly happy if it were not for the fleeting pain of trying to probe the secret of that happiness, so as to be able to find it again tomorrow and always. But perhaps I am confused and my happiness lies in that pain. Once more I find myself hoping that, tomorrow, the memory will suffice.

2nd December

Today you have talked too much.

4th December

Practical-minded people always have a sense of humor. The man who turns his back on life, absorbed in his naïve contemplation (and all contemplation is naïve), does not view things as being detached from himself, endowed with their own free, complex and diversified movement due to their individual origins. Contemplation, by its very nature, dwells on the lively, sentimental impressions inspired in us by the things we come across. Hence the excuse all contemplative people make: they live in touch with things, and so, necessarily, do not feel they are odd or singular; they simply *feel* them and that is all. Practical men—and this is a paradox— live detached from things, not feeling things, just understanding how they work. Unless a man is detached from something, he cannot laugh at it. There is a tragedy implicit in this: when you have fully mastered a thing you draw away from it and consequently lose interest in it. Hence the breathless pursuit of something fresh.

Naturally, no one is wholly contemplative or wholly practical, for one cannot experience everything in life. Even the most efficient people have something they are sentimental about.

You have trusted your life to a single hair; don't struggle, or you will break it.

Ingenuousness has a craft of its own, derived from its very simplicity: "You are such a fool that nobody opposes you." Under a variety of curious devices, an *all-pervading* air of stupidity is the best policy.

5th December

The mistake sentimentalists make is not in believing that "tender affections" exist, but in laying claim to those affections in the name of their own tender nature. Only harsh and resolute natures have the knowledge and ability to surround themselves with tender affection and they—tragically— are least able to enjoy them.

Understand clearly, once and for all, that to be in love is a personal matter which does not concern the beloved object, even if you are loved in return. Symbolic words and gestures are exchanged, in that event, but each reads his own feelings into them and supposes, by analogy, that the other feels the same. But there is no reason, no necessity, why the two should coincide. It calls for a special art to receive and interpret these symbols favorably, and arrange your own life accordingly in a satisfactory way. All one can do to the other is to proffer these symbols and cherish the illusion that they are reciprocated. But at the back of one's mind there must be a reservation, a practical device: a decision to make use of this offering (made by the loved one for his or her own satis- faction) to satisfy one's own needs. A man clever enough to correlate these reactions will never be troubled by vicissitudes, for he can arrange everything to his own advantage and create a world of crystal in which to enjoy his beloved. But he will never forget that this crystal ball is a vacuum, and will take care not to break it by any inept attempt to intro- duce air. Raptures, renunciations, children, trust, devotion, these are personal symbols from which the air—the mystical intrusion of one's partner in love—must always be excluded. Between these symbols and reality there is the same connection as between words and things. One must be astute to give them their due significance without mistaking them for the real stuff of life. Therein lies the solitude every man knows, cold and immutable.

7th December

If it were true that man has freedom of choice, would he talk so much about it? Who can say this is not merely an assumption? In some things one can be free, if one so wishes; in others, one is bound by the effects of previous action. But the initial choice?

A man who has not come up against the barrier of some physical impossibility that affects his whole life (impotence, dyspepsia, asthma, imprisonment, etc.) does not know what suffering is. In fact, such causes bring him to a decision of renouncement: a despairing attempt to make a virtue out of what is, in any case, inevitable. Could anything be more contemptible?

A man who feels no temptation because he does not do that sort of thing, is in a fine position; not so the one who is tempted, but renounces it. In realistic terms, the first is peace, the second, torture. Whatever heroes may say, it is stupid to suffer.

Before being shrewd about others, you must learn to be shrewd with yourself. There is an art in so arranging things that the sin we commit becomes virtuous to our conscience. Any woman can teach you that art.

The art of making oneself loved consists of tergiversation, irritation, disgust, miserly little concessions that seem wonderfully sweet on the surface, but which bind the unlucky fellow like double ropes; but at the bottom of his heart and instinct they inspire and foster a furious resentment that expresses itself in scorn and a fierce determination to be avenged. To make slaves is bad policy, as we have seen before and will again.

62

The usual tragedy: only the man who can make himself hated can make himself loved—*by the same woman.*

Youth ends when we perceive that no one wants our gay abandon. And the end may come in two ways: the realization that other people dislike it, or that we ourselves cannot continue with it. Weak men grow older in the first way, the strong in the second. I was among the first group. Oh, well! Make the best of it!

A true man, in our day, cannot reserve his opinion as to the *inevitability* of war. Either he is an out-and-out pacifist or a ruthless warmonger; saint or butcher. How we have fallen!

Why is it inadvisable to lose your self-control? Because then you are sincere.

11th December

It is not true that chastity is sexually alluring, for, if it were, women would be avid for young novices and newly ordained priests, who may be supposed to take their vows seriously. Instead, women go for elderly swine, men with plenty of experience, bald-headed and bad-tempered.

And you, too. You have never dreamed of nuns, have you?

13th December

Try to do someone a good turn. You will soon see how you will hate his radiant, grateful face.

15th December

That life is one long fight for existence is very plain from the sexual relationship between men and women, in which, in spite of all the restraint of chivalrous ideals, in spite of social insistence on conformity and obedience to convention, *in spite of everything,* it inevitably happens that a partner who fails to provide the longed-for thrill of liberation will be rejected.

And one can understand the innate, ravening loneliness in every man, seeing how the thought of another man consummating the act with a woman—any woman—becomes a nightmare, a disturbing awareness of a foul obscenity, an urge to stop him, or, if possible, destroy him. Can one really endure that another man—any man—should commit with any woman the *act of shame?* Noooo. Yet this is the central activity of life, beyond question. See the falsity of all our altruism. However saintly we may be, it disgusts and offends us to know that another man is screwing.

16th December

Cursed be the man who "mingles frankness with the things of love." The same thing applies to the things of art. The reason is that art and the sexual life stem from the same root.

Yet, just as a great artist is one who constructs, amorally, a sound and moral world, a great lover is one who brings an extraordinary moral intensity to each and every one of his erotic worlds. The artist is always sincere with himself, on pain of failure in his work. The great lover, the same, on pain of not *feeling* his love.

17th December

First love: "when we are grown up, we shall be able to say these things to women."

18th December

There is something even sadder than falling short of one's own ideals: to have realized them.

22nd December

Each of your stories is a combination of figures moved by the same passion expressed in different ways in their individual titles. *Notte di festa,* celebrating the festival of the Saint; *Terra d'esilio,* all men imprisoned; *Primo amore,* all men moved by the discovery of sex. I am speaking of the long stories. The short ones strike you as the least realistic.

Your real muse, in prose, is dialogue, because in it you can express the absurd-ingenuous-mythical outpourings that cunningly interpret reality. Which you could not do in poetry.

23rd December

The child who passes his days and nights among men and women, knowing vaguely but not believing that this is reality, troubled, in short, that sex should exist at all, does he not foreshadow the man who spends his time among men and women, knowing, believing that this is the only reality, suffering atrociously from his own mutilation? This feeling that my heart is being torn out and plunged into the depths, this giddiness that rends my breast and shatters me, is something I did not experience even when I was befooled in April.

The fate reserved for me (like the rat, my boy!) was to let the scar heal over, and then (with a breath, a caress, a sigh) to have it torn open again and a new infection added.

Neither deception nor jealousy have ever given me this *vertigo of the blood*. It took impotence, the conviction that no woman ever finds pleasure with me, or ever would. We are as we are; hence this anguish. If nothing else, I can suffer without feeling ashamed: my pangs are no longer those of love. But this, in very truth, is pain that destroys all energy: if one is not really a man, if one must mix with women without being able to think of possessing them, how can one sustain one's spirits and vital power? Could a suicide be better justified?

To accord with such a dreadful thought, it is right that I should have this terrible sensation of being crushed, annihilated, in my breast, my muscles, my inmost heart. So far, it lasts only for an instant, but what of the day when it will last longer? When it will endure for an hour or all day long?

25th December

With love or with hate, but always with violence.

Going to prison is nothing: coming back from it is frightful.

The average man ought to be well disciplined, not a street-loafer. I am neither the one nor the other.

There is something sadder than growing old—remaining a child.

If screwing was not the most important thing in life, Genesis would not have started with it.

Naturally, everybody says to you "What does it matter? That's not the only thing. Life is full of variety. A man can be good for something else," but no one, not even the men; will look at you unless you radiate that power. And the women say to you: "What does it matter," and so on, but they marry someone else. And to marry means building a whole life, a thing you will never do. Which shows you have remained a child too long.

If you got on so badly with her, who was everything you dreamed of, with whom could you ever get on well?

Do you remember your dreams of workmen's bright little houses; those woodland walks above a meadow; your city, cold below the mountains; the red neon signs facing you across the piazza; your Sunday strolls towards this piazza, over the cobbles; and then your heart-rending dream of Piedmontese-international friendships, of girls who live alone and work for their living, the charm and serenity of the common way of life; and then all the poems you wrote in that first year. Are all those things destroyed for ever by what happened on 9th April? All your youth, spent in the cinema and the Piazza Statuto? Dead, utterly dead?

Do you remember how, at Brancaleone, you were always thinking of the Piazza Statuto?

It had to happen to you, to concentrate your whole life on one point, and then discover that you can do anything except live at that point.

After all, today is the 25th. And she is in the mountains. There was one 25th when she did not go there. Really?

What good is there in living with others, when each man scorns the things that are really important to any other individual?

To be pleasing to men, one has to profess what each of those men, in his secret being, views with repulsion and hatred.

Sincerely. I would rather die than hear from her like this. Now, truly, I wish I believed in God, to be able to pray to Him that she will live, that nothing will happen to her, that it is all a dream, that there will still be a tomorrow. Far better if I were the one to disappear.

One woman can teach you more than a hundred.

30th December

Why should I give up? In this past year, 1937, I have recovered from the ruin of 1936; the awful collapse ('35—'36) has become merely a crisis encountered on the road to maturity. Oddly enough, I have again found a love that may last a while, that has touched the depths of my heart; again I have sought to express myself in poetry, and succeeded with *La vecchia ubriaca;* acquired a sound reputation with a certain journal as a thoughtful critic; written several novels, all significant and promising—one of them outstanding. I have regained a sense of the rhythm of creation.

Translated four books for 6,200 *lire*, done a good deal of teaching and found a sequence of pupils. I have hopes of doing as much in 1938.

This is hardly the moment to look ahead, for war may break out and blow us all up. That would be a fine stroke of cosmic irony. Provided that stupid farce does not happen I can answer for myself, and for her, and for everything.

And in this present year my long and secret shame has been straightened out. In that other year, 1934, there was a 13th August. Yet I am still alive. Isn't it a miracle?

There is only one vice, *desire,* which some call ambition, others lust. Genesis, in its obscurity, propounds original sin as an act of ambition that could be interpreted as lust. The tragic thing in life is that good and evil have the same motive force, desire, but colored in different ways. Like colors seen at night, that can be distinguished only by instinct or from prior knowledge, never by clear perception. The charm and thrill of vice is the same tremor of excitement we get from seeing a color at night, taking it to be one thing and then finding it to be something different.

We handle masses of indeterminate color, often thinking one is red when it is blue and always agitated as soon as we try to tell one from another. The tragedy of well-meaning people is the tragedy of a little man gathering all the blue he can find by the light of dawn, and then, at dusk, groping about in his collection afraid of picking up red, which may, in any case, turn out to be yellow. Conscience is nothing more than a *flair*, trying to recognize a color by the feel of it.

There is this much truth in "art for art's sake": we sit down at our little table and revel in our freedom to produce whatever we choose. The need to obey hidden rules is a salt that adds savor to our choice and induces, out of our inmost soul, our finest work of composition and selection, a creation that springs, quivering and sparkling, from our very conscience. Once the work is finished there comes a sense of detachment and, at bottom, of dissatisfaction. This choice of ours, this composition, is now presented to the outside world. We can no longer change a word of it, but must accept it as a natural reality. We feel like a father, not a lover. We scrutinize our work with cautious curiosity, a slightly hostile anxiety: as if it were a child leaving home.

Is there any man who does not feel a sense of stupefaction and resignation when he sees how far his work falls short of his dream? Or who does not find in it things he did not know?

All your serenity, your altruism, virtue and self-sacrifice fall away from you in the presence of two people, a man and a woman, who you know have screwed each other, or will screw. Their little secret seems improper, insufferable. And if one of them is all you dream of? What then?

To love someone is like saying: "From now on she will think more of my happiness than of her own."

A man who is not jealous even of his mistress's pants, is not really in love.

Is there anything more profound than the childlike action of a lover who sucks the breast of his beloved?

Two things interest you: the technique of love and the technique of art. In both you have met with success, by dint of ingenuity and a clumsy persistence that was not devoid of pleasure. In both you began with heresies, but in both you created a masterpiece or two. But the day will come when you will discover, in art, the disaster you found in love.

(Cf. entry for 20th November, para. 2.) The autobiographical origin of related thought in your poetry is on a par with the autobiographical origin of the objective novel, as you have found in Cellini and Defoe. To present real experiences in the form of an account by a third person is a refinement of technique, but surely it must always (?!) begin with reality as known to the writer, and therefore be autobiographical. As happens in your own novels, too.

Then poetry and the novel must surely spring from the same root as drama? However many characters speak, isn't it the writer speaking?

One banal, complicated variation on this theme is the modern technique of having the different characters in the novel all telling their own life story. (*As I Lay Dying,* Faulkner.)

Hitherto you have made the protagonist speak in the first person, without bothering to characterize him and give him his own mode of expression. Now you must also concern yourself with his individuality, create him as a person, not leave him a neutral version of yourself (and that will be *Volgarità* or *Suicidi*).[1]

Timidity   *Suicidi*
      A woman cashier
         nobly passionate remorse

                                 or

      Timid Streets
A story and its effect   *Volgarità*

[1] The titles of two stories in the volume *Notte di festa,* published posthumously in 1953. Ed.

This Business of Living

(Epigraph:)

> Pour obtenir la moindre rose,
> pour extorquer quelques épis
> des pleurs salés de son front gris
> sans cesse il faut qu'il les arrose.
> L'un est l'Art, et l'autre l'Amour. . . .

La Rançon

1938

3rd January

The real fundamental reason for our incompatibility is that she welcomes things spontaneously, uncritically, eagerly, and her view of their relative importance follows broad, traditional lines. She accepts everything, body and soul, as one should. Look at her frank delight in mountains; the very way she fritters away her days, quite happy to be doing just that; her capacity for giving herself up completely to whatever she has that moment decided to do.

But you have let slip the bonds of harmony between your body and your mind; you live amid contradictions—voluptuous-tragic, craven-heroic, sensual-idealistic—without being master of yourself, merely observing these excessive swings of the pendulum in stunned amazement. Your eyes drank in her beauty while she ate her *brioche*. She wished you all the good in the world, as far as her nature allowed. But to you she is life itself, and death. Yet, of the two of us, she will always be the one to be penalized.

She is sound and well balanced, while you lean all in one direction; she is more stable than you, because you live on thoughts, she on reality, and reality is never unbalanced, never at fault. It is always from the unreasonable partner that harm comes, not from the one who is realistic. I can never, in spite of all that has happened, be victimized by her. She by me, yes, in a thousand ways. But that is cold comfort.

4th January

You, if you plan some act of self-denial, want it to be so intense, so highly individual, that in the end it means nothing to anyone. Don't forget that at your first communion you would not even swallow your spittle so as not to break your fast.

5th January

One cannot change one's nature. You know how simple-minded you used to be, incapable of lying, showing your feelings in the hope that, when shared, they would be more complete. And you think you have changed your tune because now you display gloomy convictions that lying is necessary.

This much is certain: you can have anything in life except a wife to call you "her man." And till now all your life was based on that hope.

The art of living is the art of knowing how to believe lies. The fearful thing about it is that, not knowing what truth may be, we can still recognize a lie.

8th January

There is nothing ridiculous or absurd about a man who is thinking of killing himself being afraid of falling under a car or catching a fatal disease. Quite apart from the question of the degree of suffering involved, the fact remains that to want to kill oneself is to want one's death to be significant, a *supreme* choice, a deed that cannot be misunderstood. So it is natural that no would-be suicide can endure the thought of anything so meaningless as being run over or dying of pneumonia. So beware of draughts and street corners.

15th January

The penalty of a man who allows himself to act against his nature is that when he wants to be natural he no longer can be. The story of Jekyll and Hyde.

All those characters who became famous for their Olympian calm (Shakespeare—Goethe, even Sturani)[1] never acquired their serenity by overcoming tumult, as a reward for some heroic effort. The simple truth is that they were born Olympians and never had to make that effort. If they seem swayed by the tumult of passion, they have a judicious means of coping with it that leaves them immune. This to console you for your own efforts to remain calm. You are not born an Olympian and never will be one. Your efforts are futile, for a man who has once succumbed to turmoil may do so again. It is a problem of engineering. Every bridge has a limited span. Beyond that it would collapse. It is a question of strength. Will power is only the tensile strength of one's own disposition. One cannot increase it by a single ounce.

Your salvation—a nice little flower to offer you at thirty—lies solely in timidity, creeping back into your shell, never running any risk. But if the risk seeks you out? And how long will your shell last?

Another thing to know: however terrifying your trials have been so far, you are so made that they will be worse tomorrow. In your case the only thing that grows with the years is your capacity for detachment, not for resistance. For your shell—and today you see this clearly—gets thinner and thinner, even as far as material things are concerned. You are ill and out of work.

And so are thousands of other men. Don't flatter yourself you are outstanding, even in that. You always were a poor fish, and the worst of it is you still are.

For people to feel sorry for us we must "keep smiling" and not be too dirty, so that we represent some advantage to anyone who cares to be bothered with us. But the man who truly calls for pity and benevolence—one who is downtrodden, obsessed, impotent, verminous, filthy, ill-spoken, hopeless, a mere husk—who would devote their life to him? I mean

[1] Mario Sturani, one of Pavese's few intimate friends, was his fellow student at school and the university. Sturani, a painter, was a leading member of the intellectual, anti-fascist group in Turin.

absolutely, as a woman who married such a man would do, unreservedly. Plenty of people, out of charity, would feed him, reason with him, wash away his filth, but who would be willing to link their life to his?

Has there even been a saint who saved *one person only?* They all saved multitudes, fulfilled their mission, sought out many poor unfortunates, but was there ever a saint who stopped at *one?* And even a man noble enough to lay down his life for another, would he have been willing to spend his life yoked to that other, him and him alone?

16th January

I wish I could always be sure, as I am this morning, that since the will power of an adult is conditioned by the hundred thousand decisions he took as an irresponsible child, it is ridiculous to talk of free will. One gradually acquires characteristics without even knowing how, and beyond question, one acts in this way or that according to one's personality. Where, then, is any freedom of choice?

Is it conceivable to murder someone in order to count for something in his life? Then it is conceivable to kill oneself so as to count for something in one's own life.

Here's the difficulty about suicide: it is an act of ambition that can be committed only when one has passed beyond ambition.

The "illusions" of Leopardi have come down to earth again.

17th January

This can happen: with an immense expenditure of patient sincerity, the sentimental man arrives at the same conclusions as any rake. You can laugh, but love is like that. Nothing in life is worth having at a price beyond its value. But sentimentality is nothing more nor less than a distortion of values.

Prostitutes work for money. But what woman gives herself unless she knows the reason why?

(Night, insomnia.)

Many men on the point of an edifying death would be furious if they were suddenly restored to health.

> "Yet we all kill the thing we love,
> By all let this be heard.
> Some do it with a bitter look,
> Some with a flattering word."

To love without mental reservations is a luxury for which one pays and pays and pays.

19th January

There is absolutely no one who makes a sacrifice without hoping for some recompense. It is all a question of buying and selling.

If suffering is the only way of learning, I wonder why it is forbidden by philosophy to injure one's neighbor, thereby educating him in the best way?

If you tell me that in this jungle of self-interest, the world, there exists one power for good—enthusiasm for ideals —I ask: "What ideals?" For you idealists are the first to attack or treat as a criminal any man whose ideal is not the same as yours. We admit, then, that one can be mistaken as to what is ideal. Once the possibility of error is admitted, what does your own pursuit of an ideal become, if not a problem of self-interest and calculation? And in that case, since one man is born shrewd and another not, where does responsibility lie?

Why does a man who is truly in love insist that this relationship must continue and be "lifelong"? Because life is pain and the enjoyment of love is an anesthetic. Who would want to wake up halfway through an operation?

Cruelties forbidden by law are petty, commonplace things compared with the secret, agonizing cruelties one inflicts by the mere fact of being alive and trying to get along as best one can.

Loneliness is pain; copulation is pain; piling up possessions or herding with a crowd is pain; Death puts an end to it all.

The shrewdness of a virtuous man! Is virtue possible without shrewdness? I call shrewdness the capacity for assessing values. And, without calculation, no one is good. Because a man who is "pure and simple" is merely a simpleton, or, rather, an imbecile.

But, unconsciously, I am convinced that without forgetfulness-of-self, one is only an egotist. Look at women! You could strangle them, but never will they forget where their interest lies. And would you call them virtuous?

21st January

A woman is adept at arousing a man's desire, but she is scandalized if this capacity of hers is recognized.

The decadent poetry of France, and therefore of Europe, has been largely influenced by long familiarity with English songs and the works of Poe. Hence, surely, its fondness for phonetic effects, its feeling for "the magic of words," since the habit of reading foreign poetry, never more than half understood, depends for its pleasure on the sound, the glamour evoked by those mysterious syllables.

22nd January

It is conceivable that, by making himself insignificant, colorless, invisible, a man can spend the best years of his life with a woman, untouched by misfortune. But one cannot imagine a conqueror, a braggart or a great lover escaping the irony of life.

Who would ever have thought that, after having studied every possible method of sexual isolation—"self-sufficiency"—I should find it in me to want to get married, chiefly as a proof of confidence in me on the part of a woman? And for sexual serenity?

If you were born a second time you should be very careful, even in your attachment to your mother. You can only lose by it.

They tell me: "To understand that carnal jealousy is nonsense, you must have been a libertine."

24th January

The sentimental man, the dreamer, he who distorts values, begins by believing that his inaptitude for practical things is a small price to pay for the ineffable consolations and triumphs he will find in his dreams.

Then he discovers that the world of dreams also calls for skill in management, a practical aptitude. But he learns this only when it is too late for him to overcome his inveterate artlessness, and that is the real price he has to pay.

Basically, all I am looking for in life is every reason I can find for treating her like a cow. Who? Life?

Here's something to learn from her: every time you read her some undoubtedly true but unpalatable thought, she smiles tolerantly and refuses to discuss it. As all crafty people do, especially with themselves.

We store up things—rage, humiliation, cruel impulses, agony, tears, frenzy—and in the end we find we have a cancer, nephritis, diabetes or sclerosis that reduces us to nothing. It would be amazing if it were otherwise.

The worst thing about misfortunes is that they give you the habit of interpreting everything as a misfortune even when it is not.

They are right—fools, idiots, stubborn, violent men, everyone except reasonable beings. What else does one do, in history, but invent reasonable explanations for one's own follies? Which is tantamount to calling in a lot of other fools to turn sense upside down. One should be a fool, not a dreamer; on the far, not the near, side of conformity. A fool can still grow sensible again, but all a dreamer can do is to cut himself off from the world. The fool has enemies; the dreamer has only himself.

Christianity cannot die, because it contains the possibility of every form of discipline.

76

A précis of any love affair: one begins by thinking about it (exaltation), and ends by analyzing it (curiosity).

What can a woman matter to me unless she is prepared to sacrifice her whole life to me? This is every man's unspoken demand, otherwise he would not marry, or wish to. Isn't that what one expects of marriage? Yes, yes of course, we men are ready to reciprocate. But with a difference. If the lady changes her mind, naturally we shall, too; but if it is the man who gets a different idea (a little adultery on a Sunday, for instance), it does not by any means follow that she has the right to do the same. Do you agree?

25th January

Actually, I am living like the most contemptible wastrels that ever roused my scorn when I was young.

26th January

One cannot escape one's own character: a misogynist you were, and still are. Who would have thought it?

It's clear, isn't it, that without her you no longer find life worth living? Clear, too, that she will never come back to you. Even if she did, we have hurt each other too deeply for us ever to live together again. Then what?

Why write these things that she will read, and that may well make her decide to intervene, to walk out on you? And what sort of life would you lead in that event? October, '37 over again?

Remember that it is all written: February, '34, when you climbed these stairs for the first time, and stopped to think that perhaps it was the beginning of the end.

The fetters of Sapri. Every time the wheel turned you repeated her name.

Can't you face the fact that one day soon, tomorrow, perhaps, she will go off with him in a train and you will never hear of her again? Never again. As if you were dead!

You felt like this as a child when you saw two grown-ups gazing at each other, shy and shamefaced but blissfully content. In those days you didn't quite understand what they were thinking of doing, and you were not thirty years old. You're just the same now, except that you know the dreadful truth behind their embraces, and you are thirty. You will never grow up.

Didn't you once act just as badly yourself? Remember how you got rid of E. . . . But there are two sides to everything. Was it for moral reasons you threw her over, or out of cowardice?

A consoling thought: what matters is not what we do, but the spirit in which we do it. Others suffer too; so much so that there is nothing in the world but suffering; the problem is simply to keep a clear conscience. Kant's philosophy is senseless and gloomy: if God does not exist, everything is permissible. Morality is not enough; the only creed worthy of respect is compassion—charity to one's neighbor. The teaching of Christ and Dostoievsky. All the rest is nonsense.

The moral is shrewdness. Charity is only towards yourself. *But charity* is a euphemism for the *annihilation of self*.

26th January

(Another sleepless night.) When women are God-fearing, people call them sanctimonious hypocrites. Other women claim intellectual freedom, which merely serves to increase their price.

1st February

It is easy to be good when one is not in love.

2nd February

The women who are most careful to choose a rich lover are those who protest that money means nothing to them. Because, to despise money, one must have plenty of it.

Would you like to know what a woman thinks of when you propose to her? Read *Moll Flanders.*

3rd February

Oh, my dearest. In spite of these months of horror; in spite of this senseless, unintentional destruction of every incentive that remained to a poor wretch who knows only how to suffer; in spite of the waste of all the good things we could still have had by going on living together; in spite of all the harm she has done me—I still yearn for her in her sadness, her helplessness; I love her body and her brooding eyes, all her futile, eager efforts, her radiant past as a penniless beauty in love with life. Poor little girl; let this be my farewell to you, my prayer for you.

5th February

Why should this numb, deep-seated cheerfulness surge up through the veins and into the throat of a man who has made up his mind to kill himself? Face to face with death, nothing remains but the blunt consciousness that we are still alive.

9th February

The origin of all violence between man and man, and for all that between man and woman, lies in the fact that only very rarely do they agree on the value of a fact, a thought, a state of mind: what is a tragedy for one is a joke to the other. And even if at first they are both disposed to take a situation seriously, it always happens—since there is always some slight difference in their intensity—that the more serious one exaggerates his concern and the less serious one tends to make light of it, because of that love of eurhythmy, coherence, "absoluteness," which every man has within himself.

A man might be able to escape that destiny if he knew how to hold himself aloof and exhaust all his demands within the closed circle of his own person. But we are so made that even our most intimate emotions are affected by our need for other people's approval. Even those who live most alone are moved by a response from a fellow being, and throw themselves into their work with increased enthusiasm, increased exclusiveness, as if to create a multiple solitude of souls. That is why one can never sufficiently persuade a man who is convinced of the essential loneliness of his fellow men, to lose himself in innumerable social entanglements, for they have little attraction for him.

True loneliness, when one has to endure it, brings with it a desire to kill.

15th February

How many times have we made this sound and good resolution to "stand on our own feet and be self-sufficient"—to act as though everything was just beginning, but with the indescribable advantage of knowing every little move? And how many times have we fallen short? Let us see why. We have *fumed* at our solitude, and consequently been totally incapable of taking advantage of it. One should be calm and alert in its presence; occupied in solitude, be the rock and no longer the wave. Re-create the inner soundness you possessed in '33, while in your boat. Fill your secret reserves with fresh sap. Yield, make no demands, wait. You know where every impulse leads. Master all those that would carry you into situations you know and despise. If you cannot do that, you will never do anything.

16th February

I am glad that I have always expected something from Pinelli.[1] With his *Ippogrifo*, he shows an understanding of many modern trends that he used to seem unaware of, and he is sensitive to the rhythm of the city. This technique has infinite possibilities. It allows one to tell a story with all the conciseness of a scene in a play. It corresponds with the cinema.

It is fine to see that, underneath this vitality, he remains a Catholic; or, rather, that his faith is his very backbone.

[1] Tullio Pinelli, a writer who had been a fellow student of Pavese. Ed.

But it is futile; at all periods of history, only people of good sense are truly modern.

We have our weaknesses. We are convinced that no man can alter his own make-up, his personal equipment. We try, with what cunning we have, to change our weaknesses into something of value. But what if one has no cunning in one's make-up?

You like things to be absolute, complete? You cannot construct a totalitarian love affair. You can build a totalitarian goodness. But don't play the fool: keep sex out of it.

17th February

The moral judgments in *Madame Bovary* ignore every principle except that of the artist who violates and dwells on every human action. Some people revel in the way *Madame Bovary* depicts love, taking it for a sound criticism of romantic rubbish, put forward by a robust conscience, and they do not see that this *robust conscience* is nothing more than a close scrutiny and a showy parade of sordid human emotions. How could one live on the lines of *Madame Bovary?* In one way only: by aping the artist shut up indoors.

Be careful not to take seriously Flaubert's reviews of reality. They are based on no other principle but this: all is filth, except the conscientious artist.

19th February

Those philosophers who believe in the absolute logic of truth have never had to discuss it on close terms with a woman.

20th February

If you have to lose your dearest love, would you not rather she died, instead of simply going away and living somewhere else? Can we endure that she who was our whole life should cease to be so for us and become so for others, or for herself? Even supposing the distance is such as to preclude every possibility of her return, of a fresh start?

You have never been able to put up a barrier in your own life, and you want to channel and describe the lives of others?

You have chewed over the things of the spirit (art, morality, dignity, knowledge) long enough to leave the taste of them in your mouth, and then you have gone back to your bread and potatoes.

You are always forgetting that you were born a slave. You think you are always being wronged. But can a slave be wronged?

Kindness that is shown because we are weary of suffering is something more horrible than the suffering itself.

21st February

Why be jealous? He doesn't see in her what I saw myself. In all probability he sees nothing. One might as well be jealous of a dog or the water in a swimming pool. In any case, water is more *all-pervading* than any lover.

Why has almost everyone been deluded by love? Simply because they fell in love so eagerly that it was bound to play them false, by the law that lets us have only what we ask for with indifference.

23rd February

One must have cunning, to gain tragic love. But it is precisely those who are incapable of cunning who thirst for tragic love.

25th February

When there comes a pause in a tumult of passion, as today (the last, perhaps?), the desire to write poetry is reborn. In the slow lassitude of a silent collapse is born a wish to write prose.

The violent, exhausting ending of a passion is like your arrival at Brancaleone. You looked around you, dazed and battered, and you saw space, a few houses, a low, sandy beach, all in sharp, tender colors, like a rose on a rough-hewn wall. And you breathed a sigh of relief.

They were fine, those first days. But then? As soon as you realized you were alone?

You must confess you have thought and written many banalities in your little diary, these past months. I agree, but is anything more commonplace than death?

A lover's reasoning: if I were dead, she would go on living, laughing, trying her luck. But she has thrown me over and still does all those things. Therefore I am as dead.

1st March

Glamis hath murdered sleep.

5th March

To avenge a wrong done to you, is to rob yourself of the comfort of crying out against the injustice of it.

Love interests the loved one by reason of the *things* it brings with it. The man who devotes himself to loving sincerely, utterly, has hardly ever had time in his life to acquire the things (riches, power, influence) that would make his love acceptable. As for love itself, no one knows what to make of it. And let us be fair: what is love, in itself, that is more than the libido of an ape?

10th March

When a man is suffering people treat him like a drunkard: "Get up, now; come on; that's enough; be on your way; not like that; that's it. . . ."

23rd March

No one ever lacks a good reason for suicide.

What you could not do when you were twenty-five with all your strength intact, how can you possibly do now you are thirty and full of failure?

To get someone to love you out of pity, when love is born only of admiration, that's a really pitiful idea.

This much is clear: you will never succeed in establishing yourself in the world (with a job, a normal way of life); never win a woman's love (or a man's friendship), as much for the above weakness as for another you know of; never become obsessed by one of those ideas worth dying for, as you know from past experience; and you will never have the courage to kill yourself. Look how many times you have thought of it.

26th March

What use has this long love affair been?

It has uncovered all my shortcomings, tested my quality, passed judgment on me. Now I see the reason why I isolated myself until '34. Subconsciously I knew that for me love would be a massacre.

Nothing is salvaged. . . . Conscience is shattered: look at my letters and homicidal temptations. My character is warped: look at my imprisonment. The illusion of my genius has vanished: look at my stupid book and my translator-traitor's mentality. Even the hardihood of the ordinary man in the street is lacking. At thirty I cannot earn a living.

I have reached the point of hoping for salvation from outside myself, and nothing can be more obscure than that. I still think that, with her, I could have battled on, but she herself dealt with that illusion and laughed in my face.

". . . We are full of vices, eccentricities and horrors, we men, the fathers. . . ."

Exactly. Only we haven't even been a father.

Even physically I am no longer the same.

Still, many men have been destroyed by love. Am I perhaps so handsome that it shouldn't have happened to me? Now it is no longer a choice between survival and deciding to take the plunge; but between taking the plunge alone—as I have always lived—or taking a victim with me so that the world will remember.

To be thinking like this every day, every day from morning till night! No one believes it, naturally. Perhaps this is my real special quality, not genius, not goodness, not anything else. To be so obsessed by this feeling that not a single cell in my whole body is unaffected.

That's really the ultimate thing to be proud of: no one else could have endured such torture for nine months. Any other man would have already killed her by now.

The thing we secretly dread the most always happens.

When I was a little boy I used to tremble to think what it would be like to love someone and see her married to another. I exercised my mind with that thought. And you see!

27th March

I remember spending one Sunday brooding over the idea, like a fly caught in a web, till my mind, my very soul, was utterly distracted and I shook with rage, feeling the grip of Fate's iron hand or soothed now and then by a faint, vague hope of a less atrocious future.

I notice that pain stuns, dazes and crushes. Every tentacle I once used to sense, test and barely touch the world is like a gangrenous stump. I spend my day like someone who has bumped into a knob and hit the nerve of his knee: the whole day like that unbearable instant. The pain is in my chest, which seems caved in. The blood draining out as if I had a gaping wound.

Naturally it is all a fixation. But, by God, that is why I am alone. Tomorrow I shall have a brief happiness, and then the quivers of anguish will come again, the feeling of constriction or of being torn apart. I no longer have the physical strength to remain alone. I did manage to, once, but then I had a relapse and, like all relapses, it was fatal.

Another source of suffering aggravates my condition, like a person cut in two who still has a toothache. It is that I could write a letter like the one of February 2nd about the scab. What was my life like then? Was it worth it to be so abject. What did I gain by it? More wounds, more gangrene, more ridicule.

I must be mad. Over and over again I ask myself: what wrong did I ever do to her? Courage, Pavese. Take courage. . . . There is one good thing. No one else is affected by your collapse. That's something in your favor.

25th April

When one has made a mistake, one says: "Another time I shall know what to do," when what one should say is: "I already know what I shall really do another time."

6th May

There's a cure for everything. Think about the last night you spent in prison. Take a deep breath, look around your cell, grow a little sentimental over its walls, its bars, the dim light coming in through the window, the noises you hear all around you, that now seem to belong to another world.

Why does the thought of your cell make you sad? Because it has become a personal thing, your very own. But if someone were to tell you suddenly that there has been a mistake and you will not go out tomorrow but stay there indefinitely, would you still be as serene?

Let us be frank. If Cesare Pavese were to appear before you, talk to you, try to make friends with you, are you sure you would not find him objectionable? Would you feel confidence in him, be willing to go out for a gay evening in his company?

11th May

Consider how many things please and stimulate you simply because you find them strange and somehow shocking. Not so much with people but in nature. The garden, striped like a tiger; the little clouds in spring; the downward sweep from Turin to the plain of the Dora; the smell of gas among the trees bordering a road.

Basically, all the delirious pleasure you find in your

walks comes from your appreciation of the *bizarre*. "There is no excellent beauty that hath not some strangeness. . . ." The secret lies in that "strangeness." But the phrase continues: ". . . in the proportion." That is to say: there must be something striking and unexpected in the way the elements of beauty are assembled, not in the elements themselves, which are often commonplace. To discover merely that there is a strangeness in certain things is easy and means nothing. You must find something strange in their association. That will teach you to recognize the *bizarre,* and show you how that quality of strangeness can spring to life and persist even amid universal, commonplace dullness.

Indisputably, art is wholly concerned with "the marvelous," or, better still, with "pointing out marvels." If one is awed by the "how" and not by the "what," one can always be as awed as one likes.

13th May

Since God *could* have created a freedom in which there could be no evil (i.e., a state when men were happy and free and certain not to sin), it follows that He wished evil to exist. But evil offends Him. A commonplace case of masochism.

Don't forget that the poet is concerned with the "how," not with the "why." "You fooled X; you will fool me; then Y; like him, me, and so on."

Friday the thirteenth—beyond question, we are no longer children.

16th May

Turning over the pages of *Lavorare stanca* again, you feel quite depressed. The construction is lax and there are no moments of sufficient intensity to justify describing it as "poetry." Where are those celebrated flights of fancy that were to be the whole imaginative structure of the work? Was it worthwhile to spend six years of your life composing it, from twenty-four to thirty? In your place I should be ashamed.

24th May

It is a fine thing when a young fellow of eighteen or twenty stops to think about his own confused state of mind, clenches his fists and tries to grasp reality. But it is not so good to be doing it at thirty. And doesn't it turn you cold to think you will still be doing it at forty or later?

26th May

The only period when you found rich veins of material was in the years from six to fifteen. Then stories and poems full of maturity and atmosphere came readily to your mind, and the reason is this. During those years you were living *in the world,* apathetic as a calf but aware of the world around you. Your ego took an interest in your practical contacts with the world, but left intact the current of sympathy between yourself and things.

At fifteen, your ego emerged from that simple, uncomplicated way of life and began to pass judgment on the world, even though until then you knew it merely as an onlooker. And everything became sterile, confused, sensual.

The problem of how to emerge from your present, thirty-year-old adolescence is this: you must regard the stratagems of manhood with a practical eye, just as a child views childish things; but plunge yourself, equally artlessly, into a current of sympathy for this vile world.

The only reason why we are always thinking of our own ego is that we have to live with it more continuously than with anyone else's.

Talking of those "veins of material": out of all your many childhood experiences, you chose certain ones with a family resemblance, midway between dreams and harsh reality, and you chose them during the long development of your adolescent years. How was that? They, and they alone, repeatedly come back to mind. You cannot stop dreaming of them. But were your tastes already formed when you chose them, or did they determine what your tastes would be? The usual answer, that they were born together, doesn't seem to me to mean much.

30th May

When a thing depends on you alone it is sufficient to want it badly enough and you get it. Anything that depends upon the consent of others is a *do ut des,* in which it is absolutely essential to reveal no particular desire. Only by seeming indifferent can you get what you want and keep it.

Human intercourse is governed by the same laws that apply to trading. To make good deals you must seem not to care whether you do or not. Be frank with yourselves, misleading to others.

The only way to make a woman stay with you—if that is what you want—is to place her in such a position that public opinion, the respect of her own circle, and her self-interest, all prevent her from going away. A man who thinks he can hold her to him merely by his devotion and sincerity is a fool. Make sure accepted customs are on your side: that's the way to settle revolutions or keep women. Cast aside every noble impulse and settle down as a righteous citizen, a fat bourgeois. Look how all your acquaintances have found themselves good positions, enjoying their screwing, and their meals even more. That pleases everybody.

And such a man would be extremely surprised if you were to cast any doubt on his willingness to sacrifice himself for his ideals. The practical way of life is a matter of shrewdness, nothing else. Like the high-minded shrewdness of the engaged girl who feels she ought not to give herself to her lover, lest he should jilt her.

31st May

As long as you feel this bitterness within you, trying not to daydream for fear of losing your reason, it is plain you will do no more work. At least you must learn to like *things,* if you are to create anything, live alone and produce something worth while. A man who hates someone is never alone.

The one he hates is always with him. But to like things you must also like people. There's no way out of it. In fact, the logical conclusion of your present state of mind is suicide. Then do it, once and for all, or decide to forgive the world, and the one who is all the world to you. Forgive her, then you can be alone again—alone with her. You see! There's calculation in that thought, too!

Your attitude is completely false, that much is evident from the terror you feel at the thought of her death, her suicide. If you really hated her, the idea would make you smile. But it horrifies you, therefore you do not hate her. Then forgive her. Be the man you have always pretended to be, and find peace.

2nd June

In sexual matters it seems to me that the man, having satisfied himself, grows calm and detached; the woman then responds more warmly, to arouse his desire anew. The reason for this natural fact is that the woman always tries to leave the man with his desires unsatisfied, so as to keep him bound to her. It would be pointless for a man to refuse himself to a woman in the hope of binding her to him.

Furthermore, a woman finds her peace in conception, in carrying her child; but a man who did not find peace in the simple act of coition would never find it at all.

3rd June

When writing poetry, it is not inspiration that produces a bright idea, but the bright idea that kindles the fire of inspiration.

In summer and in springtime, along the avenues, in the cafés, through the arcades, the elegant women strolling up and down always make me think of the beauties of ancient Babylon or Alexandria. Probably it is all the effect of their make-up, their crimson fingernails, their bare legs glowing from the sun, their atmosphere of serenity and leisure, but there is something barbaric and exotic about them that, to my mind, is exactly typical of those two civilizations.

7th June

It is dangerous to be too angelic: when the world treats you as it has always (and legitimately) treated angels, with cruelty or off-hand amusement, you at once become the worst and most depraved of demons. One, for instance, who, incapable of doing harm, takes a whole day to kill a rabbit, because every now and then he stops to reproach himself, and doesn't go on until he convinces himself that the whimpering rabbit is making a fuss about nothing. Nothing is more warped than a fallen angel.

Among the other profound teachings of Christianity, include this: real evil comes from someone who once was good, not from a spirit that has been wicked from all eternity and so cannot possibly grow more malignant but will, one fine day, shrivel to nothing from its own corruption. One confirmation of this is the tradition that says Nero, as a youth, but for his hypocrisy and affectation, was a positive Saint Louis.

What a shame that all this is just romantic interpretation (the Pirate, the avengeful Bandit), as worthless as all the things you discover.

What has happened to you so far, should have happened before you were twenty. That's the only unusual thing about you, not genius or anything like that. In this discrepancy between your potential and actual experience of life lies the reason for your apparent fertility at twenty-five and your present decadence. Countless things passed you by in those years, and you tried to make up for them by your passionate devotion to solitude and poetry. Now you have had these experiences, but too late for you to be still capable of judging their solid worth. You have twisted everything around.

Naturally, though, such a prejudicial state of affairs did not come about by chance, but from your own initial deafness to the call of life that, at twenty, confused your sense of values and made you seek out unfamiliar things in an unusually tortuous way. But he who seeks, finds; our experiences spring from within us, and the adventures we have are those we choose to have.

The sublimation and "angelification" of women in the *Stile Nuovo,* was it not simply a method of ridding oneself of the need to bother about them? One paid homage, and then was free to give one's mind to more serious, vital things.

Death is repose, but the thought of death disturbs all repose.

I am at least eight years behind my contemporaries. Normally they, at twenty-two, are convinced of things I am still undecided about at thirty.

It is ridiculous to suppose that one's *vital* relationship with another person can ever change.

11th June

I notice I have almost stopped expressing resentment towards her. I think that is a good sign of perseverance.

Even something harsh and difficult is a comfort if we choose it ourselves. If it is imposed on us by others, it is agony.

It is an old truism, but I am pleased to have rediscovered it for myself. Believe only in the love that costs a sacrifice: the rest, in the majority of cases, is nothing but empty words. Even Christ, our divine example, asks no less from mankind.

From a man who is not ready—I do not say to shed his blood for you (that is a quick and easy thing to do)—but to bind himself to you for life, renewing his dedication every day, you should not accept even a cigarette.

My darling, one does not play jokes on children. I was a child, too (for the first month).

12th June

The third afternoon since she died.

A heroic, not voluptuous, life.

If poetry comes more rarely from me now, that does not mean it is ended, but that I am less easily satisfied as to subjects and their treatment.

All our "most sacred affections" are merely prosaic habit.

13th June

Could anything be more in the pure style of Alfieri than this letter? Does this account reveal my whole attitude? And all my ravings, outbursts, rantings? It is the story of Saul over again; it wasn't worth the trouble of being born in a later century.

For me, the French Revolution is still to come, and when it comes it will disgust me.

16th June

There is a type of man who cannot bear to leave any woman who has made him jealous without banging the door in her face. I do not think this is out of spite. It is simply his need to do, loudly and thoroughly, something that would otherwise seem half-hearted and indecisive.

It is out of weakness: concentrating on the external signs of the parting—harsh words, insults, blows, scandals—out of sheer distrust of one's own inner resolution. It is out of fear, the dread of being made to look a fool, the thought that now things will be as they were before the affair started, that all the suffering the separation has caused will be a dead loss. It is not out of evil spite, but certainly it can lead to wickedness, if all wickedness is born of frustrated ambition.

With your definition of sacrifice—living with someone and never turning away from them—the result is that you wrong anyone who wants nothing to do with you. But why, after all, should one make sacrifices?

Don't you see that—if you indeed reject a sane and normal moral structure—what is left is the *cult of morality,* shorn of every point of application, historical or transcendent, i.e., mere rhetoric.

17th June

The effect of mental suffering (humiliation, grief) is to create a barbed-wire fence in your mind, to compel your thoughts to keep away from certain areas and so avoid the agonies that reign there. In this sense, suffering limits spiritual efficiency.

To say that, when the suffering is over, your faculties will have grown stronger is not so gloriously true, after all. Primarily because there will always remain a certain numbness in that area, a tendency to avoid the bad patch; then because, if nothing is gained while suffering lasts, how can anything be gained later, when one is normal again?

The fact is that all you have gained is *experience,* the most vague and futile thing there is. As for your intellectual caliber, that can only be weakened. No character, after suffering grief, has the same quality it had before; just as no physical body, after being wounded, is as healthy as before, though there may be a hardening, a callosity.

All these great spiritual teachers talk, in the last analysis, of material results: ideas about oneself, about life, the maxims to follow, etc. Efficiency, the temper of the material, the "span of the bridge"—all those things, as anyone can plainly see, have only a limited activity when subjected to strain—to sorrow or pain, for instance. And when they once again have free rein, they do not even have the advantage of being reinvigorated by their rest, for suffering is wearying and wearing, even when one does not give it free play.

20th June

It is worth noting that, once we are adult, we do not learn new ways of doing good, or being good, only of doing evil and being wicked. In that, yes, we never finish learning. Why? Perhaps because our most earnest desire for goodness does not go beyond our *remembered* innocence as children. I say "remembered," because in actual fact we were probably little beasts, even then.

22nd June

The world lives by craft, and gets on very well. Only the crafty ones know how to indulge in sharp practice and get away with it. A man who is penalized by this state of affairs and decides to be a bit of a swine himself to get his own ba k, must not forget that from then on he should always be crafty, otherwise his single lapse will serve only to torment him by its very contrast with his normal non-craftiness. His error is in running counter to his own custom. It disrupts his balance. Hence it comes about that when a man has done wrong (something that troubles his conscience, otherwise it is no wrong), all his personal life seems called into question.

Advice to wrongdoers: never stop halfway, but immerse yourself in it completely; make a habit of this changed course, see things in quite a different light, *especially your own past*.

It may seem the contrary, but what most horrifies any man is to wake up in the morning, different than he was the night before. He loses the sense of his own structure.

What is the difference between a crime that is actually accomplished and one that is brooded over, savored, gloried in but not committed? This: the first is a fact and cannot be undone, while the second leaves us with the illusion that our character is unaffected. We ought to feel the same prick of conscience in both cases, the same remorse, but we do not, because in the second case nothing hinders us from reverting to what we were before. However, Christianity expresses its view of the matter in no uncertain terms: "he who looks on a woman to lust after her has already committed adultery. . . ."

In short: a good conscience is nothing else but the expression of a desire we all have—to be ourselves and feel comfortable. Those who tell petty, occasional lies suffer far more than great criminals, simply because the latter are thoroughly used to it.

When we feel remorse for an evil action, it is not the

harm done to others that troubles us but the disquiet it brings on ourselves. (Cf. Rasknolnikoff.)

The art of living, granted that living means making others suffer (as we do in our sexual life, commerce and every other activity), lies in developing an aptitude for playing all sorts of dirty tricks without letting them disturb our own peace of mind. A natural capacity for guile is the best endowment any man can have.

23rd June

The fine formula "I must not," that by its very finality seems the most certain sign of an exaltation of imperative morality, what more is it than an efficacious ellipsis, implying full consideration of a complex calculation?

8th July

"He has found a purpose in life in his children." So that they in turn may find the same in theirs? But what point is there in this endless procreation? We care so little about other people that even Christianity urges us to do good *for the love of God*. Man prefers to punch his fellow man in the mouth, and is such a fool that to give himself an object in life he has to produce a son.

9th July

In any course of action it is not a good sign if a man starts with a determination to succeed in it, for that implies rivalry, pride, ambition. He should begin by loving the technique of any activity for its own sake, as one lives for the sake of living. That alone shows a true vocation and promises genuine success. All the social passions imaginable can follow later to amplify that single-minded love of technique—in that way they are bound to come—but to begin with them is a sign of indolence. In brief, one must devote oneself to an activity *as if there were nothing else in the world*. The moment of significance is when one begins, and the things of the world (social passions) do not exist in respect of that activity. Any one of us is capable of devoting himself to a work when he knows what he will get out of it; it is difficult to devote oneself gratuitously.

13th July

A sin is something that inflicts remorse.

It is natural that the selfsame things may be a sin for one man and not for another (Cf. 5th May, '36): if one feels no remorse, that is enough. What are we to do? Do as I said on 22nd June, '38. Get it out of your head that remorse is an absolute reality that infallibly descends upon us. Only specially educated consciences can feel it at all. In that case one could be so educated as *not* to feel it. They say that to feel remorse for countless little acts that the uninitiated would never notice is a guarantee of inner quality, an inner richness. But is it true? Cannot one conceive an inner richness that does not lead to the rejection of states of conscience, but accepts them all for what they are, even those that usually give rise to remorse? But this is a sophism, for if any state of conscience, no matter what, is an enrichment, then a state of remorse is also an enrichment, and we are back where we started.

But if we speak of *enrichment,* we are speaking of *pleasure.* Then we shall say that even the state of remorse is welcome, not in itself (for, like all suffering—cf. 17th June— it makes one poorer, limits one's movement, turns one to stone), but as a premise of the pleasure given by repentance, and by the determined choice, from then on, of new, good actions that will cause no more remorse.

The fact remains, however, that this stipulation ("only actions that will cause no more remorse") seems to tie our hands and so leave us poorer.

Which is not to say that, if remorse and relative compunction and a resolution to do good are a positive step forward (an enrichment), it seems that we ought to sin so as to mount that particular step towards inner richness.

Conclusion: in fact it is permissible to sin in ways one has not heard of, with a view to making discoveries, for that will bring us remorse and consequently to resolutions new to us (= an enrichment).

It is a sin only when we do again some act that has already caused us remorse and inspired us to make new resolutions, because, having enriched us once, it cannot do so a second time. Right?

14th July

To understand why a woman seems thoughtful, embarrassed and apologetic when she is with several young men, think how you feel yourself among five or six prostitutes, all watching you and waiting for you to make your choice.

22nd July

Beware of the man who is never in a temper.

Once the first line of a story is written, the whole is already decided—style, atmosphere and the sequence of events. After that it is a question of patience. All the rest should, and must, develop out of that first line.

28th July

The motive force in every plot is simply this: To discover how such and such a character extricates himself from a given situation. Which means that every plot is invariably an exercise in optimism, in so far as it is a research into how a character responds. It goes without saying that even if he fails, that is still a reaction. If the failure is the author's fault, if, that is, he did not manage to get out of the difficulty, the unspoken question arises as to what he should have done to bring matters to a successful conclusion. Here is the message in every plot: this is how one ought, or ought not, to act. It follows that if immoral works exist, they are works in which there is no plot.

Modern art, which seems to avoid a plot, simply substitutes for it an artless account of current affairs, a host of infinitesimal details about domestic incidents; instead of *characters* it has one character only, *the average man,* who can be any one of us and, indeed, is, under the old clumsy psychological classifications.

The highest peak of this art is attained by a cunning device. Instead of the "average man," presented as an exceptional hero (as in the first period of modern art), the vogue now is to take for our hero an extraordinary character and present him in his normal state, his "averageness." In that way the old conventional classifications are avoided; the writer chooses an abnormal, pathological hero (that being the common conception of "extraordinary"), and follows his activities with a sort of uncritical homeliness (Faulkner? O'Neill? Proust?).

7th August

A really lovely bosom consists of the entire chest, culminating in two peaks whose roots spring from the ribs. They are beautiful additions, but beneath them lies the chest.

28th August

The subtle charm of convalescence is that we return to our old habits with the illusion of discovering them for the first time.

The thing to do with our incorrigible faults is to make a virtue of them. I very much like acting to myself, and I can make good this stupid waste of effort by learning to throw myself into the part of some humble character or other and see what the natural development may be. Fundamentally, this is a foretaste of poetry.

30th August

The great thing about Vico—apart from the fact of his being well-known—is this carnal feeling that poetry is born of all historical life; inseparable from religion, politics and economics; lived "popularly" by a whole people before becoming a stylized myth, a mental conception of a whole culture.

In particular, the feeling that one must have a special disposition ("poetical logic") to be able to write it.

This, in fact, is still the theory that best revives and explains the creative epochs of poetry; the mystery whereby, at a given moment, all the vital forces of a nation surge up in the form of myths and visions.

My stories are always about love or loneliness. For me, there seems no way of escaping from loneliness except by "picking up" a girl. Possibly nothing else interests me? Or is it that the erotic association is more easily successful when I link it in my mind with mythology instead of with any particular person?

1 7th September

What matters to an artist is not experience, but inward experience.

An argument *they* put forward is that a man takes refuge in solitude in order to sin.

Is it a comfort to reflect that weakness may be a strength, just as those who are always ailing never seem subject to serious illness?

As the years go by, the skull becomes more noticeable behind the face of every man.

What, for Svevo, is *senility,* to me seems adolescence.

A Christian would say that in seeking pleasure one discovers instead one's own shortcomings. The providential function of pleasure-seeking is to make a man forget prudence. Hurling himself against the walls of his cell teaches him to be humble. It is only by avid pleasure-seeking that a man learns what grief is.

The proofs of the existence of God do not lie primarily in the harmony of the universe, in the marvelous balance of everything, in the wonderful colors of flowers, but in man's lack of harmony with his surroundings, his capacity for suffering. Because, in brief, there is no reason why a man should suffer in this world unless there is such a thing as moral responsibility, that is to say, the capacity, indeed the duty, to give significance to his suffering.

18th September

In one's dealings with other people, a moment of candor is enough to ruin for us whole days of service to others. *Candor* is not kindliness, not *charity*. It exposes our own egotism and may cause offense. Charity, on the contrary, can never take offense.

19th September

Men who have a tempestuous inner life and do not seek to give vent to it by talking or writing are simply men who have no tempestuous inner life.

Give company to a lonely man and he will talk more than anyone.

21st September

We ought not to complain if someone we dearly love behaves now and then in ways we find distasteful, nerve-racking or hurtful. Instead of grumbling we should avidly hoard up our feelings of irritation and bitterness: they will serve to alleviate our grief on the day when, in one way or another, she has gone and we miss her.

But that is helpful only up to a certain point. To have something to blame on the one who has vanished does not sweeten the grief of her disappearance, but complicates it. The fact that she has made us suffer horribly does not loosen the bonds that bind us to her; to our present bereavement it adds an aching bitterness that can nevermore be relieved, a torture of helpless inferiority, the seal of irretrievable loss.

All sins have their origin in a sense of inferiority, otherwise called ambition.

The condensation of a novel does not consist of cramming the details one into another like Japanese boxes. The tone of it must preserve the flow of events as something that comes about after due thought, over a reasonable period, and must be full of the implications suggested by that spacing.

A novel of the type of *Due amici,* one, that is, in which matters of thought and feeling, all on the same moral level, are implacably exposed, is an unhappy compromise with play-writing, which *watches* psychological developments as they occur, by means of its highly specialized "immediate" technique. The province of story-writing, on the contrary, is to *rethink, reconsider* events, some of which are highlighted, some left in obscurity; not just letting them all happen under the same unreal, diffused light.

22nd September

At one time, giving a naturalistic touch in the second line ("It was a cool day with a little fog") was enough to start off pages and pages of ruthless naturalism; no longer narrative but documentary; a work, that is, in which every event is arranged on the level of that naturalistic touch, and so cannot be reconsidered separately.

Such opening statements serve a purpose only in the case of a novel with a limited compass, dealing with a short, clearly specified, period of time (*Notte di festa*); novels, in short, which have a scenic quality and could be played on a stage. In fact, on a stage everything happens in documentary fashion, the decor and the actions taking the place of descriptions.

The true novel (*Primo amore* and *Campo di grano*) treats time as a material, not as a limitation, shortening or lengthening it as it chooses, in no way concerned with stage directions, which are the time and vision of real life; rather, it resolves the temporal atmosphere into an impulse (a fundamental thesis or creative idea) of construction (time and space seen in perspective or reconsidered).

Every man over thirty identifies his youth with the worst fault he thinks he has discovered in himself. (Cf. 31st October, '37.)

29th September

I shall have to stop priding myself on being unable to find pleasure in the things ordinary men enjoy—high days and holidays; the fun of being one of a crowd; family affection and so on. What I am really incapable of is enjoying out-of-the-ordinary pleasures—solitude and a sense of mastery, and if I am not very good at sharing the sentiments of the average man it is because my artless assumption that I was capable of something better has rusted my natural reactions, which used to be perfectly normal. In general we feel rather pleased with ourselves when we do not enjoy common pleasures, believing this means that we are "capable of better things." But incapacity in the one case does not presuppose capacity in the other. A man who is incapable of writing nonsense may be equally incapable of writing something pleasing.

We hate the thing we fear, the thing we know may be true and may have a certain affinity with ourselves, for each man hates himself. The most interesting, most fertile qualities in every man are those he most hates in himself and in others, for hatred includes every other feeling—love, envy, ignorance, mystery, the urge to know and to possess. It is hate that causes suffering. To overcome hatred is to take a step towards self-knowledge, self-mastery, self-justification, and consequently towards an end of suffering. When we suffer, it is always our own fault.

3rd October

We know many things that, in our everyday life, do not work out in the way we might expect. The *man of action* is not the headstrong fool who rushes into danger with no thought for himself, but the man who puts into practice the things he knows. Similarly, a poet is not a vague dreamer, but a keen mind bringing to life with his own special skill the things he knows.

From what I wrote on 29th September it follows that hate is necessary. Every contact with a new reality begins with antipathy. Hate is an essential preliminary to knowledge. Diffidence and reluctance do not amount to hatred, except in so far as they go outside the sphere of interest and become an aversion to facing something unknown, which in every case they do, more or less.

(Cf. 21st September, IV.) The difficulty about time, in a story, lies in transforming *material time,* monotonous and crude, into *imaginary time* in such a way as to retain the same consistency as before.

The eternal falsity of poetry is that its events occur in a time that differs from reality.

5th October

You cannot insult a man more atrociously than by refusing to believe he is suffering.

In the same way that we do not think about other men's sorrow, we can avoid thinking of our own.

9th October

The art of discovering trivial motives to bring ourselves to accomplish the important deeds we have to do. The art of never letting ourselves be discouraged by the reactions of other people, bearing in mind that the value of a sentiment is a matter for our personal decision, since it is we who will feel it, not anyone else. The art of lying to ourselves, knowing that we lie. The art of looking all men (ourselves included) squarely in the face as though they were characters in one of our own novels. The art of remembering that, though we count for nothing and so does every other man, we count for more than anyone else, simply because we are ourselves. The art of regarding a woman like a loaf of bread: a problem of cleverness. The art of plunging like a thunderbolt into the depths of grief in order to rise above it on the rebound. The art of putting ourselves in another man's place and so learning that each is concerned only with himself. The art of attributing any action of ours to someone else, to see at once whether it is a sensible thing to do.

The art of dispensing with art. The art of being alone.

10th October

Naturally you consider that the most hateful man you know eats enough for four and thoroughly enjoys life; you agree he has the loveliest wife and lives with her in perfect harmony; he has a beautiful home and excellent taste; is a happy father, holds an important position in the world and enjoys a reputation for fair dealing. Furthermore, you must concede him the pleasure of feeling unhappy now and then, supremely unhappy, so that he can feel noble in his suffering. What, then, can you deny this most hateful of men? You can deny him nothing whatever.

Immoderate laughter is a sign of weakness, just as much as weeping. They both leave you utterly exhausted. In general, everything that robs you of your senses is a sign of weakness. The greatest weakness of all is to die.

13th October

If a woman does not betray you, it is because it does not suit her convenience.

Every luxury must be paid for, and everything is a luxury, starting with being in the world.

It is stupid to grieve for the loss of a girl friend: you might never have met her, so you can do without her.

Religion consists of believing that *everything that happens is extraordinarily important*. It can never disappear from the world, precisely for this reason.

It is not true that death comes upon us as an experience in which we are all novices (Montaigne). Before being born we were all dead.

15th October

Certainly, by suffering one can *learn* many things. Unfortunately, suffering robs us of the strength to make use of them, and merely knowing them is less than nothing.

To accept suffering (Dostoievsky) is, in essence, a way of not suffering. So . . . . When a man sacrifices himself, is it not with the purpose of alleviating someone else's suffering?

Which amounts to saying: it is all right for me to suffer, provided others do not. But if every man took care not to suffer himself, would that not be a more efficient method?

But Dostoievsky's theory is that one ceases to suffer only by accepting it. And it seems that one can accept suffering only by sacrificing oneself.

In such matters, the error lies in trying to take a longer steps than one's legs can manage. One accepts suffering (resignation), and then realizes that all there is to it is that one has suffered. It has done us no good, and other people are not in the least concerned. So we grit our teeth and grow cynical. The thing that always hurts us most is to feel we have been fooled, to see our suffering denied, rendered of no account. (Cf. 5th October, '38.)

16th October

It is not the actual enjoyment of pleasure that we desire. What we want is to test the futility of that pleasure, so as to be no longer obsessed by it.

18th October

Describing nature in poetry, is like describing a lovely heroine or a stalwart hero (as some writers do).

Success in anything, no matter what, is an act of ambition—sordid ambition, so it is logical to resort to the most sordid means.

19th October

While we are in pain, we believe that outside our circle of suffering happiness exists. When we are not suffering, we know that there is no such thing as happiness, so we feel even sadder at having no pain to endure.

Cosmic pessimism is a doctrine of consolation. It is much worse for a man who believes in the ambivalence of the existing order of things but finds himself unsuited to it, and so condemned to suffer.

There is a thing we call *conscience*, but it is not, as we

imagine, an omnipresent eye watching us: it is the protest made by our self-respect, which knows what our future opinion will be of any deed we commit, and wants to prevent us from putting ourselves in a position counter to the conclusions of our own experience. Each man's conscience allows or forbids different things, and with differing intensity. These variations always result from experience.

To pass judgment as to the morality of another man's action is to reveal the uneasiness we should or should not feel ourselves, if we, constituted as we are, had committed it. It is not a matter of logic. How are we to know whether his conscience is disturbed by it and to what degree, since an experience is always incommunicable? Or, which comes to the same thing, if disclosed it would change, because it would merge with our own previous experience?

An interesting experiment is attempted in *Spoon River Anthology*, in which each dead man judges himself on the basis of his own experience. Rightly speaking, that idea is obviously absurd, from what I have already said: it is the writer himself judging each of them according to his own experience. But this is an absurdity that arises with any writer. Naturally, all his *dramatis personae* are one and the same character—the author. The interesting fact is that Lee Masters views the world as a place where every man evolves, out of his own experience, his own condemnation or justification.

It is futile to add that, for each of us, the value we attach to other people's opinions forms a part of our experience.

22nd October

The character and the things pertaining to him are always visualized as being real. There is no need to be afraid, in the periods before imagination takes hold, of watching them live and act. Instead, one should let them do all they can.

At a certain point, go back over what they have done.

(This means that *style* should have no influence on the formation of the story: before the tale can exist at all, there must be a nucleus of reality and of characters that have already taken shape. Once that is settled, you can tackle the main structure and break it up in the way you think best. "Literature" is when style precedes the imaginative nucleus. [See my comment confuting this on 24th October.]

The man who feels he must never display interest, and has a horror of seeming interested in anything, will also be detached in his dealings with relatives and friends, and will always shrink from joining with them in an organized *bloc* of common interests, will cultivate a coolness towards them. Which means that indifference to material things leads to self-isolation and egotism.

To resume. The epic poet *believes* that what he is telling *really* happened. The beginnings of a creation that *knows itself to be a product of the imagination,* are also the beginnings of "literature." In Greece, comedy and romance. (It goes without saying that there is "literature" in Homer, too.)

In this connection it is appropriate to note Leopardi and the fact that great books are not written with the *purpose* of creating poetry. When one proposes to reproduce a reality, it is with the intent to employ this reality to some other end. In direct contrast, to give free rein to one's imagination and conjure up visions, means having the intention of creating poetry. And the advantage does not lie with the visionaries.

(This, too, is refuted in my note for 24th October.)

23rd October

Gertrude Stein's idea is that every human being possesses a certain energy; when that is used up, they "have had it." Here we see her medical training. She is catholic in the sense that all doctors are, fondly compiling rules. Like all the rest of them, she knows how to identify and diagnose a fundamental, matter-of-fact normality.

She overlooks the drama of a man who admits, as she does, the "measurability" of every one, but will not resign himself to it; the drama of infinite will power. In her pages, life is terribly clear. Instead of an awareness of things that cannot be measured—fantasy, imagination, she brings us the magic of a tranquil stream, the assurance that a rose is a rose is a rose. "Then I am unfortunate through no fault of my own or of life in general" is the ruling of this tragic "measurability," and once my energy is exhausted I can die in peace.

24th October

Resuming my earlier train of thought. But *now* what happens is that the mere presentation of an event and a character is, in a half-hearted way, a work of imaginative creation, because the traditional concept of poetry is reduced to such a presentation. To write with any other aim in view, one now has to labor with the style, i.e., to try to create a way of understanding *life* (time and its influence—cf. 3rd October, III), which shall be new knowledge. In this sense, my earlier craze for making imagination the subject of the composition, narrating the thought, getting away from naturalism, becomes acceptable.

This is not imagining, but *knowing:* knowing what *we* are in reality. And this satisfies the need that what we are to tell has really happened: then it remains true that only what we think actually exists (our style, our time = the object of our knowledge) is worth writing about. If we are aiming at pointing out a new way of seeing things, and, therefore, a new reality, it is evident that our style must be accepted as part of that truth, making its influence felt beyond the printed page. Otherwise, what serious value would there be in our discovery?

(Which refutes my note in parenthesis on 22nd October.)

One must tell a story, knowing that the people in it have a given character, and that things will happen in accordance with predetermined laws, but the *point* of our story must lie neither in these characters nor in those laws.

25th October

Human imagination is immensely poorer than reality. If we think of the future, we always see it unrolling itself in a monotonous progression. We forget that the past is a multicolored chaos of generations. This can help to console us for the terrors inspired by the *"technical and totalitarian barbarization"* of the future. In the next hundred years it may well happen that we have a sequence of at least three moments, and the human spirit will be able to live consecutively in the streets, in prison, and in the papers. The same can be said of one's personal future.

26th October

If only we could treat ourselves as we treat other men, looking at their withdrawn faces and crediting them with some mysterious, irresistible power. Instead, we know all our own faults, our misgivings, and are reduced to hoping for some unconscious force to surge up from our inmost being and act with a subtlety all its own.

27th October

It is possible not to think about women, just as one does not think about death.

28th October

For any misfortune we may suffer, we should blame no one but ourselves (cf. 28th January, '37).

Suffering serves no purpose whatever (cf. 26th November, '37).

Suffering limits spiritual efficiency (cf. 17th June, '38).

Suffering is always our own fault (cf. 29th September, '38).

Suffering is a weakness (cf. 13th October, '38).

At least there's one thing to set against all that: if I had not suffered I should not have written those fine phrases.

29th October

It is one thing to remember my own counsels about *technique* when I am sitting at my writing table deep in thought, debating my choice of words; it is quite another to remember advice about *life* and act as I ought when, distracted by joy or grief, I have to deal with rapidly changing situations.

To complain to the world at large is futile and harmful, that much is certain. It remains to be seen whether it is not equally futile and harmful to complain to ourselves. What can we hope to gain? Sympathy? That would be meaningless, for sympathy is the voluptuous union of *two* spirits. A concession? The only concession a man can make to himself is to permit indulgence in his own lamentable weakness, and anyone can see how harmful that would be. The only other excuse is that we do it to delve for truth in our own heart while it is softened by compassion. But experience teaches us that truths are exposed only by a calm, rigorous soul-searching that halts our conscience in some unforeseen reaction and *looks* at it like a film that has suddenly stopped, paralyzed and motionless.

—Before being astute with others, we must be astute with ourselves (7th December, '37).

—The art of looking all men squarely in the face, ourselves included (9th October, '38).

—If we could deal with ourselves as we do with others ... (26th October, '38).

—It is equally futile and harmful to complain to ourselves as to the world in general (29th October, '38).

In all this I find: an urgent need to regard our own ego as being no more important than that of other men, so as to free us from the false advantage that our own personal singularity gives to our ego; to banish maudlin self-pity and the cancerous importance that our every humor assumes in our own eyes; to deal objectively with ourselves, as we do

with others; to pity others, perhaps, but never to pity ourselves.

30th October

We forgive others when it suits us.

1st November

Characters that are depressed at a mere nothing are
the ones best suited to endure heavy blows. They accom-
modate themselves more easily than forceful men to living
in an atmosphere of tragedy. Their powers of resistance are
soon exhausted and they muddle along somehow. The habit
of considering every scratch as a calamity robs a real disaster
of its power to hurt. When misfortune comes, the self-confident
optimist suffers horribly; the man for whom things always
go wrong, suffers in moderation; the out-and-out pessimist is
pleased to find his expectations confirmed.

In order not to suffer we must convince ourselves that
everything is suffering (Leopardi could have had a happy
life), and that we must "accept it." But to do that we must
know an alchemy strong enough to turn filth into gold. We
cannot "accept it," and that is that. Why should we? We
shall be told: (1) one becomes a better man; (2) God is won
over; (3) it will inspire us to write poetry (the feeblest excuse
of all); (4) we are paying a score that all men pay. But
when it comes to the final suffering, death, (1) and (3)
collapse: what remains is the conquest of God or the common
destiny of mankind.

2nd November

Misfortunes cannot suffice to make a fool into an
intelligent man.

Dante was wise in punishing misers and spendthrifts
together: only spendthrifts are truly avaricious. It hurts them
to spend. The miser thinks he is prodigal, the prodigal dreads
being miserly, and both are in torment.

112

3rd November

We are all capable of evil thoughts, but only very rarely of evil deeds. We can all do good deeds, but very few can think good thoughts. (Cf. 20th June, '38.)

Men's good opinion of us is a stronger force than conscience. Who would not choose to yield to the basest temptation within himself, rather than commit, even innocently, a base action, always provided, of course, that he could not pass on the blame?

4th November

Since all states of passion have their own decisive chemical reaction that, by the play of cause and effect, lead to sudden exasperating situations, contradictory, created in error by ourselves, it is essential to counter every kindhearted passion with a firm determination to crush it as a roller crushes a blade of grass, pleasing itself and refusing to turn aside. As for voluptuousness, crushing such an impulse gives just as much pleasure as giving vent to it, and is much more sound. The pleasure of breaking every restraining bond of joy or irritation, for oneself alone.

Your very exclusiveness and sameness will make this pleasure voluntary and not something imposed upon you. Or, at least, its motives will be decided once and for all, not gone through over and over again.

The man who has not had this firmness of purpose is the one most determined to acquire it, for he knows how much it is worth (= Alfieri).

The snag lies in the fact that *without* charity and attachments life becomes deadly, but *with* charity and attachments it leaves itself open to a waste of passion and to the consequent exasperating chemical reaction. The roller and the blade of grass.

In poetry you feel the same necessity. The close, garrulous interest in a complicated, passionate plot (Proust!) is very different from the strong, assured grasp that seizes and gains command of a whole life (Lee Masters).

You do not like submitting yourself to the determinism of analyses. But you want to choose a swift action that could be a myth, i.e., a voluntary happening imposed on the variations.

You do well to know all the exasperating, involuntary intricacies of passion. But you must select them, i.e., not approve them all, as other analysts do, notwithstanding their ironies against the generic mechanism of passion.

Yield as you have yielded to passion in life, but seeing clearly what its design is—the myth of marriage—and crushing the blade of grass as soon as this conclusion appears impracticable, undesirable. You have the temperament to do so: look at the times you have drawn back and your frigid refusals in April, '36 and August, '38.

To maintain that our successes are due to Providence and not to our own cleverness, is a cunning way of increasing, in our own eyes, the importance of those successes.

When a man has an innate love of luxury, abandon, enervating softness and also has an inflexible determination to root it out, clenching his jaws and concentrating every effort on mastering it, he can be sure his inner life will be unceasingly productive.

5th November

The prose used in essays, descriptions, moral and social studies is, to the novel, what lyric poetry is to epic.

The sixteenth, seventeenth and eighteenth centuries had the essay, then came the novel. The fact that, during decadence, this kind of prose is coming back, confirms the parallel: the lyric, too, is doing the same.

At one time, if a husband went wrong his wife had the blame for it, which proves that, in sexual matters, public opinion was based, not on ethics (ethics being a man-made creation), but on self-preservation. What matters to a man is keeping his wife to himself, not obeying some absurd idea of justice. The fortune of war, in which it is a disgrace to be conquered, and the conqueror's conception of justice is subjection. (Cf. 15th December, '37; 31st December, '37, III; 19th January, '38, V; 1st February, '38; 5th February, '38, II; 20th February, '38.)

The art of family life lies in reconciling our egotism with our need to see ourselves from the outside, our need to love, i.e., to sacrifice ourselves.

The style of the twentieth century deepens the breakaway from Leopardi and Stendahl which began earlier, with the impressionism of the realists. And it does so by reverting to and augmenting the conception of style whereby its creators see in Leopardi-Stendhal the last champions of stylized construction. But this concept is no longer in line with the universal humanistic pattern: it accords with the ideal model by which each spirit can express and harmonize its own reality: a magic self-revelation of thought, of inner life, in which there can be no initial calm, no "language of reason," no abstract thought. It is a style that expresses but does not explain. Its origins lie in the researches of story-writers of the past century, not (as with Leopardi and Stendhal) in the pages of humanistic essayists who were concerned with restoring the logical style of treatment.

The researches of realistic story-writers had destroyed style (as in Dickens and Dostoievsky), giving the world, instead, sensations and fine shades of meaning (Balzac, Tolstoi, Maupassant, etc.). It was necessary to revive the individuality of every inner life, but it was not style. Anti-realism began to emphasize that all the impressions of a single consciousness are similar in tone (the aesthetic styles of Pater and Wilde, the carnal quality of d'Annunzio, the psychological musings of Proust, the studied vulgarity of Joyce, and so on), and finally gave way to writers who rediscovered the living, rhythmic pattern that, by reviving one's own thoughts, explains them. A pattern, incidentally, already met with in the work of a few anti-realists, particularly Verga.

This is why the play of imagination, in styles of the

past, interests you so much, the transition from it to reality, their interpenetration. At such moments we glimpse the style of the twentieth century, which is a never-ending revelation of inner life, manifesting it in moments when the subject of the story is the link between reality and imagination, i.e., rendering inner reality expressive. Putting that more plainly: as the imagination unfolds, it is interesting to see how its development reflects, corrects and re-creates the original term of comparison, i.e., how the narrative reality becomes stylized in the imagination.

6th November

I spent the whole evening sitting before a mirror to keep myself company.

Naturally (as you prove in *Eremita*), it is unnecessary to make imagination depend on the "how" or its equivalents. The image is formed for you (and that is the only thing that matters) when you allude to a different experience that helps to define the character or the situation by giving it a background. For example: the sea and the lightning. But let us be clear. These touches when, without pausing in your story, you seize an opportunity of using memories to deepen the total experience, are more symbolic than descriptions. Although they may be imaginative, in the sense that they recur at moments when it seems natural to clarify an inner reality, they play the same part in your story as the recognized attributes of a god or a hero do in a myth (the white bodies of the Oceanids, the murderous hands of Achilles, the belt of Aphrodite), stories within the story, alluding to the hidden reality of the character.

So leave the name of images to the touches about the little goat in *Eremita* or the dynamo in *Fedeltà,* honest, old-fashioned bits of imagery.

8th November

One cannot know one's own style and consciously employ it. One always uses a pre-existent style, unconsciously molding it into something fresh. One discovers what one's style is at any given moment only when it is past and clearly defined, when one reviews it and can interpret its meaning, deciding how it has come about.

While actually writing, we are blind to it. We cannot, at that moment, know whether it is developing well; whether, that is to say, we shall consider it successful when we go over it again. We simply live it. Our craft, the skill we bring to it, is obviously part of our previous style, quite different from what we are that moment evolving. As we write, we efface our errors of style by practice. It is dangerous to go back over what we have already written, to correct it; different ideas would have intervened.

Then is there no such thing as technique? There is, but what really counts, the new growth, is always a step ahead of the technique we knew, born of what flows unconsciously from our pen. To be conscious of our style means that we have finished expressing part of our mystery. Also that from then on we cannot write in that style. The day will come when all our mystery has been revealed, and then we can write no more, can create no new style.

10th November

Literature is a defense against the attacks of life. It says to life: "You can't deceive me. I know your habits, foresee and enjoy watching your reactions, and steal your secret by involving you in cunning obstructions that halt your normal flow."

The other defense against things in general is silence as we muster strength for a fresh leap forward. But we must impose that silence on ourselves, not have it imposed on us, not even by death. To choose a hardship for ourselves is our only defense against that hardship. *This* is what is meant by accepting suffering. Not being resigned to it, but using it as a springboard. Controlling the effect of the blow. Those who, by their very nature, can suffer completely, utterly, have an advantage. That is how we can disarm the power of suffering, make it our own creation, our own choice; submit to it. A justification for suicide. Charity has no place in all this. Unless, perhaps, this act of violence is in itself the truest form of charity?

11th November

My observations of 5th November about the state of war between the sexes appear in a fresh light if we broaden them to apply to all instances of material pleasure. When we see a man making love we shudder and hate the lucky man, who always seems to us a fool or a beast, but we feel just the same if we see him guzzling his food or indulging in an act of cruelty. Perhaps the indignation we feel when we see or hear of political atrocities springs from this: we can tolerate the idea that we—or those belonging to us—might employ such measures, but not that they should be used by someone whom we cannot, even in imagination, invest with our own egotism. In an absolute sense, we cannot endure the sight of a man enjoying himself (we always think of his pleasure as merely physical) without being filled with spite. Now and then we feel the same about ourselves, when we catch ourselves in the act of enjoying some physical pleasure. Then we hate the coarseness of that pleasure, the vulgar insolence of it, namely the quality we connect with it when others enjoy it. Hate is always a clash between our own spirit and someone else's body. (And at the same time, maybe it is the suspicion that that body has a spirit, and that body and spirit get on exceptionally well, better than our own, or in a way unknown to us? cf. the end of 29th September and 3rd October.) Also there will be the suspicion that his body, for him, possesses a spirit that can do without us. What we all want from others, in short, is their docile, devoted agreement to our pressing needs (even to the need we feel most strongly—to humble ourselves at their feet). That alone, when it is constantly with us, can make us take pleasure in the joys of others.

In this sense, to hate one's neighbor is really to ignore him, or, rather, to know one is ignoring him, seeing him only from the outside. And since to be aware of knowing nothing implies a desire to know, hatred is a thirst for love. Charity is all a question of nerves.

13th November

In a story told in the first person one can be realistic without lapsing into realism. When it comes to realism, a song in the first person is more convincing than one in the third.

Proust is obsessed by the idea that every hope, once realized, is replaced exactly by a new state that consequently cancels the preceding one (Swann's dream that he was to be married. Dreams of the "I" who will be received in Swann's home). Beyond the impossibility of communication between souls, there is the same impossibility of communication between different states of soul. Hence the feeling that everything is relative and empty—short of recapturing time that has been lost. Hence the taste for flights of fancy, noting sardonically how they vanish whenever they encounter reality, and realizing, therefore, the need for a law to serve and perpetuate every dream.

What we desire is not to possess a woman, but to be the only one to possess her.

17th November

A class gets the better of a teacher by taking advantage in almost imperceptible ways that the teacher tolerates out of generosity, knowing that his presence should be sufficient to impose silence, without the need to call for order. But, little by little the hubbub becomes general and the teacher has to intervene, calling one of the class to order. Then they all understand that the teacher is not invulnerable, that someone spoke and it could be any one of them. Other calls to order follow and the class gets used to them. Since they cannot all be punished, general disorder develops to whatever degree they know will be tolerated, and will excuse any pupil in particular. Now the teacher demands silence with greater vehemence; the result is that the din becomes more determined, more malicious, assuming that the teacher is reluctant to punish or fails to find penalties that will quell them. The uproar becomes from then on the normal state of affairs, a distraction, an outlet for high spirits, open warfare, now that they know the limits of the teacher's reactions. His mere presence is no longer sufficient to maintain silence; he is compelled to call for order, but his commands have proved themselves ineffective.

21st November

To hear people of the same profession, trade, sex, religion talking about it among themselves arouses a disgust for that profession, etc., unless the listener belongs to the same group himself. The reason is that efficiency transforms even the most exciting occupation into mere habit, a matter of precise detail, and so robs it of all mystery, all those delusive veils born of that mystery, which are for that sphere of activity what legend is to history. Thus far, Leopardi would agree.

Going beyond Leopardi, we will say that incompetence is a much more unhappy state than competence, because, one fine day, it must inevitably reveal its own emptiness and disturb its fanciful illusion with the sorrowful conviction of its own stupidity and ineptitude. Still, there is a robust, stoical pleasure in getting out of that state and moving, as though between the cogs of a machine, into the pitiless world of hard facts. A pleasure, incidentally, that Leopardi enjoyed (without having justified it) in his cruel dissections.

24th November

All those boys of your own age that you knew when you were a lad, you hear young N. describe them now as "old relics," and you agree with him. "But why are they still around, those old relics?" he says. How could they escape this verdict? Obviously by no longer doing what they did when they were young, not "being around," not going on saying the same things, not spiriting up by their mere presence an impossible, long-vanished ghost of the past. How can someone of thirty *not* feel a relic? By ceasing to live on hope; ceasing, that is, to believe that some friendly, mutual contact might change something in his life; seeking a point of application in his own concerns, a broadening of his own personality.

They say that youth is the age of hope, simply because then, in a confused sort of way, one hopes for something from other people as well as from oneself, one does not yet understand that they are precisely "other people." We stop being young when we can differentiate between ourselves and "others," i.e., when we no longer need their company. And we grow old in two ways: either by having no hope, even from ourselves (fossilization, lapsing into second childhood), or hoping for nothing except from ourselves (industry).

During our mature years there are two ways of treating other people: as if we were all young but being careful not to get involved, and well aware of it; or as if we were all old, and therefore well aware of each man's need for isolation.

Why does marriage mark the step from youth to maturity? Because by that act we select one woman from all the rest to be our constant companion, to stand between us and other women, identify herself with us, become the circumscribed arena of our social life, in which we no longer look for company outside ourselves. It puts the seal on the egotism needed to live soberly, an egotism whose excuse is that it creates duties.

Of these two ways of becoming mature, the first is terribly difficult, precisely because it gives us the foolish illusion of being still young ourselves, still hoping wearily that some contact with others will bring us what we no longer believe we can find in ourselves. That is, it creates skeptical old relics. The second seems easier, but it is nerve-racking and places you in most disagreeable situations, and eventually leads you to plunge even more blindly into the vain hope of establishing some contact with your fellowmen. That is, it creates ingenuous old relics. It is pointless to add that in both cases the motive force is egotism, just as it is with grown-ups who fight against their maturity.

Not a trace of charity. What young people feel is not yet charity, precisely because it will become one of these egotisms, by thirty at the latest. (All this discourse is an illustration of the fine maxim of 31st October, '37.)

26th November

Still in a stupor and just out of prison in an unfamiliar town, you see someone else—already dear to you—go to jail, and the obsessive idea of this second prison is colored by the strangeness of the town that shows its hidden face in your new loneliness. The Genoese, with vulgar assurance, who talks loudly about the unusual things in the town, protesting and condemning, is not receptive but demanding and thus approves when the town agrees with him.

To go back to 24th November—to be serious makes you naïve.

29th November

Knowing about the invisible cell makes us feel that everything is provisional, even in the human circle to which we belong. Who can feel at home with a cell?

30th November

I) There are two stages in writing a novel. The first is as though a sheet of water were becoming opaque and dark with mud; there is violent movement, upheaval, foam; then there is a calm, a period of quiescence; the quivering water grows still, begins to clear and suddenly is transparent again. The depths and the sky reflected in them are motionless.

The novel came into existence quietly, during this elimination of all motion and every impurity. Remember: it happened quietly.

II) So a novel is born; the agitated water trembles, grows clear and then is still. Those are the two stages: I) cloudy and disturbed, II) calm and serene.

3rd December

When we read, we are not looking for new ideas, but to see our own thoughts given the seal of confirmation on the printed page. The words that strike us are those that awake an echo in a zone we have already made our own—the place where we live—and the vibration enables us to find fresh starting points within ourselves.

What a great thought it is that all *effort* is futile! It is sufficient just to let our ego blossom, go along with it, take it by the hand as though it were someone else, have faith that we are more important than we realized.

4th December

The *Fioretto* of the Sermon to the Birds can show any-one what symbolic construction is. St. Francis is uncertain whether to pray or preach, and sends to ask Sister Clare and Brother Silvester (the one who had seen a cross of gold pro-ceeding from the mouth of St. Francis to the extremities of the world). The reply is that he should preach. (Accordingly, with great fervor of spirit, he preaches at Carmano [Savurni-ano], commanding the swallows to keep silence. All the people want to follow him and St. Francis makes them minor friars.) Then he preaches at Bevango to his "little sisters," the birds, and when they have listened to him and received his blessing, they fly away in the shape of a cross, carrying the significance of his teaching to the four ends of the world.

The symbolic interest links Sister Clare and Silvester, the cross-bearer, with the birds, who are also "sisters" and "cross-bearers" (by means of the sermon at Carmano, when, under the sign of the swallows, all the people were transformed into minor friars). It is this device of making the birds per-sonify sisters and cross-bearers (Clare and Silvester) which makes the story, and creates, out of a simple, charming detail (the behavior of the birds while St. Francis was preaching) a rich, profound imagery of inner life. This may be a symbol, but it is certainly poetry. Clare and Silvester (the companions) give their own significance to the birds and receive fresh significance from them—and this is what I call imagery. (The devotion of the people of Carmano and the silence of the swallows are clever touches that unite the two extremes of the greater imagery.)

To suggest, by a repeated action, a descriptive name, some cross-reference or other, that a character, an object or a situation in the story has an imaginative link with another, is to take away the material nature of both, and to substitute an account of that link, that imaginative connection, instead of a story based on their individual, material nature.

"This imaginative link" must be something more than a mere similarity. It must give its own color to the whole subject, present it in a certain light, with a certain meaning, which then is the truth it has to convey: the "little sisters and the cross" changes the companions and the birds into "creatures of charity bearing witness to God," i.e., "imparting a message of active charity."

View in this way the symbols of Dante, not so much the Cross and the Eagle (those are the most banal ones), but, for example, the atmosphere of twilight in all the cantos of the *Purgatorio,* which gives meaning to the visions and awakenings, and expresses the *message* of "a world that is glad to conceal itself in shadow."

6th December

Old age—or maturity—falls also on the external world. The clear, freezing winter night etching the outlines of houses against a snow-laden sky, once it touched our hearts and opened up a whole world of heroic restlessness.

As time goes on, we no longer need to move amid the outside world and share its anxieties. All that we want is a brief recognition of it, knowing that it exists in itself and also in us, and waiting for a world composed entirely of an inner life, that thenceforward takes on the freshness and fecundity of nature. Maturity is this, too; no longer seeking outside

ourselves, but letting our inner life speak with its own rhythm
—the only thing that matters. Then the outside world seems
petty and materialistic, compared with the unforeseen, profound maturity of our memories. Our very flesh and blood
has ripened and become imbued with spirituality, its rhythm
has broadened. Maturity is an isolation that is sufficient unto
itself.

Youth does not possess its own body, or the world at
large.

As for the old idea that genius is synonymous with
creative fertility—eighty tragedies, twenty novels, thirty operas,
and so on—genius is not a matter of discovering some external theme and treating it skillfully, but of finally achieving
complete possession of one's own experience, own body, own
memories—one's own rhythm, and expressing this rhythm,
above and beyond the limitations of plot or subject matter,
with the perennial fruitfulness of inexhaustible thought.

Youth has no genius and is not productive.

8th December

Anyone who denounces the immorality of venal love
must leave all women alone, for, apart from the rare occasions
when one of them offers her body for love's sake, even the
woman who has loved you merely allows the act of love to
happen, giving herself out of courtesy or for some personal
advantage, as apathetic as a prostitute.

The same thing, though perhaps less often, can be
said of a man.

The only way out of this farce is to condemn sincere
love, too, in as much as its object is self-gratification. The
fact remains that screwing, with its plea for caresses, smiles,
complaisance, sooner or later becomes a bore to one of the
couple, who no longer feels inclined to kiss, caress, or give
pleasure to the other. Then their love-making is as false as
venal love. You can't deny it. Even if their purpose is to
produce a child.

The conclusion of 6th December confirms the state-

125

ments of 24th November about youth. "We stop being young when we can differentiate between ourselves and others." "Youth is not possessing one's own body." Maturity is isolation that is sufficient unto itself.

10th December

Idleness makes hours pass slowly and years swiftly. Activity makes the hours seem short and the years long. The busiest time of all is childhood, because it is fully occupied by finding out what the world is and getting used to it.

Years become long in our memory if, when thinking of them, we find they contain many events that add to their imaginative appeal. That is why childhood seems so very long. Probably every period of life is multiplied by our reflections upon it in the next. The shortest is old age, because we shall never be able to think back on it.

Everything that has happened to us is of inexhaustible value; each time we think about it makes it more far-reaching, endows it with associations, gives it a deeper significance. Childhood is not only the childhood we really had, but the impressions we formed of it in our adolescence and maturity. It seems the most important epoch because it is the one most enriched by our long succession of thoughts about it.

The years are a unit of memory; the hours and days, of experience.

20th December

Get rid of your taste for the significant, extravagant remark and replace it with the significant, extravagant thought, no longer expressed in dialogue but deepened to form the connective tissue of the tale. The first is descriptive realism, the second is construction. Stop making your characters say intelligent things; the intelligent things are what you should know yourself, amplifying them in the construction of your story.

26th December

Imprisonment is bound to seem like the end of every kindly impulse, the point when human sympathy congeals. In fact, during the ascending phase, one's mind soars beyond those walls. (Do not take the strangeness of that new world as final. Use it as a means of stimulating wonder and curiosity), and in the descending phase one thinks with sympathetic horror of the next prisoner to be confined there, for whom that strangeness will increase the burden of loneliness.

27th December

Although, in reality, childhood is made up of long periods of vague uncertainty and rare contacts with the world (the first we have), it seems very long in retrospect, simply because we know that there were long pauses between our important discoveries.

The art of living is the art of behaving in such a way that we have no need to invite people or things, but still they come to us. To achieve that result, it is not enough to despise them, but we must *also* despise them. Just as with women, it is not enough to be stupid, but we must *also* be stupid.

1939

1st January

This past year has been a period of much reflection, of release from bondage (half in, half out); few new works, but a great and growing urge to find freedom and understanding. *Now I can begin.*

My active work, now organized on a practical basis, should no longer be chaotic; a life of sensible seclusion will follow, and all my energy be devoted to creation.

Remember that the self-confidence of 30th December,

'37 was an illusion, and that six months later I was still raving. Remember.

7th January

Though a young man tends to be reserved—out of timidity—he is naively full of confidence that to be on cordial terms with other people would bring him everything he wants —but this worries him even more, because he cannot attain this cordiality. A mature man, on the contrary, accepts with equanimity the social life that comes his way, but does not dream of basing his own serenity upon it.

19th January

Any suffering that does not also teach you something, is futile. Remember that, seeing how painful it is. Instead of sorrowing over the extent of a disaster, grieve for its uselessness. Enduring a dreadful calamity passively, like an animal, does not make it any less. Instead, one should look at it calmly, and get something useful out of its futility by means of contemplation.

There still remains the actual reality of death, that by annihilating the subject also abolishes his powers of contemplation. But then it is even more useless to suffer it. To contemplate it up to the last moment without batting an eyelid is still the most practical method. . . . *"Wouldst drink up eisel? Eat a crocodile? . . ."*

23rd January

Only a thought that has become automatic, instinctive, can serve as a *credo* and inspire action. There is danger in analyzing oneself too much: it brings too clearly to light the living veins of one's own temperament, and by familiarity their reactions become mechanical. Instead, one must acquire the art of giving free play to one's spiritual impulses, allowing them to react automatically to stimulation. There is a reaction due to orthodox beliefs—the catechism, false and known too well—and a reaction due to instinct. One must foster instinct, seek it out, recognize it, rely on it, without dulling it by reflection. But thought is needed, too, to act in accordance with it and take its place in moments when we are deaf to it.

29th January

The most banal thing, discovered in ourselves, becomes intensely interesting. It is no longer an abstract banality, but an amazing co-ordination between reality and our own individuality.

2nd February

If inner progress comes only through conscious convictions that coincide with things we knew unconsciously already (cf. 3rd December, '38), then all that really counts is our unconscious mind, in which lies our true nature, our temperament. What we learn in life, what we can teach, is the technique of the path to conscious knowledge, which thus becomes the simple *outline* of our nature.

Religions and doctrines all claim that it is possible to teach not only the path to knowledge but also the structure of knowledge, and, as if that were not enough, they all add a good deal about *grace,* inspiration, zeal, to supplement the warmth generated by the contact of the unconscious mind with reality.

5th February

To believe in things means leaving something behind us to exist after our own death, and having the satisfaction, while we are still alive, of being in touch with something that will outlive us. But does it give us any satisfaction to think that *things* were in existence before us, and that in the course of our life we come into contact with what went before? The same meager satisfaction is all we shall have after death, knowing that something of ours will continue to exist.

7th February

Those who seem most passionate in their youth, generally become cynics later in life; young cynics develop, as they grow older, a naive ingenuousness in sexual matters. Byron typifies the first, Swann the second. It is not possible to possess only one of those two attitudes, for the one inevitably engenders the other.

I noted on 24th November, '38: young men see no difference between themselves and others; a man is mature when he can distinguish between himself and others. How then can we explain why civilizations begin with a belief in the objectivity of the world, and invent idealism when they are decadent? Thus: the *objectivity of the world* is the result of looking at it on the bright side, believing in it as a mystic, objective, organized unity; *idealism* means isolating the ego from empty, conventional pretenses (the "others" of the man of riper years).

9th February

Where juvenile enthusiasm falls short is in its refusal, substantially, to recognize its own limitations. The ability to differentiate between oneself and others, that comes as one reaches maturity, tends to convince the ego that there is no way of communicating with others. And, in fact, there is no direct communication. One recognizes the dignity of other men only through a superior being: God. That is why we are told to do good *for the love of God*. So little does the other man, as such, matter to us.

Given that to know other men is an enrichment (and the only true knowledge comes through a loving recognition), the man who refuses to love them, i.e., to know them, is that much poorer. Hence the adolescent feeling of completeness, for in the intoxication of youth one feels the never-ending thrill of universal knowledge. But since this feeling of completeness is unfounded, more mature experience regards it as a delusion. Hence the retrocession of the thirties, that can be avoided only by the man who recognizes his own limitations and does not compare himself with others. The bare, utilitarian knowledge (cynicism) of the thirties, is the reverse side of the simple, muddled love of everything (ingenuousness) of the twenties. They are both forms of poverty, and without much trouble one of them can change to the other, but a man must sweat blood to pass from either of them to true charity, or, as they say, "find God."

15th February

A discovery: when anyone "takes us down," humiliates us and treats us as servants, we attach ourselves to him, will not let him go, take his hand and bless him in our inmost heart as if we were bewitched. Is this a presentiment of the brotherhood of man, a recognition (against nature) of our need to be abject?

5th March

No matter how much a young man likes to think for himself, he is always trying to model himself on some abstract pattern largely derived from the example of the world around him. And a man, no matter how conservative, shows his own worth by his personal deviation from that pattern.

This arises from the fact that only gradually do we come to understand that our way of life is our own creation; in all its minute ramifications it is the expression of our experience. The troubles of young people are born of the impossibility of making their own experience coincide with the broad, stylized impression they have gained of the world. Any profession, any social status, seems to a young man remote and unattainable, until, little by little, he has created his own status and profession—totally different, in their slow, inner growth, from the clumsy vision he imagined and dreaded. But then he is a man. Which confirms that to be young is to be unable to possess oneself.

12th March

Note that Proust, who breaks experience down into myriads of momentary feelings, then becomes the most rabid theorist about those feelings, and constructs his book not upon memories of the reaction one feeling has upon another, but on planes of conceptualism and mystical knowledge that reduce them to material for research.

29th March

From what I said on 6th December, '38, it follows that it is more unpleasant to die old than young.

3rd April

Every man has the philosophy of his own aptitudes.

26th April

The company of a woman we love makes us suffer and live in a state of violent agitation. We should choose the company of one we do not care for, but then our relationship with her is full of mental reservations; we are always wishing to be alone, and in our own mind we abolish her.

In all these thoughts on human relationships the main thing is the contrast between passion and indifference, which makes both of them absurd and incompatible. A charitable solution: the only way to get near such women is to see them through the fire of a search for information.

In *Memorie di due stagione*,[1] as long as Garofolo wants to break down his isolation or strengthen it (the first nine chapters), he damages only his hands; when he thinks of something else, relaxes, welcomes the spring, thinks of his fantastic past, grows humble and considers himself one of many (an identification with Orestes in prison and the banished anarchist), then he grows serene and lighthearted (the last two chapters).

[1] This was the original title of the story that was later published as *Il carcere (Primo che il gallo canti.* Einaudi, 1948). Ed.

29th April

Note that in the autumn of '38 I found a style and a sequence of ideas all building up to a climax. Note, too, that then, for the first time in my life, I decided to improve my behavior, that is, I theoretically determined what I wanted to be. And immediately I was able to write a novel which experiments with that attitude. A good starting point is to modify one's own past.

3rd May

The part of us that suffers is always a minor part. So, too, is the part that feels pleasure. Only the part of us that remains serene is of major importance. Suffering, like pleasure, is yielding to emotion. The only difference is that pleasure seems like serenity and is consequently deceptive, more time-wasting, while suffering quickly toughens and exhausts us. Substantially, to transform pleasure into serenity it must have grown boring. It is always through boredom that one attains serenity. Even suffering, to become creative, must first become a bore. This is the reason why we need leisure to dream, if we are to create. Then boredom crystallizes into ideas.

4th May

Serenity can come from doing something which is not an end in itself (as suffering and pleasure-seeking are), but which is connected with our work, because this interrupts boredom without involving us in an *unexpected* sequence of thoughts and feelings, allowing us instead to take a detached view (serenity) of a structure that obeys our commands (our work).

The finest thing we can say of any human endeavor, and therefore of art, too, is that it lets us live serenely, shunning determinism and being governed by the nature of our material, forgetting self-interest as we watch that method in action.

What the Greeks used to say of philosophy, which is

contemplation without self-interest and therefore the most sublime occupation, we can say of any *techné*, which is a selfless life creating a long chain of consequences.

If we denounce pleasure on the score of the stale dissatisfaction that remains when enjoyment is past, I do not see how we can exclude the production of works that, when completed, leave us as dissatisfied and stale as any pleasure. True, the work remains, but is that enough? There is, too, the thought that the work—a detached reality—is living its own life and doing some good to our fellowmen. It seems, then, that happiness is inseparable from the dedication of oneself to others. In that case, we can be happy only by going outside ourselves (another criticism of pleasure and pain); happy only indirectly, at a tangent, going in a certain direction and finding an additional unsought, side-shoot of pleasure that does not end when our immediate purpose is satisfied. Fundamentally, this is a clever device that ensures a longer duration to our pleasure, by the very fact that its end becomes indefinite. When we can say: "I did not act for myself but for a higher principle," having been careful to choose the broadest, most longlasting principle possible—eternal, if need be, we can be sure that our satisfaction will endure until the far distant future, or perhaps for ever.

(Evening)

Note that when you want to discredit a principle you call it a device, a piece of astuteness. This fashion of not considering anything acceptable but ingenuousness, disinterested enthusiasm, is romanticism. But why reject a shrewd principle if it makes you happier? The trouble is that if it is shrewd it no longer makes you happy, because you no longer believe it absolutely.

15th May

They have told you they do not complain, they would ask little or nothing, they suffer hopelessly, but they are not moaners.

134

Politics is the art of the possible. All life is a matter of politics.

The greatest misfortune is loneliness. So true is this that the highest form of consolation—religion—lies in finding a friend who will never let you down—God. Prayer is giving vent to one's thoughts, as with a friend. Work is an equivalent to prayer, since ideally it puts you in contact with something that will not take advantage of you. The whole problem of life, then, is this: how to break out of one's own loneliness, how to communicate with others. That explains the persistence of marriage, fatherhood, friendship, since they might bring happiness! But why it should be better to be in communication with another than to be alone, is a mystery. Perhaps it is only an illusion, for one can be perfectly happy alone, most of the time. It is pleasant now and then to have a boon companion to drink with, provided that what we ask of others we already possess within ourselves. The mystery is why it is not enough to drink and fathom our own individuality alone; why we should have to repossess ourselves through others. (Sex is merely incidental; what it gives us is momentary and casual: we see ourselves as something more involved, more mysterious, of which sex is only a sign, a symbol.)

16th May

Bachelors regard matrimony more seriously than married people do.

18th May

The man who avoids having children because he does not want to support them, will have to support other men's children.

20th May

It is natural that a woman, compelled by circumstances to submit to the intrusion of another's body into her own (leaving out of it her social subjection), should have developed a whole technique of escape within herself, eluding man, nullifying his conquest of her. Quite apart from her other weapons—deceitfulness and the game of social life.

Man is, at most, the slave of vice, but the woman, after coition, is the slave of the probable consequences: hence her terribly practical attitude to these things.

12th June

Since one is bound to throw a woman over, sooner or later, it is as well to do it quickly.

People at the dawn of history had a far stronger sense of the past than those who came after them. When a race no longer has a *vital* sense of its own past, it is dying out. Creative vitality springs from what has been stored in the past. We become creators when we have a past. The youth of a race is a rich old age. (Genius is wisdom and youth.)

Creation begins when an action is repeated endlessly until it becomes a routine and therefore wearisome. There follows a period of boredom, when our mind wanders. Then the thing we have forgotten because of its banality springs to life again like a miracle, a revelation, and there is our creative urge.

One substitute for far-off-in-time (the past) is far-off-in-space (the strange and exotic). This explains why, in some races, many creative urges are born from the fusion of two different civilizations; or more precisely, that fusion is a stimulus which brings out the richness already stored in the two respective pasts. It is the essential spark that gives their combination power to achieve wonders. By "richness," whether exotic or of the past, I mean a consciousness of life itself, not historical or geographical.

In the life of the imagination there are only two phases: the reflowering of a past or the clash between two ways of life.

The muses are the daughters of memory or the Indian Dionysus. Boredom, therefore, is like the sickness of pregnant women.

136

7th July

A past should be familiar enough for us to be able to relive it automatically, yet strange enough to astonish us each time we turn back to it: then it is ready for the use of our imagination.

An experience that seemed to you commonplace—let time pass, and you will see it with fresh eyes. It will be amazing.

To spend time in silence rejuvenates men and nations.

30th July

Is there or is there not progress in history?

There can be no solution to that problem, because while what you mean by progress is bringing moral values into what is absolute (all the rest you call technical skill, cleverness), other people are quite satisfied with this technical improvement in comfortable living conditions, regarding this as progress.

One cannot reach the absolute by degrees. Therefore one cannot find the absolute through historical evolution. So progress (undeniably) is not towards the absolute, but is quantitative.

The same applies to the individual. There is technical progress, an increase in cleverness, in experience, but the span of the bridge is what it was at the age of seven. It will be the same at thirty-five, as far as the absolute is concerned.

3rd August

Sexual morality is a palliative for jealousy. It strives to avoid comparison with another man's virile capacity. Jealousy is the fear of that comparison.

Tolerance of ideas is born of the illusion that truth is something rational. But as soon as one accepts the principle that any idea is based on an initial choice, and that the will is the first organ of understanding, then it becomes impossible to agree with that policy. To think this or that is incriminating. A *practical* source of error.

27th August

To what I said on 30th July, add that by technical progress I also mean the perfecting of moral ideals that, in essence, are a *comfort*. Progress towards moral absoluteness, on the contrary, is a matter on which time has no bearing (1), necessitating a complete annihilation of self and becoming one with God. That takes place in a metaphysical sphere where progress has no significance.

(1) A man might experience this change suddenly, as if, in life, he had found a moment of eternity, but that is outside our idea of time, which is a collective conception. There can be no such thing as collective self-annihilation and oneness with God, because collectivity is an empiric conception. It would always be possible, at any given moment, for a man to be born who would refuse to merge himself with God and lose his own identity.

9th September

War makes men barbarous because, to take part in it, one must harden oneself against all regret, all appreciation of delicacy and sensitive values. One must live *as if those values did not exist,* and when the war is over one has lost the resilience to return to those values.

17th September

We give alms to a beggar to rid ourselves of the sight of the poor wretch; and if such a one upsets us by his display of utter misery, appealing to our sense of some obvious, undeniable kinship with him, then we loathe him with all our might.

1st October

Mistakes that leap to your eyes in a work, or even those that become apparent as you read, are by their very nature easily correctible and of no account. What does count is a fundamental error, a mistaken viewpoint that distorts passages correct in themselves, throwing them out of their true perspective. Such error cannot be corrected except by destroying the work. Superficial, obvious errors serve, at most, as pointers to what lies beneath.

9th October

"There is an emotion inseparable from our encounter with any man we meet." Lavelle: *L'erreur de Narcisse*, p. 31.

"Doubtless I am wrong if I complain of the treatment others inflict on me. For it is always a result, a copy, of the treatment I inflict on them. But if I grieve at not being loved enough, it is because I myself am not sufficiently loving." Lavelle: *ibid.*, p. 34.

"The terms we are on with other men are always a reflection of the terms we are on with ourselves." Lavelle: *ibid.*, p. 165.

". . . the only thing that counts is what we are, not what we do." Lavelle: *ibid.*, p. 171.

14th October

The urge to do something wicked at all costs, something that runs counter to our own nature, is characteristic of adolescence. We feel compelled to prove to ourselves that we belong to the universe and are above any conventional restriction. What is better than finding we are a hero when we've been up to a bit of devilment, on a country road in the morning, as the heavy carts go by?

The style of Berto[1] should not be regarded as peculiar to him alone, but as though it were in the third person. By its very naturalism, it must become a revealing *way of thinking*. That is something one cannot do in poetry, but it should be successful in a prose work.

We think constructively when, upset by some shock in life, we look at ourselves from the outside, like separate

[1] A character speaking in the first person in *Paesi tuoi*. Ed.

characters. Exactly the same thing happens when writing a story, for fresh thoughts and problems arise with every scene. Worthwhile thoughts are born when one strikes a pose foreign to one's real nature, and observes oneself living in the attitude *of one's choice.*

So the art I invoked on 9th October, '38, the art of "looking at ourselves as though we were characters in one of our novels," becomes understood as the way to put ourselves in a position to think constructively and reap the benefit.

18th October

Passing judgment on people, or characters in a book, means making silhouettes of them.

Philanthropic times are times when beggars are put in jail.

29th October

It is not true that in our day novels are not written because no one any longer believes in the stability of the world. It cannot be true, for the nineteenth century novel was born while a world was crashing into ruin, and even served as a substitute for the stability the world was losing. Now the novel is seeking a new code in the new world just coming into existence, and cannot be satisfied to follow its old outlines in this new world.

An idea becomes fruitful when it is a combination of two lines of thought, merging to produce something new and full of zest. In the same way a novelist creates a character.

1st November

One generally feels kindly disposed towards a woman if one finds that, in spite of all her cynicism, all her Hitlerism and nastiness, she is capable of a human impulse of pity, of gentleness. But more particularly we think kindly of ourselves in such circumstances, deeply congratulating ourselves on our own good thought. Rare though this may be ("a good deed is easier than a good thought," cf. 3rd November, '38), note

that what is commonly called "a good thought" is a sentimental impulse of which we are all capable. As is shown by
film scenarios, even German ones.

An example to illustrate what I said on 29th October:

— — Loneliness; bewitching visits by a young man
— — Two days of *fiesta*. How they pass, condensation
— — Discovery of syphilis in the young man
— — Great moment of political activity concentrated into those two days; frantic desper-
ation of the young man
— — He feels driven to commit some crime or
other, because of
— loneliness
— those days of fiesta (Pause)
— syphilis
— political substitution

Taking away the political angle (which comes from
Nizan), what remains is the bewitching visit to the upper
room, all that happened during the two days of fiesta (magical
incantation), with the torment of the discovery of syphilis—
which drives him to crime.

5th November

Why do we find any new writer tiresome? Because
we do not yet know enough about him to visualize him in a
social environment we would feel confident in sharing.

10th November

Being ashamed to indulge in a spontaneous bit of devilry is one way of becoming aware that we are no longer young
(cf. 14th October). It is an apt theme for revealing that youth
is over. One's aim should be not to mention *youth* in the
story, but let it be deduced from whether or not the character
refuses to let himself go. If mentioned at all, it could be in
the title: *Youth is past*. And, at bottom, is the thought: "See,

I will not do those things any more: the mistakes I make now will be well thought out; circumscribed, not universal."

Also because casual, high-spirited mischief calls for plenty of spare time and a willingness to put up with discomfort, which we no longer have at thirty.

18th November

You do not like Merimée, precisely because of those qualities that make him an "exquisite artist." You feel he is a man who disregards any sincerity of atmosphere, holds himself aloof, hashes up multi-colored pictures of a false, borrowed society. He changes his background like changing his clothes. He cannot bring alive a drama of *a man in his own environment;* even where it is tragic, it is tragic only by hearsay, by supposition; it lacks roots in the background (*Carmen*). The exact opposite of Stendhal, who *lives* in high society with the zeal of a fanatic, of a sainted demon.

Cf. my note on 28th July, '38, ruling that every worthwhile plot consists of "seeing how a particular character extricates himself from a given set of circumstances, i.e., his background, atmosphere." Then Merimée, who does not believe in atmosphere, cannot take a single one of his plots seriously and make it convincing.

19th November—Sunday

Reading Landolfi makes it clear that your *motif* of the goat was the *motif* of the bond between man and the animal kingdom. Hence your taste for prehistory, the period that gives us a glimpse of a community of interests between man and wild beasts. Hence your own research into the origin of imagery at that epoch: the link between a first object (usually human) and a second (usually animal) which should be something more than a simple piece of imagery: evidence of a living bond. All that was already grasped (15th September, '36) when you commented on Lévy-Bruhl and noted that imagery, to a primitive mentality, was not a play of expression, but *positive description.* (Cf., also, in *Lavorare stanca*, November, '34, your first realization that imagery could be a theme for a story, your way of escape from naturalism.) The imaginative story would be *an account of this bond,* i.e., instituting a symbol. (Cf. 6th November, '38). Furthermore, the imaginative story, looked at clearly (cf. 24th October, '38) must believe that what it relates really happened, i.e., must regard the imagery as a *truth,* existing even beyond the written page.

A somewhat similar psychological affinity occurred to you earlier (29th October, '39), when you said that an idea becomes fruitful when it is a *combination* of *two* discoveries.

26th November

In his *Purgatorio,* Dante never turns back to survey the panorama, for the reason that he is not realistically describing a journey, but expounding a creed, using the scene and making it *visible* only in so far as it serves to give his ideas a bodily form. Thus he is not obliged to respect the naturalistic logic of reality.

At the end of the century, the theme of the discord between art and life—the artist who feels ineffectual and out of touch with reality—put a stop to all the romantic autobiographies that seemed inadequate after the wild outbursts of genius and folly in the eighteen hundreds.

28th November

It could be that children are more routine-minded than adults, but we do not realize it because they live at war with adults, and are forced to follow their habits in secret. In fact, adults do their best to break all the habits of children, suspecting that they contain an element of opposition and anarchism. But in the field of games, where children enjoy relative self-government, their close observance of custom is very plain—their love of ritual and formulae, their superstition about places and so on. It even acquires, unconsciously, a special importance as a vindication of their independence of adults.

Since it is difficult for we-little-folk-to-do-things-like-grown-ups, difficult in itself and because grown-ups are so distrustful, the child tends to create rules for himself in his own affairs, to stay in the same rut, encouraging himself with what he has already done. Remember your own habit, when you were five, of crying as soon as you sat at table, quite without reason. But you liked doing it because you had tried it before and it was your own special way of behaving.

4th December

Wrote to Pinelli: ". . . reverting to some of my ideas, the work is a symbol in which the characters, just as much as the setting, are the *means* of presenting a little parabola, the ultimate root of inspiration and interest: the 'path of the soul' in my own *Divina Commedia*."

"My language is very different from a naturalistic impressionism. I did not write in imitation of Berto—the only one who says anything—but translating his meditations, his wonderment, his raillery, as he would have expressed them himself, *had he spoken Italian*. I introduced errors of syntax only to indicate occasions when his own spirit grew scornful, involved or tedious. I wanted to show, not how Berto would write had he forced himself to speak Italian (that would have been dialectic impressionism), but what his own words would be, had they been changed into Italian by some new Pentecost. In short, his thoughts."

10th December

The *symbol* I spoke of on 6th November, '38, and on 4th December (I Fioretti), is an imaginative link forming a network that underlies the discourse. I am talking of recurring points of contact ("epithets," as in the classic example of 6th November) that indicate a persistent, imaginative significance in one of the material elements of the story (a tale within a tale)—a secret reality coming into bloom. For example, the "breast" in *paesi tuoi*—a true epithet expressing the sexual reality of that countryside.

144

No longer an allegoric symbol, but an *imaginative symbol*—an additional means of expressing the "fantasy," the story. Hence the dynamic quality of these symbols; epithets that appear and reappear in the story are *characters* in it, adding their effect to the material completeness of the discourse; not substitutes that rob reality of its very breath and lifeblood, like the static symbol (Prudence, a woman with three eyes).

A parallel to this method is to be found in Dante, not so much in his allegory as in his imagery. On this point one could quote many lectures and analytical studies The 23rd Canto of the *Paradiso* can inspire you. All these phenomena of light express the luminous reality of the place, and even its hidden reality as the "meeting-place of all created things" (thunder, sunshine, birds, the moon, song, flowers, precious stones).

12th December

Every artist tries to take to pieces the mechanism of his technique to examine its construction so that, if necessary, he can use it "cold." Nevertheless, a work of art is successful only when, *for the artist himself,* it has a certain element of mystery. It is quite natural: the story of an artist is the successive improvement upon the technique employed in his previous work, with a fresh creation that imposes a more complex aesthetic law. Self-criticism is a means of self-improvement. The artist who is not continually analyzing and breaking down his own technique is a poor one. (cf. 8th November, '38.)

It is the same in all activities, the logical rule of life throughout history. But, as much in art as in life, ever since romanticism came into existence, there exists in this rule of logic an ever-living danger: that of deliberately deciding where the mystery shall lie, so as to guarantee oneself the desired creative urge. But the mystery that stimulates creation must come about of itself, through an obstacle encountered unawares during the course of our very effort at clarification.

Nothing is more obscene than an artist (or a politician) who *coldly* plays around with his own mysterious unreasoning intuition.

To take the mystery to pieces in order to use it "cold" in one's work (without the agony of creation) is the impulse behind the whole history of the spirit. Herein lies the dignity of man, but also his temptation.

14th December

We want Realism's wealth of experience and Symbolism's depth of feeling. All art is a problem of balance between two opposites.

21st December

Love is the cheapest of religions.

25th December

A true artist talks of art as little as possible in his creative works. (Otherwise he is not an artist but a virtuoso of art.) He who has merely mastered the labor of art has not yet passed the stage of preparing his tools; he is not yet qualified to speak in the world as a grown man.

27th December (Morning)

A russet acropolis. On the opposite hill, a great cluster of buildings and palaces (the city where all is planned and assured). On the walls are painted two large pictures, visible from the acropolis. One is allegorical—a throng of women and symbolic devices; a hovering female figure (typifying Venice in Verona), borne aloft on palm branches with other women circling round her. In the foreground is a calm, majestic woman letting pearls drop from her fingers into a vessel. (But one does not *see* her dropping pearls, one *knows* she is doing so.) Just as in a story when, without describing it (making us see it), the author says: "She fingers her pearls."

I suddenly realize—having already seen it in imagination—that this woman is Italy. The dancing girls and the palms are symbols of the sea that surrounds her. Here is proof that while dreaming of this figure, I attributed to her, by implication, a significance of which I was quite unaware. *Who gave her this significance?*

(The dream is certainly a result of my visit to Venice in February, '39.)

It seems to me that at other times I have dreamed of the crests of strange hills, seen from below or halfway up, and covered with mulberry trees or in the open country. Who knows when or why?

There are two possible explanations. Either this is the first time I have dreamed of this Piedmont town of paintings (by Carpaccio, as I know in my dream), and my impression that I have walked its streets before and seen it in the past (in other dreams) is due only to a recognition of the temporal nature of the dream, whereby every moment we dream is born with its own temporal, retrospective landscape. Or it really is a dream I have already dreamed on other nights, of other similar cities on the crest of a hill (not Venice, perhaps, in that case, but Siena and Genoa) reduced to the proportions of a rustic dance? Then the world of our dreams is a mine with a vertical shaft, down which we are conveyed, as in an elevator, to varying depths where there are fixed dreams that we see again each time. Even so, it cannot be said that the tempo is our normal one, or the construction of dreams (sedimentary layers, geological strata) would be even more remarkable: not a single dream creating the illusion of a past implicit in itself, but a whole temporal network underlying all our nights, all our slumbers, taken together. It would really be an *existing* world that we enter each time we sleep (and our dreams are waiting for us at different depths; we do not create them.)

31st December

When the creators of the *stile nuovo* invented the ever-present "chorus" of friends and womenfolk to whom the poet addresses his discourse, they had discovered the *justification* for their poetry which is the celebration of this community and consists of the cordial expression of one's own thoughts, returning full circle.

All national poetry begins with circles of that sort, detaching from the social body a limited, "conditioned" group made up of listeners and collaborators.

1940

1st January

Not much done. Three works: *Le due stagione, I Paesi tuoi* and *Il carretiere*. The two stories are things of the past, of some value, perhaps, in that they satisfied an impulse I had and proved that I can decide upon a style and sustain it, but that is all. The little poem is just a trifle, but shows some promise. I hope to go back to it with renewed zest when I have considered it more fully and thrown off my present mood for narrative.

As for my thoughts, I have not expressed them so expansively in these pages but I have gathered a varied, mature, rich harvest of them, and, above all, I feel thoroughly fit to make lively use of them. As '39 ends I am full of aspiration, confident of myself from now on, tense as a cat lying in wait for her prey. Intellectually I have the same agility and pent-up energy as the cat.

I no longer rave. I have lived for my creative work: and have acquired peace of mind. On the other hand I have grown very much afraid of death, terrified that my body might let me down.

This has been the first year I have lived with dignity, because I have applied myself to a definite plan.

Artists like Dante (the *stile nuovo*), Stendhal and Baudelaire are creators of *stylized situations:* they never lapse into fine phrases because they conceive a phrase as the prime cause of situations. They never let themselves go when they write because, for them, filling a page means creating an abstract situation that evolves inside a closed circle, on a restricted plane with laws of its own, quite different from real life. On the other hand their opposites (Petrarch, Tolstoi, Verlaine) are always on the verge of confusing art and life, and if they make mistakes in their art it is in their phrases, whether they are fine or clumsy, not in creating stereotyped situations as the others do. They have a tendency to extend their art into their practical life (Petrarch—a humanist; Tolstoi—a saint; Verlaine—a man accursed), and they are nearly always successful men as far as their practical life goes. (They are also frustrated in their art for existential reasons; cf. 26th November, '39, paragraph 2.) Men of the first group, on the contrary, are always failures who do not mourn their lack of worldly success (as some of those uninhibited types do to please the common herd), but they build another world where their bitter, day-to-day experience is filtered through their intelligence, and allowed to appear in their work only if it accords with the construction. Great authors of decisive works are men who never write a page to give vent to their own superabundance, but ponder over it and shape it in their minds before the work is begun.

They are great theorists about art—the problem they are always brooding over—while the others write as spontaneously as breathing, singing, living. My favorites are the solitary ones, the ascetics who ask nothing of life beyond the realization of their own clear vision of art, of morality, of political truth. All that the others ask is *experience,* and their works are merely diaries that reflect those experiences.

Flaubert is, quite unconsciously, a travesty of *my* kind of artist. (Cf. my criticism of 17 February, '38, which shows that although art, for him, is a closed circle, self-controlled, created by intelligence; man's moral nature, *considered as a whole,* does not come into it. Consequently his fine phrases are mere phantoms.)

It could be that the *stylized situations* I spoke of are not intended as actual descriptions of reality but as parables, and the characters in the story are symbols of imaginary qualities or events.

3rd January

There is a type of man accustomed to thinking that life owes him nothing, not even on the score of work he has done or an ordeal he has endured: nothing from anyone on any pretext whatever, not even from those he has helped. Consequently he gives nothing to others except for his own pleasure. Myself exactly.

8th or 9th January

The proof of your own lack of interest in politics is that, believing in liberalism (i.e., the possibility of ignoring political life), you would like to enforce it autocratically. You are conscious of political life only at times of totalitarian crises, and then you grow heated and run counter to your own liberalism in the hope of quickly bringing about the liberal conditions in which you can live without bothering about politics.

11th January

From the thirteenth century to the sixteenth, Italian poetry concerned the world of the nobility; it began with the conception of nobleness of heart (the *stile nuovo*), admired nobility of behavior and fashion (Boccaccio), recreated the idea of chivalry (Bioardo), and lapsed into irony and theorizing (Ariosto and Castiglione). As it died it gave way to Shakespearian witticism and to the neo-classical good taste of the *grand siècle*, reappearing as a nostalgia for the past and as a standard of life in certain romanticists (Stendhal, Baudelaire).

Periods of great productivity in literature are preceded by a generation of intensely active translators. The closer history approaches our own era, the more does the fusion of two civilizations take place, not by flesh and blood, but on paper. Instead of invasions we have translations.

21st January

At first, power served ideologies; now ideologies serve power.

Things which cost nothing are those which cost the most. Why? Because they cost us the effort of understanding that they are free.

22nd January

(Cf. 27th December, '39.) The features of a dream are engendered and strung together out of some dominating experience of the previous evening that grows disjointed in our mind and becomes a kaleidoscope, symbolic of the "passion" and excitements of the night before. (As Dante said: "after the dream, passion makes its mark.") This explains how it is that the world of a dream has its own temporal, retrospective setting—the reality of the experience that remains in the background of the figurative symbolism that is the dream.

Furthermore, it is understandable why the dream unfolds itself like a coherent story, one, that is, in which a particular detail comes to acquire an ulterior importance that was already implicit in its first appearance. We do not know what is going to happen, but we, ourselves, are the "passion" of the dream and the mass of impressions of the night before. We are, in short, like a narrator who knows (sees within himself) the second symbolic phase of one of his ideas, but not the first, the symbolic figuration. Little by little, as it passes before his eyes, this will come to life, full of imminent developments, starting points that the story itself will interpret, giving them meaning. Dreaming is like writing a symbolic story already known in spirit and in process of development as to the letter.

26th January

Nothing can be a consolation for death. All the talk about the inevitability, the value, the importance of that step leaves it increasingly stark and terrifying, and is nothing more than a proof of its enormity, like the derisive smile of a condemned man.

1st February

Just like Proust: when you had to do without coffee, you no longer found the serenity of nerves that you needed before you could use your imagination. Then you got accustomed to it (*Paradiso sui tetti, Paesaggio,* and the plot of *La tenda*).[1] Now there is coffee, and it seems to you to counteract imaginative serenity.

Anger is never sudden. It is born of a long, prior irritation that has ulcerated the spirit and built up an accumulation of force that results in an explosion. It follows that a fine outburst of rage is by no means a sign of a frank, direct nature. It is, on the contrary, an involuntary revelation of a tendency to foster an inner spite, the sign of an envious, introvert temperament and an inferiority complex.

The advice to beware of a man who is never in a temper (22nd July, '38) because one is sincere only when self-control is forgotten (7th December, '37), amounts to saying that, since all men inevitably accumulate hatred, you should be especially on your guard against men who never betray themselves by bursts of anger. As for you, there's no harm done if your spite is kept secret, but you are wrong to betray yourself with a fit of rage.

9th February

In general, the man who is readily disposed to sacrifice himself is one who does not know how else to give meaning to his life.

The profession of enthusiasm is the most sickening of all insincerities.

18th February

Once the fervor of a monomania has lapsed, it has no central idea that might give significance to random moments

[1] *La tenda* was the original title of *La bella estate.* Ed.

of inner reflection. In short, the more the spirit is absorbed by a dominating mood, the richer and more varied is one's inner breadth of vision.

One must look for one thing only, to find many.

19th February

The characters in your poems tend a little too much to have odd, i.e., picturesque, ways of earning a living.

21st February

It is easy to preserve a lordly manner, an aloofness, a disdainful familiarity or an aristocratic imperturbability with people from whom we want nothing. They are not of the least importance, merely a game to us, a pretext for a pose, like animals (that do not bite). That sort of behavior is called *superior*. But the moment we have to ask for something we are no longer even equal, but inferior, for the reason that the other man could refuse to give it to us.

Perfect behavior is born of complete indifference.

Perhaps this is why we always love madly someone who treats us with indifference; she represents "style," the fascination of "class," all that is desirable. Here is the answer to your endless thoughts in '37-'38 on the necessity of never giving yourself completely to a woman you want to possess— especially 16th November, '37, paragraph 2.

22nd February

The interest of this journal would be the unforeseen profusion of ideas, the periods of inspiration that, of themselves, automatically, indicate the main trends of your inner life. From time to time you try to understand what you are thinking, and only as an afterthought do you go on to link your present ideas with those of days gone by. The originality of these pages is that you leave the construction to work itself out, and set your own spirit in front of you, objectively. There is something metaphysical in your confidence that this psychological sequence of your thoughts will shape itself into a well-constructed work.

That is how lyrics are written, as you have said in *certain poems not yet finished*. Would the difference between "poems" and "thoughts" be merely illusory? Is it enough to say that thoughts are attempts to clarify a problem for yourself, and poems are attempts to create a *universal* picture? I do not see that it is enough.

The problem is the same for the collected works of a whole life: each is a construction in itself, of course, but taken all together do they form merely a succession or a constructive sequence? It is a sophism to recall that centuries in literature have no existence in factual historiography. A century is an empiric, abstract unit, but a life, an individual, is something more than that.

Certainly something more in that he lived and developed himself; but is there an implied unity of construction in his work as a whole, arising from the mechanical succession of days and his own self-criticism as each stage is completed? What one calls a metaphysical unity.

Conversely. A single work, well constructed, does it come about other than by welding together, after considering them separately (and before making the final draft, of course), the diverse fragments?

We shall see, one day, that our common faith in poetry will cause envy.

It happened that I became a man when I learned to be alone; others when they felt the need for company.

23rd February

The superhuman greatness of Shakespeare is plain, not only from his works, but also because he died leaving two thirds of them unpublished, including *Antony and Cleopatra, Macbeth* (?) and many comedies.

Such an extraordinary thing leads one to imagine that at the beginning of the seventeenth century the idea of publishing was not yet very widespread and that it was believed that once a book was written it would naturally go down to posterity. But then, how can we explain the texts in the form of parts for individual actors, that Shakespeare *knew* were left in that disjointed, corruptible state? It cannot be said that he lacked the time or leisure to attend to it. There you have wisdom so vast that it borders on cosmic irony. A superhuman gesture.

24th February

The persons or the institutions that we make responsible for keeping us happy have the right to complain if we remind them that we nevertheless still consider ourselves free, with power to rebuff them if we so decide. Everything we fall short of achieving for ourselves, makes our liberty that much less. The patient in the hands of the doctor is like society in the hands of a deliverer, whether a hero or a political party.

What? You commission him to reorganize society—that is, yourselves—and yet you claim to remain free?

For the very reason that no such thing exists as a purely economic society, every scientific economic organization carries with it the affirmation of a subtle power, that is, a government manifesto that intrudes upon the inner life, and just as the organizer should eliminate every economic heresy, so will he have to eliminate every heresy of private opinion. The society, completely controlled economically, is a contradiction of a society with complete spiritual freedom.

"Moral idealism" is a collective notion. The individual has no moral ideal, because in his absoluteness (the eternal present) he does not conform to a standard but just *is*. (Bergson, *The Two Springs*.)

If society cannot become absolute, inasmuch as one of the individuals it contains can always rebel against it, neither can an individual become absolute for any length of time, because though he may reach that state at one moment, he can lapse from it the next.

This goes back to what I said on 22nd February, '40, and denies, in short, that a life composed of a mechanical succession of moments, even those of which it is most conscious, can shape itself like a metaphysical construction. In fact, the mechanical succession of thoughts falls into the same pattern as time, realized empirically. For an experience to have a metaphysical value, it must be dissociated from time. In practical life that seems to happen only in an isolated moment—an escape from time.

The "falseness of poetry" (3rd October, '38)—the substitution of absolute for empiric time—becomes more entrancing than the "kingdom of heaven," because the latter is realized only for brief instants, but the former is experienced in constructions that, though they count as a single absolute moment, give more prolonged pleasure and sometimes embrace lengthy periods of empiric time.

* * *

The unity of a work will therefore consist of the interdependence of all its moments at one and the same period, absolute, or metaphysical.

Hence the difficulty of determining it, apart from the indicative development of its own events and phenomena, for us who are accustomed to examine life always according to the pattern of empiric time and who, in practice, know absolute time only as the negation of empiric time, in matters of ethics. (Hence, by the way, the *individual* nature of a work of art, as of a moral act: experiences that by their very nature are non-collective because they are absolute.)

It is easy to create a "momentary" work of art, a "fragment," just as it is easy to live a moment of morality, but to create a work that transcends the moment is difficult, just as it is difficult to live for longer than a single heartbeat in the kingdom of heaven. The art of organizing the kingdom of heaven for longer than a moment (saintliness) is on the same level as organizing the work of poetry beyond the fragmentary stage.

You have defined the first as practically impossible (in so far as you consider morality, basically, as being composed of isolated moments), but you hope to succeed in the second, which shows that your vocation is poetical, not ethical. Satisfied?

156

26th February

As in time, so in space. Poetry and Painting. In a poem, empiric time should not exist, just as, in a painting, empiric space should not exist.

To create a work is therefore to make absolute one's own time, one's own space. One of the best accredited methods was always to introduce some sentimental intensity which, as is well known, transforms empiric time and space. (An hour filled with strong passion is longer than an hour by the clock. Note that boredom is a strong passion, and therefore *having nothing to do* makes time longer, in so far as it fills it with tension.)

What you call contemplation (your own poetic character) is the transition from the empiric plane to the poetic plane.

The hypothesis that evolution progresses (De Vries) by means of sudden mutations of the germ (which then perpetuate themselves by natural selection [J. Rostand, *Heredité et Racisme*]), accords with your own experience that the inner life (the creation of concepts and imaginative ideas) does not progress by developing one thought from another (one individual from another, in biology), but by sudden intuitions (invariably transmutations of the germ), which only *later* reveal their connections with previous intuitions and their ability to perpetuate themselves (by inner selection).

My notes on 29th October and 1st November, '39, show another parallel between the inner life and biology. Two concepts or two imaginative ideas, once they are considered jointly, produce something of more value than one concept or one such idea, considered singly. A cross between widely divergent races often produces extremely happy individuals.

27th February

The analysis of 24th February, in which you deny the possibility of a life being a metaphysical construction, inasmuch as the total of its significant moments would be an empiric succession, is false.

There remains the possibility that the empiric succession of eternally significant moments (moral actions, poetic creation, imaginative perceptions) may *afterwards* be interpreted or used to form a vital construction.

All the more so since it is admitted (22nd and 26th February) that *any* work of construction is *always* made from sudden flashes of illuminating thought—metaphysical moments—that are *later* fused together, i.e., shown to be capable of unification.

It might be that no thought, however fleeting, however secret, passes from the world without leaving a trace. That is certainly true for every single individual. Still, it would be interesting to know if it leaves a trace on *things,* not only to the extent that the individual, affected by that thought, whatever it may be, may use it differently, but actually on the things themselves—in the case, for example, when the individual dies in the very act of thinking. Which is a way of believing the world has a soul, and that is another matter.

1st March

The balance of a story lies in the coexistence of two things: the author, who knows how it will end, and the group of characters, who do not. If the author and a protagonist become merged, as with a story in the first person, it is essential to increase the stature of the other characters to restore the balance. Therefore the protagonist, if he relates the story himself, must be primarily a spectator (Dostoievsky: "in our district"; *Moby-Dick:* "Call me Ishmael").

If the story is told in the first person, it is evident that the protagonist must know, from the beginning, how the story is going to end. Unless you make him talk in the present tense.

Your conception of style as one's inner life working itself out (cf. 24th October, '38; 5th November, '38) tends to transport the story to the present tense and the first person, thereby nullifying the balance between the one who knows and the one who does not. Hence the impossibility of a construction devised as a game of perspective between the present and the past (or the future). The fine thing about the theatre is that all the characters appear in the first person and the present, but do not know how it will end.

9th March

Naturalism has taught novelists—and by this time we all have 't in our blood—that nothing that is not action should come into the story. Once it was usual to describe the setting that was part of the action, and the events, objectively; now all that is described as seen through the eyes of the character; but everyone has grasped that one must no longer digress. Just as in naturalism the author had to vanish for the sake of reality, so he now has to vanish from the sight of the character.

17th March

If it were possible to have a life absolutely free from every feeling of sin, what a terrifying vacuum it would be!

It can be said that this feeling ("the forbidden thing") is in life what the difficulty of the material is in art; that we should all be bored to death, and artists first, if it were not difficult.

Naturally, the joy of life is in one's struggle with this feeling, the expedients, the compromises. Better to have it and disobey it, than not to have it at all. To know that there are certain things we cannot or should not do is most alluring, (cf. your *Adamo e Eva* and the 17th September, '38, para 7).

25th March

It is not true that a man, like yourself, who is used to living on little, liking simple things taken quickly, suffers less when he finds himself reduced to the austerity and privations of war or some similar event. Why? Someone used to refinements, profusion, a wide choice, when faced with harsh reality will discover the charm of what is simple and plain; you, on the contrary, cannot go lower and have nothing more to discover.

The *living,* vital balance of a book arises from the contrast between the naturalistic logic of the events that unfold beneath the writer's pen, and his preconceived idea, kept in mind, of an inner logic that dominates him like a legend. The first struggles inside the bonds of the second and becomes over-burdened with symbolic feeling—stylistic conceptions, as one calls them. The farther apart these two ways of living are, the more exciting and thrilling is the publication of the book (cf. 14th December, '39).

28th March

The geographical adjectives of Latin poetry (*"ante tibi Eoae Atlantides abscondantur"*) are, when considered, the finest possible way of *making* a myth, submerging the imagined reality in the long ago and far away. This is the only exotic thing that the mind of antiquity was capable of producing: legend turned into definition and limited to the symbolic meaning—for everything had limitations, then. This shows exactly how the symbol (the allusion?) became style. (Cf. your earlier thought.) Cf. especially the note on 10th December, '39, defining the *symbol.*

29th March

You must acknowledge that the magnificent promises of science-to-come terrify you and you would gladly see them come to nothing. Not because science creates murderous weapons of war (some equivalent defense will always be found; and, anyway, it is not the *killing* of men that worries you: one comes into the world to die), but because science will one day be able to provide similar means of control over the personal and physical life of the individual ("sincerity test," sterilization, and so on); or will find substitutes for man himself (robots); or interfere with his inner and physical life (artificial insemination, the classification of his habits, statistical control of his actions à la Taylor, etc.), so that life will no longer be worth living. The typical conclusion of the futuristic novels is, in fact, after a description of the highly controlled mechanism of life on those lines, a *climax* of sheer boredom that drives the masses to break loose, killing themselves and going mad to escape from the nightmare. In short, to die, whether by the sword or a death ray, is nothing; to live scientifically seems appalling. One comfort is my thought on 25th October, '38.

7th April

One man may seem to you older than his age, and another always appears younger than his actual years. They are two distinct types of men; probably they have other differences. You belong to those who are younger than their years. At thirty, you do not believe you are so old.

16th April

It must be important that a young man always intent on studying, turning over pages, satisfying his eyes, should have produced his great poetry in moments when he went out on the balcony, into the woods, over the hill, or strolled on green turf. Poetry is not born of "our life's work," of the normal course of our occupations, but of those moments when we lift our head and are stunned with our discovery about life. (Even normal routine becomes poetry when we meditate on it, that is it ceases to be mere normality and becomes something wonderful.)

So one understands why adolescence is great poetic material. It appears to us—when we are men—like a fleeting moment when we had not yet bent our heads over our jobs.

19th April

Generations do not age. Every youth of any period, any civilization, has the same possibilities as always.

The Empire did not fall through the decadence of the race (how true that is, is shown by the fact that generations that witnessed the fall, and those which followed, have built out of it a spiritual empire, the Catholic Church), but through changed economic and social conditions that wasted their strength (economic atrophy, provincial decentralization, the admission of barbarians, and so on).

20th May

The *Paradis artificiels* describe Baudelaire's real *paradiso,* they are his plan of campaign: only, they repudiate any suggestion that it might be permissible to attain this paradise by trickery; rather do they insist that all this inner world should be a work of intellectual toil and sweat. In short, they argue against the concurrence of drugs, yet reaffirm their virtues. (Especially the 4th chapter of *L'Homme-Dieu,* which is his authentic poetry.)

21st May

If it is true that a man marries, for preference, his opposite (the "law of life"), that is because we have an instinctive horror of being tied to someone who displays the same defects and idiosyncrasies as ourselves. The reason is obviously that defects and idiosyncrasies, discovered in someone near to us, rob us of the illusion—which we formerly fostered—that in ourselves they would be eccentricities, excusable because of their originality.

28th May

Faulkner's figures of speech (*Sanctuary*) are dialectic and imaginative: for example, "crazy as a cow on a bicycle," or when he describes the eyes of a deaf old man as being "turned inwards to show the backside of the eye-balls," or Temple who thinks about becoming a man and feels like a tube fallen over as does the finger of a glove—flop! They are all Elizabethan metaphors; "Fate is a spaniel; we cannot beat it from us"; narrative images, not contemplative, substituting for the object an expressive indication; the images that create a language.

29th May

Tourneur's *The Revenger's Tragedy* could have been the story of an embittered avenger who, as he sets to work, discovers that everything he values dearly is corrupt or on the point of corruption, and that is how it looks in the scene with the mother Graziana (Act II, Sc. I) and the speech of the daughter Castiza in Act IV, Sc. IV. Except that the mother quickly repents and the daughter pretends to do the same. Thus the tale is reduced to a game of intrigue and bloodshed between the avengers and ambitious luxury-loving courtiers; Vindice does not, in the course of five acts, make a single ethical discovery or gain a new experience, but mechanically carries out his revenges and then is punished, just as mechanically. His last words are by no means the inspired swan song of Shakespeare's characters, or of Flamineo and Victoria in Webster's *White Devil,* but a flash of spiteful pique after a rash action that destroys him and which, with any sense, he could have avoided. "We die after a nest of dukes" is too paltry.

Tourneur's imagery, of the type in 28th May:

". . . 'Sfoot, just upon the stroke
jars in my brother; 'twill be villainous music";

and, about a poor man, he says:

". . . hope of preferment
will grind him to an edge. . . ."

1st June

Why do people adopt poses, play the dandy, the skeptic, the stoic or the careless trifler? Because they feel there is something superior in facing life according to a standard and a discipline they have imposed on themselves, if only in their mind. And, in fact, this is the secret of happiness; to adopt a pattern of behavior, a style, a mold into which all our impressions and expressions must fall and be remodeled. Every life lived according to a pattern that is consistent, comprehensive and vital, has a classic symmetry.

5th June

Grief makes one live in a dreamlike world of fantasy where banal, everyday things take on a bewildering, *thrilling* aspect, not always displeasing. It makes one aware of the gap that separates the spirit from reality; uplifts us, lets us view reality and our own body as something remote and strange. Herein lies its educational effectiveness.

The reality of war suggests this simple thought: it is not sad to die when so many of your friends are dying. War gives one a sense of being one of a group. Welcome! Come on in!

9th June

The man who has a dominating passion consequently hates the human race because they all seem to him, as far as his passion is concerned, rivals, usually opponents.

12th June

War raises the tone of life because it organizes everyone's personal, inner life in accordance with a very simple pattern—the two opposing camps—giving one the idea that death is imminent and so investing the most banal actions with an air of importance more than human.

13th June

A declaration of war is like a declaration of love. One becomes the equal of the enemy, to rise or fall with him (or her). We blame the enemy for the same spiteful outrages that—once we are in love—we are more than ready to commit ourselves, and for the same reason—offended humanity. What you said on 12th June about war you can say again about love.

14th June

The reason why any dirty trick is permissible in politics, where the crucial test is clever or stupid, not good or bad, seems to be as follows: The political body does not die and so does not have to answer for itself before any God. The sole exclusive reason for individual morality is that one day we will die and we do not know what will then happen.

16th June

(Air-raid warnings.)

These shrieking noises, the dull, heavy thuds, the explosions that make us all tremble nowadays, were not only taken calmly, before the war, but were not even noticed. Every passion—in this case, terror—creates a particular sensibility towards its own stimuli and pretexts, and reveals a whole province of objective life that formerly passed unobserved. As long as we have passions we never cease to discover more about the world.

The abstractly descriptive nature of Doeblin's *Giganti* shows that *Berlin-Alexanderplatz,* even in the passages that seem crammed with human experience and meditations, was composed only of blunt, commonplace, everyday truth, described, not dramatized; a defect common to much of the narrative prose of today, your own included.

Doeblin, Dos Passos, you; if you want to escape superficial realism, you fall into abstract expressionist construction. Above all, you lack a sense of drama.

You must learn not only to *be* many different characters (Dos Passos succeeds in that), but also to create these characters, *choosing* them and selecting their individual features (the portraits Dos Passos gives can be transposed from one of his characters to another).

18th June

The creation of parliamentary government provides a focus for the conflicts between king and nobles. The need for parliamentary government is felt when oligarchies become decadent, not when monarchies (or dictatorships) fall, for then oligarchies are born.

21st June

To animate nature by describing it in terms of human behavior ("the field was relaxing under the water") is originally a dialectic device, in so far as it reverts to the most instinctive imagery ("the rain was murmuring") and, substantially, reduces the description of things to the presentation of eccentricities. We can say, then, that impressionism is a matter of caricature.

The point of conflict between your work and life is your need for expression in the first, and your need for contact with your neighbor in the second. As long as there is a man who is hated, unappreciated, ignored, there will be something in life to do: draw near to him.

Your poetry is necessarily dramatic because its message is the meeting of two people—the mystery, the charm and the adventure of such encounters—not the confession of your soul. Till now you have preferred contrasts of setting (north against south, town against country) because these vividly accentuate the contrasts between the two people.

23rd June

To express life, one must not only renounce many things, but must have the courage to remain silent about that renunciation.

The aestheticism of English literature in the nineteenth century—the fine imagery from Keats to Hardy, the sustained Oxonian atmosphere—is a reflection of Elizabeth.

There is a connection between Dostoievsky's simple, rambling phraseology and his inventions, all of them clever and closely reasoned. The force with which he feels life is expressed not in vivid imaginative ideas but in dramatic, visionary realities made of the stuff of daily life. Compare with Plato: the logic, the myths (the dialogues and the visions of Dostoievsky).

Defoe is the greatest English novelist because he is the least affected by Elizabethan influences. His voice is *unmarred*. The others, even Dickens, reflect the seventeenth century, either in their poetry or in their humor. They are imaginative and express themselves in images, but no longer have the lusty instincts and wit of the Elizabethans. They indulge in rhetorical phrases and keep nothing concealed from their characters, consequently they are not dramatic.

A story can be dramatic even when there is only one character visible (Defoe). But in this case it is really a contest between a man and his surroundings.

24th June

Tess of the Durbervilles does not come alive because not one of the characters, not even the eccentrics, has his own way of speaking. How does Tess talk? And Angel? In the language of the author. That envelops everything, but still it is a rich, abstract, and sometimes sober method of description which serves to present a most powerful scene (the meeting of Angel and Tess at Sandbourne) (Ch. LV.) in which the pathos comes alive, but not the characters. (Melodrama.)

Melodrama is when the characters speak through the external pathos of the scene, existing not as persons but as lay figures that lend a verisimilitude to the emotional drama. But the characters should be treated with respect even in the story, otherwise it tends towards melodrama, which is, in art, what ambition or hedonism are in life.

Of course one has the right to use characters, not so much to produce an effect but rather as a means to construction; just as in life, not for sentiment or experiment, but to realize a significance.

27th June

From an old race one expects a great solidarity, respect for the law and so on. To a young race, many things are permitted. Youth and age in peoples, are youth and age in the ideologies from which they have sprung. It follows that a young ideology may do many good things badly, for the simple reason that we do not yet see clearly how far they are wrong, or whether, on the other hand, they are surgical interventions. But from the old, all one asks is obedience to the law.

28th June

Even in history it happens that when a thing would be pleasing, it does not come about: it will appear when it no longer makes any difference. Old empires fall when they have become peace-loving, civil and beneficent; but when a power is impertinent, illegal and violent, no one can stop it.

3rd July

All this talk of revolutions, this craze for seeing history in the making, these monumental posturings, are the consequence of our being saturated with history. We have grown used to treating the centuries as if they were pages in a book, and claim that we hear the trumpet blast of the future every time an ass brays.

Furthermore, seeing everything through the eyes of history, we judge by ideas, abstractions which ought to triumph in the end, more or less, and we no longer know what a man may be. We have reverted, that is, through our broad doctrines, to the times when the very name of enemy was hated, the most religious of all barbarous customs. But there is a difference from those times: we are not precisely religious.

6th July

We teach only that which incontestibly exists, as techniques do. For the rest, to teach a thing we must believe in its absolute value, which exists even without us; we must believe in it objectively.

7th July

Aesthetic values, the essence of morality, the light of truth, cannot be taught. Each man must create them within himself. They are *absolute,* outside of time and of society (cf. 27 August '39 and 24th February '40), and therefore cannot be communicated. Words can convey only an outline of them.

8th July

The heroines in Dostoievsky's books can never decide which suitor to take. (Nastasia Filippovna hesitates between the prince and Rogozin; Katerina Nikolsievna between Versilov and the young man; Grusegnka between Dmitri and

Feodor Karamazov.) The negative pole at one time (Rogozin) is positive at other times (Dmitri). The women are
never protagonists; they are always *seen* by others.

The Adolescent is weak, not because it talks more than
is usual about consumptives, but rather because it is the most
panoramic of Dostoievsky's great novels. It lacks that scene or
series of scenes which epitomizes and absorbs the whole feverish story, a kind of unexpected jungle in the desert; and the
story is long drawn out, watered down into a *chronicle;* i.e.,
there are continual outbreaks of crises, intrusive and imposing,
but they are continual recapitulations, never decisive; like a
car engine that roars and never gets into gear.

9th July

It is not through reflection and knowledge of myself
that I am unhappy, but rather when those things are lacking,
as Leopardi did *not* say.

10th July

This war has produced perhaps the richest crop of
treacheries that has ever been known; which indicates a revolutionary climate—a climate, that is, where the initial state
of things is gradually changing and the general standard of
discernment is beginning to differ from the views of this or
that group.

13th July

Of *The Decline of the Middle Ages,* Gerson, Chancel-
lor of the University of Paris, says: "the contemplative life is
full of dangers and has driven many men into melancholia
or madness." First, he makes a distinction between the man
who blasphemes for the sake of doing something wicked, and
one who speaks without thinking about the seriousness of it.
He judges the religious life by its respect for dogmas, but
feels that is not enough and introduces psychological yard-
sticks, reviewing individual cases to assess whether their intensity may not be pathological.

He condemns John of Varennes who, because of his craze for purity, said that an unworthy priest administering the sacraments made them null and void, thus blowing sky high the whole complex ecclesiastical structure. He analyzes the *dulcedo,* the fervor of the modern devotees of the Low Countries (retired bourgeois who maintained the rapt ecstasy of exalted religious emotion with a tranquil air of friendliness and unction), and finds that the faithful content themselves with that, forgetting God. Ruysbroeck's idea of self-abnegation to become one with God does not suit Gerson, because then one may claim to sin no more and so lose one's responsibility.

Historically, these mystics live on visions of hunger, thirst and luxury. From the *dulcedo* they pass to pleasurable, carnal acts of devilry—witches' revels. That is the reason for the spread of witchcraft in the sixteenth century, and the decadence of true piety, the belief in symbols in materialistic fashion.

14th July

The medieval tendency to see something universal in every object or individual—not Fra Dolcino, but *the heretic;* not Henry VII, but *the Emperor,* and so on—is like our habit of viewing individuals according to their class or nation. With the difference that then there was the absolute dignity of the individual soul (the problem of salvation), but that exists no longer.

Extremely perceptive is the discovery of Huizinga (pp. 300-301) that medieval realism, where everything is crystallized into essential realities, even the most fleeting thoughts and phenomena, is, in essence, materialism. (Cf. the Thesaurus of the Good Deeds of the Saints.) Sin is a corruption of the blood; Christ washes away sin with His blood. Metaphors that become real.

21st July

In Dostoievsky there is never the story of a natural reality (man, family, society) but rather fragments of an over-emphasized, keenly-reasoned mass, strung together like anecdotes in the course of a discussion (the myths of Plato). The only story that is more natural is *Crime and Punishment*.

22nd July

To dream that you come home from prison to a princely dwelling with salons and staircases and find there a group of family friends to whom you are introduced, while you wait with the utmost curiosity for the arrival of your father and mother so that you can see what types were selected to produce you, is another instance of a dream like a novel that one reads without knowing how it will finish; where, that is, the reader and the central character coincide. A dream is a creation of the intelligence, the creator being present but not knowing how it will end.

23rd July

Another strange thing about dreams is that, unless one immediately seizes upon them, thinks them over and relives them, one does not remember them. A dream is not so much our own as a story composed by others, because while listening we are never as passive as while dreaming. Yet, beyond all doubt, we create the dream ourselves. We create without being aware of it, that is the extraordinary thing about a dream.

25th July

A case in which tyrannical injustice meets with no opposition and goes smoothly is when it is exercised against a group which is clearly defined and not very numerous.

Writers who please us by their very existence, by their attitude to life in general (Stendhal, for example) are usually stylists even in their writing.

Artists are the monks of the bourgeois state. In them the common man sees, actually functioning, that life of contact with the eternal that the peasants of the middle ages saw in the friars.

26th July

Spent with Gognin.

27th July

The things of this world (the things we do, nature not being included, of course) are symbols of reality, our own or that of others. It follows that the wiser one is, the less one is disposed to sacrifice one's sensual life to do honor to a vain and arbitrary symbol.

Here is a case where the apparent realism of thought is shown to be defeatist and where, instead, transcendentalism is wholly a matter of discipline, giving the symbol a tremendous significance. The believer will let himself be killed rather than commit an action which is a symbol of evil. To a fervent spirit, everything is a symbol. Look at a man in love.

Or perhaps it does not follow that actions are symbolic in idealism, and natural objects in transcendentalism? A thing can be a symbol only when it is brought into the world by a creative spirit.

Anchorites used to ill-treat themselves in the way they did, so that the common people would not begrudge them the beatitude they would enjoy in heaven.

28th July

We do not remember days, we remember moments.

1st August

All libertines are sentimentalists. First, that stems from their long, verbal pretense to be so; then, from their contact with women, which makes them used to all that is delicate, soft and formal; but above all it arises from considering the relations between men and women as a field, not of duties, but of emotions. The cure for sentimentalism is to become, not cynical, but serious-minded.

172

2nd August

In dreams, the dreamer is always very cowardly and puts up with things he would not tolerate in life. He completely lacks any moral or social sense, and becomes a cluster of instincts.

5th August

We must never say, even in fun, that we are disheartened, because someone might take us at our word.

It is a certain sign of love to want to know, *to relive,* the childhood of the other.

We feel moved and full of tenderness when someone feels his state is inferior to our own, just to *our own.* If, instead, he envies and covets another man's condition, he does not interest us and may even wound us.

7th August

Gognin's way of life. Freedom of judgment in sexual and social affairs; as though living among *viveuses* and *viveurs.* But inside, reserved, bashful, virginal. Any breakaway is usually at times of transition: new forms, but the spirit as of old. Not, as people think, vice versa.

Forms change first, then the things of the spirit. The power of the word, the form, the style.

8th August

Life is not a search for experience, but for ourselves. Having discovered our own fundamental level we realize that it conforms to our own destiny and we find peace.

11th August

One of the most unpleasant things in life is to strike the wrong note, even in a simple phrase. Thus it is easy—too easy—to give a certain tone to a character in one's art and never be able to change it. This is why there are many "ideal" types in novels, and readers love them.

We hate a person when her tone is wrong.

Happy marriages are apparently few, for novelists find nothing to say about a happy marriage.

There is no doubt that you prefer people who do a thing because they *must,* to those who do it by instinct. Of course, this *compulsion* is not only their present trend. A confirmation of your theory about style and tone (25th July and earlier, on 1st June).

12th August

Love and poetry are mysteriously linked, because both are a desire for self-expression, for talk and communication, no matter with whom. An orgiastic desire for which there is no substitute. Wine can induce a fictitious state of the same sort, and, in fact, a drunkard talks and talks and talks.

14th August

A man succeeds in completing a work only when his qualities transcend that work.

16th August

The idea that mistakes do not exist, that, instead, they may be "portals of discovery," postulates the other idea that it is one's duty to be lucky; that is, the intelligent man never makes mistakes, which means he is lucky. Or he makes them and they turn to his advantage. Ideas suggested by Gognin, who says that for women it is a duty to be beautiful.

17th August

Gognin's way of talking at random, capriciously putting a subject aside and going back to it when the fancy takes her, has become a style. Anyone who accepts and adopts it she treats as a friend. She likes doing it and makes a habit of it. The power of a style!

174

19th August

". . . like all sensual men, a coward." "Sensual" does not mean a hot-blooded man, but one who has no idea of self-control and considers that the only pleasures are those of the senses. He lacks inhibition.

Sensuality is sentimentalism. In fact, the most sentimental songs and music are born in the corrupt atmosphere of the smart café.

21st August

To sit on a bench with a man, except in a café, is taboo for a virgin.

Whatever people say, the fastidious, formal manner of the upper classes is preferable to the slovenly easy-going behavior of the common middle class. In moments of crisis the first know how to act, the second becomes an uncouth brute.

31st August

There is nothing more stupid than thinking one can make a conquest of a woman by showing off one's own cleverness. Cleverness cannot compete with beauty in such a matter, for the simple reason that it does not arouse sexual excitement; beauty does.

At the most, one may win her in that way when one's abilities seem a means of acquiring power, riches, social position—advantages that, by yielding, she will also enjoy. But cleverness itself, like an immense impersonal machine, leaves any woman quite unaffected, a truth you must not forget.

6th September

As for love affairs, we only tolerate our own.

7th September

The central idea in Proust—that situations and people are forever changing in ways one cannot grasp, so much so that by the time we achieve our desire we find it fails to satisfy us—is like Croce's view that situations and people are the consequence of practical causes; they never control us fully, but, once reached, change to the opposite of what they were at first.

The difference is enormous: for Proust, it is an incentive to withdraw from life, for Croce, to fling oneself into it.

9th September

I can see the scene. She is always wandering off, changing her mind, getting up from table, interrupting the conversation, going to the telephone, and so on. If anyone reminds her of her duties, she replies: "It is your fault if you fail to interest me and keep me sitting."

Such an answer presupposes that inner hardening of adolescence, because it implies that things would have been different if her companion had been different. A fallacy one is prone to credit, in youth, but not later, when one grasps the truth that *whatever happens is one's own fault*.

12th September

Practical life evolves in the present; contemplative life dwells on the past. Action and memory.

21st September

There are certain trivial, commonplace actions that, when I am out of humor, I ought to find soothing—making my bed when I stay at home in the morning; spending money lavishly to entertain someone who expects it; washing myself with plenty of soap, and so on. But they give me an instinctive revulsion, and to do them—when I happen to think of them—I have to make a great effort. This is the effect of a stern upbringing upon a nature that was extremely sensitive and shy. Yet my parents were not cruel or exceptional. Children who have really been ill-treated, what state must they be in?

I always find it strange, even astounding, to realize,

176

all of a sudden, that there are some things I can do peacefully without anyone forbidding them or grudging me the pleasure they bring; there is nothing to stop me enjoying an action instead of just doing it. This explains my poetic capacity: after being hardened, I am discovering the thrill of melting and growing tender, a thrill that will last until all my childhood problems have vanished into thin air. (Thoughts inspired by a kind word from Gognin.)

The night of 29th September

Pf ! ! ! !

30th September

The best defense against a love affair is to tell yourself over and over again till you are dizzy: "this passion is simply stupid; the game is not worth the candle." But a lover always tends to imagine that this time it is the real thing; the beauty of it lies in the persistent conviction that something extraordinary, something incredible, is going to happen to us.

After all, the events of 25th-29th September carry out what I said in my triumphant thought of 4th November, '38. The only trouble is that in practice it is not too triumphant. My affair with Gognin (provided it is all over) has been a repetition of '34-'38.

5th October

No, it is not all over.

7th October

Can it be true that you fall in love only with women who are very popular (the ballerina, Gognin) and that what pleases you about them is that they are desired by everyone, that you suffer because you are not the only one to possess them? The really clever thing, in affairs of this sort, is not to win a woman already desired by everyone, but to discover such a prize while she is still unknown. (Cinderella.)

10th October

There is an art in taking the whiplash of suffering full in the face, an art you must learn. Let each single attack exhaust itself; pain always makes single attacks, so that its bite may be more intense, more concentrated. And you, while its fangs are implanted and injecting their venom at one spot, do not forget to offer it another place where it can bite you, and so relieve the pain of the first. Real suffering is made up of many thoughts. You can think only one thought at a time, so learn how to dodge from one to another, and you will relieve each seat of pain in turn.

12th October

Love has the faculty of making two lovers seem naked, not in each other's sight, but in their own.

14th October

To see again the woman you have been desperately longing for, the one you have been thinking of every single moment for a fortnight, has almost the effect of disillusionment. The real woman is different from the one you have been dreaming of, more definite, yet more evasive.

Women are utterly, fundamentally, indifferent to poetry. In this they are like men of action, and all women are "men of action." It seems that they are interested in it, from adolescence, for one subtle reason only: poetry is born of a bacchanalian exaltation, an exaltation that lies at the root of all that women regard as real. Even when they are inexperienced or superficial, women never confuse any other emotion with the real, active, vital emotion that seizes them when confronted with life itself.

Great lovers will always be unhappy, because, for them, love is of supreme importance. Consequently they demand of their beloved the same intensity of thought as they have for her, otherwise they feel betrayed. It does not please a woman that a man thinks of her day and night, for she does *not* think of him all the time.

178

It is not true that, with the passing of years, love becomes less dreadful. To all the usual pangs—jealousy, desire and so on, is added the terrifying thought that time is slipping by beyond recall.

No one renounces what he knows; we renounce only what we do not know. That is why young men are less egotistical than adults or old men.

15th October

We obtain things when we no longer want them.

To console a young man who has met with some misfortune, we say: "Be strong; bear it pluckily; you'll know better in future; it happens once to everybody," and so on. No one thinks of telling him the truth: "The same thing will happen to you twice, four, ten times—it will always be happening, because if you are so made that you left your flank unguarded once, the same thing is bound to occur again."

Classification of women: those who exploit others, and those who let others exploit them. Classification of men: those who love the first type, and those who love the second.

The first are honey-tongued, well-mannered, fine ladies. The second are sour, discourteous, incapable of being self-possessed. (What makes them rude and hasty-tempered is their thirst for tenderness.)

Both types confirm the *impossibility* of human fellowship. They are servants and masters, not equals.

The sole heroic rule is to be alone, alone, alone.

When you can pass *one* day without assuming or involving the presence of others by a single action or a single thought, you will be able to call yourself heroic.

Another way is to be as Christ, that is to annihilate self. But, as you said yesterday, no one renounces what he knows, and you know too many things.

17th October

One cannot belie one's own nature. You wanted to do something strong, to withdraw like a self-possessed stoic, and you have put yourself in the position of not having withdrawn, and not being able any longer to enjoy the natural company you had before.

The bitterest lesson of this new kick fate has given you is that you have not changed at all or *corrected* anything by your two years of meditation. You have even lost the consolation of thinking that you might still be able to get out of this slough by meditation.

20th October

Your particular trouble—which all poets have—is that, due to your vocation, you cannot have more than one public, yet you keep looking for *twin souls*.

Artists interest women not as artists, but in so far as they have achieved worldly success. That is natural. To marry is to make a social position for oneself, and what man—even the most altruistic—would involve himself from choice in a business that was not sound? So with women, and rightly.

Even self-sacrifice (or renunciation) is a problem of astuteness. You are always talking of astuteness, you who were born for something very different.

What distinguishes a man from a child is knowing how to master a woman. What distinguishes a woman from a child is knowing how to exploit a man. (The second group of women I spoke of on the 15th is, substantially, a group of children, souls incapable of self-mastery.) But then, children or adults are born; they do not change. So console yourself.

21st October

Since what a man seeks in his pleasures is that they should be infinite, and no one would ever give up hope of attaining that infinity, you see why *all* pleasures end in disgust. It is nature's device for tearing us away from them.

22nd October

A person counts for what he *is*, not for what he does. Actions are not moral life; the way we treat others is only well or ill. Moral life is the eternal, immutable existence of the ego. Actions are only the ripples on that sea whose real depths are revealed only in tempests, or not even then.

23rd October

I am not ambitious; I am proud.

The active life is a feminine virtue; the contemplative, masculine. One significance for my presence in this century could be the mission to explode the theory of Leopardi and Nietzsche that the active life is superior to the contemplative; to show that the dignity of the truly great man lies in *not* giving himself up to toil, social life, the mere *trivia* that pad out existence. Without, of course, ceasing to follow Dostoievsky's advice on the way to live. Whatever passions may come. But not forgetting that one counts for what one is, and not for what one does (22nd October).

24th October

Only a man in love knows how to employ love's strategy.

30th October

Suffering is by no means a privilege, a sign of nobility, a reminder of God. Suffering is a fierce, bestial thing, commonplace, uncalled for, natural as air. It is intangible; no one can grasp it or fight against it; it dwells in time—is the same thing as time; if it comes in fits and starts, that is only so as to leave the sufferer more defenseless during the moments that follow, those long moments when one relives the last bout of torture and waits for the next. These starts and tremors are not pain, accurately speaking; they are moments of nervous vitality that make us feel the *duration* of real pain, the tedious, exasperating infinity of the time pain lasts. The sufferer is always in a state of waiting for the next attack, and the next. The moment comes when the screaming crisis seems preferable to that waiting. The moment comes when he screams needlessly, just to break the flow of time, to feel that *something* is happening, that the endless spell of bestial suffering is for an instant broken, even though that makes it worse.

Sometimes there comes the suspicion that death and hell will also consist of pain like this, flowing on with no change, *no moments,* through all time and all eternity, ceaseless as the flow of blood in a body that will never die again.

Oh! The power of indifference! That is what has enabled stones to endure, unchanged, for millions of years.

31st October

Here is the proof that you are wholly made of pride: now that she has given you permission to telephone or write to her, you not only do not do so, but you do not even feel any burning desire to contact her. Which could also be a proof that, in everything, we seek only future possibilities. If we know we *can* do a thing, we are satisfied, and perhaps do not do it at all.

1st November

Fernanda expects to find in a poor man the virtues of the rich (refinement, delicate feelings, all the social graces), and in a rich man the virtues of the poor (seriousness, simple expediency, labored kindness, etc.).

2nd November

If a man does not save himself, no one can save him.

I have often noticed that what I eventually find most valuable and full of meaning, always displeases and repels me at first.

8th November

If we accept Freud's *Essays on Psychoanalysis,* all thought is born of our instinct about death. It is a force that binds all the fleeting, Dionysiac, libidinous emotions of life into a pattern that satisfies the self-love of our ego. The ego

182

tends to revert towards calm, to be self-sufficient in its immobility and absence of desire.

That is a truth one can appreciate when one is suffering and trying to analyze, understand, *settle* one's own crisis, and, in fact destroy it.

9th November

Everything our body does, other than the functioning of the senses, escapes our notice. We know nothing of our most vital processes—circulation, digestion, and so on. It is the same with our spirit; except for the superficial pattern of ideas, we are ignorant of its activities and changes, its crises.

Nothing but an illness makes us aware of the profound workings of our body. In the same way we realize those of our mind and spirit when we become unbalanced.

12th November

We feel pity only for those who have none for themselves.

24th November

Hemmed in by railings and iron grilles, separated into many different groups (= swimming pools). F. lets in three men (the three Sicilians from the shelter tonight), self-possessed, taciturn, their smiles threatening. As she opens, F.'s expression grows hard. I am the prisoner of these three—I feel fully aware of it, and every now and again I glance at F. who says nothing and looks hard. I think of how she has for so long tried to trap me, make me fall into these men's hands (= intelligence mysteriously obtained from the general public, but also perhaps a brother). Which brother darkly promises himself to get to grips with me on the matter of his sister F. and her studies. Their fists are heavy and they joke among themselves, watching me out of the corners of their eyes. The sense of danger coming from them is extremely strong and keen.

Until I swing open a barrier and furtively dash away, calling to F. that I'll be seeing her and will explain then. Meaning that I do not think she has betrayed me.

30th December

Foscolo, *Prose letterarie*, Le Monnier.

Vol. II, p. 65: "then the man who is capable of the strongest feelings has the liveliest ideas."

Lessons in eloquence:

p. 129: "In the history of literature, so many men who could congratulate themselves upon gaining some real, tangible honor have nevertheless, after their initial, noble efforts, set aside their work and preferred to remain unknown, even though they may not have found, in leisure and obscurity, the contentment and peace to which they so modestly aspire."

p. 19, note: "R. Cartesio states, as an axiom: *"Nature has endowed men with equal reasoning faculties (Disc. de Methodo,* no. I): Jean Jacques Rousseau begins his *Contrat Social* with this phrase: *Man is born free.* Both errors are always extremely prejudicial to literary philosophy and to good government."

p. 152: "so you would fall into that very disillusion, the one error that a man ought carefully to avoid."

On the text of the Decameron:

Vol. III, p. 20: "Nor is it any less true that the various dialects have always played their part in the formation of a national literary language in Italy, a language never spoken by anybody but always understood by everyone, and written more or less well according to the skill, the artistry, and above all the heart, of the writers."

p. 38 (dialects as literary language): "The old comedies of Tuscany, and the Venetian ones by Goldoni, are the best: but they would be very coldly received by the people of Rome, Lombardy, or the kingdom of Naples."

p. 41 (Boccaccio): "All the others wrote in ways

that were different from his, but will anyone maintain that he wrote exactly as he spoke, and that the language in his writings was the dialect of the Florentine people, neither more nor less?"

p. 42: "—if only because this art, essential with every language, is most difficult for Italians, for they have no Court, no capital city, no parliaments where the language may be enriched by the flow and modification of ideas."

p. 43: "by its literary essence, Italian is the only modern language that has preserved almost all its harmonious, clear and graceful words, all its elegant turns of phrase, for five centuries and more."

p. 58: "Elsewhere I have, I hope, established that the language of Homer was not devised as a mosaic of different dialects, as is generally supposed. But it was indeed studied by poets and historians to impart a literary quality to the dialects of their towns, so that by writing in the same way they would be more acceptable to the whole of Greece (*History of the Aeolic Digamma*)."

p. 76: (*Crusca*): "However, it still remains the dictionary of a dialect and not of a language."

On the text of Dante's Poem:

p. 117: "Greek and Roman writers . . . not because they taught theories of natural liberty and inalienable rights, when, for them, it was rather that all rights and all obligations were decreed by fate and by victory."

p. 120: "opinions can never prevail except when they have the backing of governmental power, which alone enables them to progress."

p. 321: "Languages, when there is a nation, are a public inheritance, administered by the eloquent; and when there is no nation, they remain an inheritance for men of letters; and authors of books write only for authors of books."

p. 382: "I think, and I am sure it is true, that very many passages, especially the didactic and allegorical passages in the *Paradiso*, were thought of first, and composed some long time before the Poet was really master of his language and his art. For seldom in the *Inferno,* and still more rarely in the *Purgatorio,* does he have to be satisfied with the crude latinisms, ambiguity of syntax and uncouth expressions that now and then spoil the *Paradiso*."

p. 453: "from which of those ideas does poetic fantasy more naturally spring?"

p. 458: "D. made use of them: and with them the more common meanings of the same word, about the duration of time, constancy and the increasing power of the action. This explains what he said to his Interpreter, which otherwise would seem an enigma: "that many a time and oft he made words in his *Rimes* mean something different from what later writers used them to express" (*L'Anonimo*). As a consequence, the conflict of concomitant ideas springs spontaneously and powerfully from his speeches."

p. 479: "Nevertheless, the language, for those who founded it, was written, never spoken; and consequently, since books do not conform to successive pronunciations, the vocal organs have to obey the eye."

Sulla Lingua Italiana (written in England, in Italian):

Vol. IV, p. 180 (The Language of Homer): "the progress of its words is always simple and naturally grammatical. Its phrases are never overburdened with metaphors, never applied to metaphysical ideas, nor to thoughts or feelings which are, so to speak, intangible. So that, if one were to take away the meter from the verses, and if the *Iliad* and the *Odyssey* were reduced to prose, they would seem romantic stories full of marvels, like thousands of others written today in language and style a thousand times worse. . . ."

"Dante's poetical language . . . has never been, and never could be, used as a model for prose compositions."

p. 197: "Finally, Thucydides uses words as if they were passive material, and sometimes forces them to condense more passions, more ideas and reflections than they can contain; he handles his language like a tyrant. While Boc-caccio caresses it like a lover. . . ."

p. 210 (Petrarch): "But his language is that of the author, rather than of the nation."

p. 211: "Villani, the most idiomatic of Florentine writers."

Cf., for his trends and his analytical capacity as a novelist, his *Saggio d'un Gazzettino del Bel Mondo* (addressed to the reader and expressing the resignation of the forties) and his Fragments, especially the 10th: ". . . I, with my heart hardened by experience"; the preface to the great translation (*Didimo Chierico a' lettori salute*) where he describes Sterne: ". . . and his eyes, sparkling with desire, lower their gaze as if ashamed"; the whole of his *Notizia intorno a Didimo Chierico*; the *Lettera Apologetica*; the extracts from his *Atti dell'Accademia de' Pitagorici* (a humorous, doleful essay of the same type as *Bel Mondo*); his translation of *Sentimental Journey*, and of *Degli effetti della fame e della disperazione sull' uomo*, taken from Crevecoeur's *Voyage en Pensylvanie*; and, lastly, his youthful attempt in *Jacopo Ortis*. He did not become a novelist, perhaps because he found himself in Sterne and was content to translate him, but his type of humor was exactly the same, as is shown in *Bel Mondo*, the *Atti* and various fragments.

1941

14th January

To perceive what style is, it is sufficient to read any prose passage of Foscolo and then some of his prose translated from English, even by Ugoni. Better still: *first* read the trans-lation, then a piece of his original prose—the *Lezione In-augurale*, for example.

If, this year, you have not examined your conscience,

it is because there was more need for you to do so than ever before. You were in a state of transition and lacked clear inner vision.

30th January

This gentle benevolent feeling of love for humanity that comes over you on a cold day—when you are spending a few moments in a café and notice one man's thin, sad face, another's twisted mouth, the kind, sorrowful voice of a third —and you give yourself up to a sentimental, luxurious surge of pity and grief at so much daily suffering, that is not real love for your neighbor, but complacent, expansive introversion. At such moments we would not lift a finger for anyone: we are, in fact, blissfuly happy in our own tranquil futility when faced with life.

If even the *silent reading* of a poem, to get to know it, is a form of interpretation, then I no longer see how one can form a historical judgment of a poem, if knowing it means creating *another* poem in one's own mind. Should we be judging this other one? And what of the universality of historical judgment? Its truth? (On reading Pugliatti, *L'interpretazione musicale.*)

2nd February

Friend P. is filled with a good-natured, obstinate sense of his own merit, which shows itself even in the characteristic way he holds himself aloof from anyone else's affairs, his impenetrable reserve like that of a peasant who tolerates no intrusion by others into his own field of activity. He is a man who never has a doubt about his own behavior, and so knows nothing of the nervous tension others feel when brought into contact with the world. If he were not an "artist," if, that is, he had not cultivated his innate aptitude for observing, with keen, impersonal interest, the manner and appearance of any man he meets, he would be a typical yokel. A good deal could be said about this "disinterest" of his. Can you call a faculty "disinterested" when he employs it unremittingly in

the active building up of his own world, permitting no un-
productive deviations, such as reading anything that has no
bearing on what he imagines to be the culture of the theatre?
Has he ever known a vital experience, some contact with
real life that shattered him because it was outside his original
plan for his career, made when he was young?

He is a Catholic, and presumably believes that humility
is a duty, yet he is so made that he accepts all the distinctions
of life as his due, without excitement and without surprise.
That is as he planned. When I tell him he knows nothing of
psychology, I do not mean he is ignorant of the mechanical
human reactions on which he builds his play, but that, outside
the "possible" psychology used in art, he has never, in reality,
lived through a time of psychological doubt, an illness of the
spirit—one of those maladies that alone can make us probe
and glimpse the depths of consciousness. One would say that
he rejects these experiences *in corpore sui,* possibly for the
reason that he sees no practical advantage to be gained from
a malady. One thing is sure: even if he were to let himself
go tomorrow, work up a psychological crisis and probe into
it, his purpose would be to glean material for a tragedy, not
to satisfy a vital necessity. His vital necessities are already
satisfied by that inexorable "schema" of his, so typical of a
catholic peasant and, for what the word is worth, egotistical.

Hence the melodramatic tone of his best pages. His
writing, precisely because it is pure dramatic art (due perhaps
to this tone), has always been—until now—literature. I do
not see how he can change.

Perhaps P. has never known adolescence—of the sort
that makes one meditate on suicide. And the penalty for this
deficiency is a special, perennial adolescence of the spirit,
which, underlying all his virile achievements (dignity, family,
sense of responsibility, success) makes him, not a creator, but
a *man of letters* of a new type. That, after such an exposition,
I still love him, almost as much as I could love a woman, is
quite understandable: P. is the antithesis of myself and of
my experiences.

P. has something feminine in his calm, sensible egotism. That, too, belongs to adolescence—the adolescence that means simplicity and calm, refreshing grace.

3rd February

What is there, really, in my fixed idea that everything lies in the secret, loving "inner self" that every creature offers to anyone who knows how to reach it? Nothing, for never have I been able to attain that loving communion of spirit.

Basically, the secret of life is to act as though we possessed the thing we most painfully lack. In that lies the whole doctrine of Christianity. To convince ourselves that everything *is* created for good, that the brotherhood of man *really exists*—and if that is not true, what does it matter? The comfort of this vision lies in believing it, not in whether it is real. For if I believe it, and you, and he, and everyone, it will become real.

On 18th January, '41, I finished *La Spaggia*.

10th February

Marcel Raymond: *De Baudelaire au Surréalisme:*

After the three "lighthouses": "But the real thing, the absolute, if you like, you do not dream of finding here at the end of a chain of concepts or an argument, you expect to discover it in passages that are definitely psychic. A new sensibility, infinitely delicate . . . psychological perception . . . that is the faculty a modern poet must possess." (p. 48.)

". . . the most recent poets willingly admit, in principle, that the gifts of their ego do not belong to them personally, but are manifestations of a universal spirit." (p. 261.)

"What is new is entirely a matter of surprise," says Apollinaire (p. 273).

Dada: "Only the unconscious does not lie" (p. 316).

Dada: "It is always a question of knowing whether the linguistic accidents that happen each time one breaks traditional associations without giving it a thought, in order to copy a model or express a sentiment, are only inconsequential trifles, or whether they may in certain circumstances, almost without our knowledge, correspond to something that really does exist" (p. 324).

Surrealism: "Every surrealist text presupposes a return to chaos; startling combinations of totally dissimilar words, new possibilities of synthesis reveal themselves sharply in a lightning flash" (p. 332).

". . . allow evidences of another nature to take shape involuntarily, unconsciously, purely psychic evidences, if that is possible, which affect us in a certain inner poetic sense that may perhaps merge itself with our deepest feeling about life" (p. 333).

Criticism of surrealism: "surrealist texts . . . we are led to regard them as products of culture, and of culture in its most advanced form—a very different thing from the result of the free exercise of that faculty of verbal invention which is more or less generously distributed to all men" (p. 335).

Surrealist definition: "to penetrate a world where freedom would be infinite" (p. 337)—"childhood is perhaps the nearest approach to true life" (p. 338).

Breton: "Everything leads us to believe that there exists a certain point, spiritually, from which life and death, the real and the imaginary, the past and the future, things we can communicate and things we cannot, and height and depth, cease to be viewed as contradictory. Now, one would seek vainly, in surrealist activities, for any stimulus except the hope of determining this point exactly" (p. 430).

Criticism of surrealism: "our dream is worth as much as our sleepless nights" (p. 365).

After Rimbaud, his pupils "subordinate poetic activity to purposes that go beyond it" (p. 391).

They view their art as less important than nature (no longer as sentiment, reason, imagination), that art which is spontaneous thought, the stuff of dreams. Poetry cannot dwell in any particular form because it is a psychic phenomenon (p. 392).

". . . the poem tends to become something other than

a more or less faithful *expression,* which one would appreciate
according to an inner pattern imagined by induction, or to
the special circumstances of a life. Ultimately, it would be
an object existing in its own right, disconnected from its
creator . . . an autonomous object, a meteorite fallen from
an unknown planet. . . ." (p. 400).

Evoke emotion not by a description, but by a fact of
nature: poetry is a sunset, a seashore, etc. *La Spaggia* was
finished on 18th January, '41.

14th February

In a dream, Fern. tells me she was just behind the
musicians and enjoyed "that divine trio."

Shortly after, we go in—I do not see her any more—
and I see my musician friend settle himself behind the two
percussion players, close against the wall, and pretend to
conduct the orchestra with his hands (the players surrep-
titiously turn round to watch him).

Evidently, the musician is a more suitable person
than Fern. to do this—*more suitable in imagination*—so an
adjustment has taken place in the story, during the dream.
It is not a case of two successive facts, the second developing
out of the first, but the crystallization of a single fact, a single
state, that is first glimpsed in an embryonic form and then,
one might say, finds a richer, more appropriate expression
(with a different person and a new significance, further en-
riching itself magically by adding coherent details which at
first sight were completely unknown to me).

Perhaps this is the explanation of the fact (27th December '39) that in the course of a dream certain details
seem to us to anticipate, in the story, other details that will
complete them. It would be simply a preliminary, embryonic
sketch which then shapes itself into something different. In
short, one would not be telling oneself a story, but conjuring
up a picture, a static situation, expressing a psychophysical
state, the *dominating passion*. The apparent unfolding of the
action, in a dream, would spring from the succession of un-

conscious, tentative efforts to define the vision more and more clearly (first Fern., then the musician, doing the same thing). Within the bounds of each separate vision there is, of course, a certain natural sequence of events.

As if someone were to show you a picture; then, immediately after, the same picture with the figures altered and retouched. If that were done rapidly and in the right way, you have a cinematographic story, but a story in which every sequence is a fresh attempt to say the same thing.

Still dreaming, I noted that there are no antecedent facts in a dream, everything is action, there is no repetition— a pattern of evocative art.

2nd March

LÉVY-BRUHL. *L'expérience mystique*

Ch. 1—Primitive man lets himself be seized by the passion for a game of chance and even loses his all, for mystic reasons; because, once launched on that course, what matters to him is not the amount he has lost, but his need to prove to himself that he is *not deserted by the supernatural powers,* and what he owns is no more than a means to secure and increase his hold upon that protection. Compare this with your own tendency, when something in life has gone wrong for you, to wallow in your unhappiness, to touch bottom, as if to find in fate's absolute condemnation a confirmation of absolute value—confirmation that your misfortune did not come about by chance, but because *in alio loco* the powers have a grudge against you, which could mean that *in alio loco* you count for something.

4th April

Nothing is more essential when beginning a work of art than to make sure of a richly productive standpoint. The simplest, most direct way of doing so is to draw on your experience for something a little unusual and sufficiently far-off, then work on the realistic complexity of associations that it offers. But there is a technical method of constructing a standpoint, which consists of arranging various spiritual planes, various times and angles, various *realities,* and deriving from them intersecting cross-currents, a game of illusions, a wealth of implications that you can devote all your energies to developing as you please. A good example would be my discovery this morning that the story of Corradino could be told in the third person, but surrounding the events with an atmosphere of the first person plural, which not only gives a setting, a background to the over-free Corradino, but —an immense advantage—would enable one to treat him ironically.

In anything, it is a mistake to think one can perform an action or behave in a certain way once and no more. (The mistake of those who say: "Let us slave away and save every penny till we are thirty, then we will enjoy ourselves." At thirty they will have a bent for avarice and hard work, and will never enjoy themselves any more. Others may say: "With this one crime behind me I shall be happy all my life." They will commit their crime and will always be ready to commit another to conceal the first.) What one does, one will do again, indeed has probably already done in the distant past. The agonizing thing in life is that it is our own decisions that throw us into this rut, under the wheels that crush us. (The truth is that, even before making those decisions, we were going in that direction.)

A decision, an action, are infallible omens of what we shall do another time, not for any vague, mystic, astrological reason but because they result from an automatic reaction that will repeat itself.

12th April

One of the least noticed human pleasures is that of visualizing a sequence of events, arranging a group of incidents to give them coherence, a logical development, a beginning and an end. The end is almost always imagined as a sentimental climax, a peak of delighted, gratifying self-recognition. This extends beyond the fabrication of a flight of fancy and becomes a *riposte*—a cut-and-thrust defying the set pattern of life. And what is that but the first step towards the art of story-telling, the art that exactly satisfies this deep-seated desire? The pleasure of telling a story, and of listening to it, lies in seeing events arranged according to a preconceived outline. Halfway through the story one can go back to the beginning and enjoy finding the reasons, the clues, the motives for the action. What else is it when one thinks over one's own past, finding pleasure in recognizing the signs that foreshadowed the present, or still foreshadow the future. This reconstruction shows the significance of *time,* and story-telling is, in brief, only a way of turning it into a legend, a myth, and finding an escape from it.

14th April

No woman marries for money: they are all clever enough, before marrying a millionaire, to fall in love with him.

27th April

Rousseau, *Les Confessions* (L.IV, 1731-1732, p. 135, ed. Flammarion):

"Besides, I was hardly tempted by dressmakers, chambermaids, little shop-girls: I wanted fine young ladies. . . . Yet it is not in the least any vanity of rank or position that attracts me: it is a complexion treated with greater care, prettier hands, more grace in adornment, an air of delicacy and fastidious cleanliness of person, better taste in their way of conducting and expressing themselves, a finer, better-made gown, a daintily shod foot, ribbons, lace, a well-dressed head. . . ."

"And why stop at permanent things, when all the follies that went through my fickle head, fleeting tastes lasting but a day, a journey, a concert, a supper, a walk to take, a novel to read, a comedy to see, everything that was in the slightest degree premeditated in my pleasures or affairs, became, for me, tantamount to violent passions whose ridiculous impetuosity gave me the most acute torment? . . ." (L.V, 1732-1736, p. 223).

". . . this mutual possession (between myself and Mme de Warens), perhaps unique among human beings, was not in the least, as I have said, the bond of love, but a more fundamental kind of possession that, without regard for sensibility, sex, age or features, was bound up with everything that makes me what I am, and that I cannot lose except by ceasing to exist . . ." (id. p. 225) (and note that Mme de Warens had already given herself to him).

2nd May

There are *vertical* types, who try everything in succession, passing from one person or one thing to another, dropping each for the next, who resent it if one of their former loves comes back to tempt them while they are devoting themselves to someone new. They are *romantics,* eternally adolescent. On the other hand there are the *horizontal* types, who acquire their experience through a wide range of values, all at the same time, and they know how to grow enthusiastic about new people and new things without dropping those they knew previously; who, out of their calm, inner convictions derive the power to dominate and temper the most varied infatuations. Such men are *classic.*

10th May

The banality of totalitarian ideologies reflects the banality of the humanitarian theories that produced them. Tolstoi, Ruskin, Gandhi, they have created. . . .

22nd May

BÉGUIN, *L'âme romantique et le rêve.* (An idea that will also be found in Schubert, Carus, Schopenhauer and Jung.)

The keen interest K. P. Moritz takes in *childhood recollections* is a method of discovering evidence of a state that existed prior to life. During infancy it is still fresh in the memory and leaves traces. It represents escape, not only from contemporaneous reality but from reality as a whole. This is the typical aspiration of the proto-romanticists. Hence the desire of poets from Shelley to Leopardi to transform themselves into natural objects (a cloud, thunder, a wave), thereby finding a pretext for participating in a life that is no longer in human form. Hence their search for dreams, not only as an escape from the reality of every day, but as a focus for prenatal experience. Hence their anxiety to identify themselves with "The Everything," which appears to be the same as pre-natal reality.

(p. 72.) "Forgetfulness of mankind, also of one's own weaknesses and doubts, can be found in gaming. Since life, when one faces it with all the gravity of its questions and its hopes, is terrible, one must gamble with it. To take a hand in someone else's game is not enough; we must play so well that we dupe ourselves; show life that we are capable of unmasking it, making it our toy, and so proving to ourselves the sovereignty of our own spirit. The Romantics will call this virtuosity 'irony,' and ally it to their poetry."

There are feminine garments so lovely that one could tear them to shreds.

24th May

It is curious that Romanticism, which passes for the discovery and the vindication of the individual, of originality, of genius, should be completely pervaded by a desire for unity and cosmic totality; that it should have invented legends of the fall from primitive Unity and sought for ways (poetry, love, historical progress, the contemplation of nature, magic, etc.) to recover it. The proof of this tendency is the creation of so many collective conceptions (the nation, the people, Christianity, the Teutonic, the Gothic or the Roman style, and so on).

27th May

By thinking of the artist as a vessel, a receptacle for inspiration that works by a power of its own, *without his knowledge,* the Romanticists discover *the unconscious,* i.e., a set of positive forces that put man into contact with cosmic reality. There will come a second generation of Romanticists who will claim to master this *unconscious,* experiment with it and learn all about it, in other words transferring its functioning to the *consciousness* (Poe—Baudelaire, etc.). Art, which was at first an ingenuous discovery of symbols of behavior, becomes the deliberate creation of aesthetic symbols (French Symbolism).

The term "dream" acquires its second meaning of "a poetic flight of fancy," "a reverie," from the romanticism that reveals the autonomy of the imagination and the auto-sufficiency of the unconscious, which is exactly what we find in the dreams we have at night.

Here is a satirical law of life: it is not the giver who is loved, but the one who takes the gift. The loved one does not love, for one who loves, gives. And that is understandable, for giving is a pleasure not so easily forgotten as receiving; the one to whom we have given becomes necessary to us, that is, we love him.

Giving is a passion, almost a vice. We must have someone to whom we can give.

1th June

Béguin, II, 152.

When we look at a lovely color, the dream within us tends to merge into a more exquisite, more mysterious dream, seeking not to explain but to understand: "to transform itself, burst into bloom, become something that really exists in the heart of an existing lover."

(Tieck. The conversations of *Phantasus,* including the *Marchen.*)

As a poet, Tieck uses free verse, according to his *mood,* and if he allows *caras rimas* it is in order to find expression in complex sounds. So he creates a whole symbolism of rhyme and strophic forms.

Tieck would like a dialogue of different kinds of sound (*Sternbald*) and invents (Fantasie) *hearing with the help of color*—broadly speaking, the substitution of one sense for another. (Wolsel, *Il romanticismo tedesco*.)

It is Wackenroder's idea that music may be a means to knowledge beyond the reach of words.

He often comes back to *irony*. Schubert noted that dreams are ironic (expressing joy in the guise of sadness and *vice versa*). The poet is a continual obstacle to the spread of *matter-of-factness*. Jean-Paul (and Schlegel) say that irony is a piece of clear reasoning in the midst of a dream or of anarchist poetry. Tieck says that taking charge when the unconscious begins to scintillate, assessing it, directing it so that it has free play, is irony. (Cf. 22nd May.) Hoffman, that irony is mixing the commonplaces of life with *revelations* of a superior existence.

13th June

If we can judge by its analogy with the day, old age is the most tedious time of all because one no longer knows what to do with oneself, just as in the evening when the day's work is finished.

25th June

Béguin, on *Aurélia* of G. de Nerval:

"This explains the apparent chronological inconsistency in the story of *Aurélia:* in spite of their chance sequence, the moments of a whole life arrange themselves according to their joint significance. A sort of timeless memory, like that of the dream, gives its instant of crisis as a starting point for a whole destiny, and even the childhood of G. de Nerval, which brings about a change in perspective, seems subsequent to the events of riper years and to be colored by them."

The night of 26th June

A dream that could be a novel. (The central atmosphere is dramatic; all the rest leads up to it, with the mystery of the plot being revealed little by little. The whole story is implied.)

I dreamed I was at an inn with a lieutenant. I had just arrived and was meeting him in connection with a job; with the lieutenant I saw a sergeant, who, they told me, was looking for me on the colonel's behalf. I tried to avoid him. There were all sorts of people coming and going. I was going on at once to Turin. (Or was it Serralunga?) As I went with him towards the door, I passed through a large underground room where a group of soldiers were all sitting at little refectory-type tables. I realized there was something strange and felt a vague fear. One of them told me that they knew the lieutenant and I loved each other, not as officers; and we liked them too, so they all asked to be made officers. I was terribly afraid that someone present might tell this to the colonel and I said with a good deal of emphasis that they ought to be ashamed to break discipline in this way. I shouted several more phrases in the same vein, that "they all knew what we thought of it, the lieutenant and I" and that, if he became colonel, I should be in complete agreement. They all fell silent, as if frustrated and threatening. (I continued to nudge the lieutenant, whispering to him to say nothing and let me carry on.) The situation developed with me talking, and the lieutenant, standing behind me, letting me speak as though I were his deputy. I shouted to them to stop, then I was taken aback to see, at the far end of the tables, the faces of men I knew, who were fraternizing with them. I gave a little wink to a soldier sitting near me; he understood and winked in reply, but I pretended not to notice. The atmosphere grew more friendly, but still watchful.

"Have you been fraternizing with my friend?" I asked two intellectual looking types at the end of the room, and found myself standing between them. I had to get away. I do not know how, but I and the lieutenant, who was now drinking wine, had left our underwear hanging on the railings of his villa, and he advised me to call and collect it. We went out, and found a traffic block of buses. Then it was pouring with rain and I was alone. I ran to look for my underwear, but it was dark and I could not see it. When I got to the gate I suddenly knew it was Serralunga and I was with my

own folk. I jumped on the step and shouted: "I'm Cesare!"
and there was Maria and even some of the neighbors (two
girls, and I notice they are pretty). I think of going to sleep
again, and M. calls out: "There are four apples left."

5th July

I do not know what to do with women who belong
to other men.

11th September

I have read Cohen's little book about *Chrétien de
Troyes* and reflected once again that narration is not made up
of psychological or even of natural realism, but of a predetermined pattern of events, created according to the style
that is reality to the narrator, the one irreplaceable person.
Cf. Erec's command to Enid that she is not to speak, and
her three failures to obey. Or the caprices of Guinevere, who
compels Lancelot to fight, now in jest, now in real earnest.
Or, again, Landine's rage because Yvain has stayed away
for more than a year, which brings about Yvain's long mar-
tyrdom. Or Perceval's unawareness that he ought to ask the
Fisher King the significance of the procession of the Grail.

By "style" I mean this development of a chain of facts
that convey psychological and natural realism and maintain
it, but are contrived on purpose, products of the intelligence
and of nothing else. Something like the arbitrary prelude to
a dream that conjures up a whole series of events, coloring
them according to a "passion" that is purposeful but unreal.

(Cf. the theory of the *symbolic-link* (4th December,
'38) and of the *stylized situation* (1st January, '40). Religion
(*I Fioretti*), fable (*Chrétien de Troyes*), modern art (Stendhal, Baudelaire, Kafka) all combine to teach me this lesson
—that once I vaguely called the *image-story*).

2nd October

Why does this naturalistic-psychological realism fail to
satisfy you? Because it is too petty. It is not a question of
discovering a new psychological reality, but of multiplying

viewpoints that will reveal the riches to be found in the normal conception of realism. It is a problem of construction.

9th October

"I like writers who always use the same theme," says Pintor. Apart from his simple preference for coherence and definability in the writer—a foothold for criticism—P. does not explain whether he means the naturalist content or the stylized treatment. Of course, variation in the former indicates an inner poverty, but the second should of necessity be an ever new development—from the simple shade of meaning to the outburst of descriptive style, otherwise the pages will lack that sense of discovery which is the true and only pleasure of the writer.

The winter of '41-'42

A man is never completely alone in the world. At the worst, he has the company of a boy, a youth, and by and by a grown man—the one he used to be.

It is not that, in our time, people are less willing to listen to a man of culture than, in the past, they listened to the theologian, the artist, the scientist or the philosopher. It is that now the masses live on mere propaganda. Even in the past, the mass of the people lived on propaganda of a sort, but in those days, since elementary culture was less widespread, they did not ape truly learned men, and so the problem of whether or not they agreed with their views did not arise.

The setting should not be clearly defined, but live through the senses of the character—through his thoughts, his way of speaking. The thing you so dislike—as "impressionism"—thus becomes (conditional upon the personage—personality) life in action. This is the norm you sought for earlier in your research on *Mestiere di Poeta*. And what else is Anderson's *story-behind-a-story,* or the *inner monologue* of Joyce, but this same imposition of personage-reality upon objectivity?

202

When a woman marries she belongs to another man; and when she belongs to another man there is nothing more you can say to her.

1942

28th January

Things are revealed through the memories we have of them. Remembering a thing means seeing it—only then— for the first time. You ought to devise a connection between the fact that in your moments of greatest truth you are inevitably what you were in the past, and the fact that only things which are remembered are true.

10th February

Traveling by train along the seashore near Pineto at night when the tide is low, watching the little fires in the distance, the thought came to you that although this scene, this reality, fills you with ideas you feel you must express, moves you like a childhood memory, yet it is not really, for you, either a memory or a constantly recurring fancy. It fascinates you for trifling reasons—literary or analogical, but it does not, like a vineyard or one of your own hills, carry the stamp of your own knowledge of the world. From which it follows that very many realms of nature (the sea, the moors, forests and mountains, for instance) are outside your province because you have not lived among them at the right time. If you had to embody them in poetry, you would not know how to move among them with that secret wealth of inner comprehension, perception and discrimination which invests a world with poetic dignity. The same thing applies to the sphere of human relationships and human beings: only those situations and those types that, little by little, have taken shape in your mind, standing out against the background of your initial awareness, have so far had time to graft themselves upon your spirit and throw out those countless secret rootlets of reconnaissance that bring blood and life to works of creation. In brief, you cannot, merely by wanting to, interest yourself poetically in a given countryside or a given sphere and make them live, except by reshaping them in the (inadequate) molds of your infancy-adolescence. Hence you cannot escape (at least for the moment) from a world already implicit in your natural perception, just as, in practical life, you cannot escape from the limitations of your natural volition, limitations which were largely determined during the period when you first came to terms with the world. It remains to be seen whether, in these two fields, the active and the creative, you should probe and understand more and more deeply the reality already given to you, or whether it would be more profitable to confront continually those things, figures, situations, decisions that are extraneous and formless to you, and to draw from this clash and this effort a continual improvement in the development and potentiality of your capabilities. The whole question is whether, once your first consciousness is formed, you can live spiritually on the income from it, or whether you can achieve a daily increase in your capital. It seems evident that, wearisome and fearful though it might be, the two paths could unite, and a childhood experience elaborated in maturity would be a different and novel starting-point.

12th February

Modern art—for what it is worth—is a return to infancy. Its perennial theme is the discovery of things, a discovery that can come about, in its purest form, only in the memory of infancy. That is the effect of the *all-pervading* consciousness of the modern artist (the notion of art as an activity sufficient unto itself, individualism) which makes him live from sixteen onwards in a state of tension, i.e., a state no longer propitious to the absorption of new ideas, no longer open-minded. And in art a thing can be well expressed only when it has been absorbed with an open mind. All that is left for artists to do is to go back and seek inspiration from the period when they were not yet artists, and that period is infancy.

21st February

My stories—in so far as they succeed—are tales by an onlooker who watches things greater than himself take place.

23rd February

This continues 27th April, 1941—reading Rousseau:
". . . Seeing through so many prejudices and artificial passions, one must know how to analyze the human heart in order to unravel real feelings about nature. A certain delicacy of tact, *which can only be learned by education in high society,* is needed to feel, if I may speak in such a way, the niceties of heart of which this work is full. Without hesitation I would place its fourth part beside *La Princesse de Cleves,* and I say that if these two pieces had been read only in the provinces, their real worth would never have been felt. . . ."
". . . every painful feeling I can imagine only with effort. . . ." (and that is why he does not introduce rivalries, quarrels, jealousy in *La Nouvelle Héloise*).
"People believed that I could write by profession like all other men of letters, whereas I could only write by passion."

26th February

(Cf. 4th April, '41.) Great modern art is always *ironic,* just as ancient art was *religious.* In the same way that a sense of the sacred was rooted in visions beyond the world of reality, giving them backgrounds and antecedents pregnant with significance, so irony discovers, beneath and within such visions, a vast field for intellectual sport, a vibrant atmosphere of imaginative and closely reasoned methods of treatment that make the things that are represented into symbols of a more significant reality. To treat a thing ironically it is not necessary to make a joke of it (just as treating something as sacred did not mean making it into a liturgy). It is enough to create imaginative visions according to a standard that transcends or governs them.

The same thing is apparent in your own initial approach to work that has turned out well: you begin with a discourse broader than the story that is to follow; you view that story with a certain nonchalance, as though your interest embraced a wider field than the story will cover; and you make it your aim to preserve this viewpoint, arranging the whole story, from the first word, the first comma, in such a way that there shall be nothing superfluous in respect of the material play of the facts. It is a matter of avoiding digression and projecting clear-cut realism on to an *enormous* imaginary screen.

24th March

Alain: *Système des beaux-arts* (1926).

Art

"The artist . . . controls his images according to what he does, I mean, according to the object which is born under his fingers. . . ."

"The work of art must be made, complete and solid . . . What is not part of the mass cannot be ornament."

"The model . . . is first of all the object and then the work."

"Every time that the idea precedes and dominates the execution this amounts to industry."

"The idea comes to the artist afterwards, just as it does to the spectator, and he is also the spectator of his own work being born."

Tragedy

"Nature's own movements have something mad about them, above all for the spectator."

"[With tragedy] one must always feel the passing of the hours, and the outside necessity which pushes the passions onwards and ripens them before they are ready. . . . One might say that the passions are the matter, and time the form, of all tragedy."

"One can try anything in the theater, except showing beforehand what comes afterwards."

"The unfolding of the drama in dialogue, and the passing of time which can always be felt, are assertion enough that the universe is present."

"In comedy the danger with what is natural and probable is that one becomes enclosed in them and cannot get out again."

Architecture

"For these carvings on cathedrals do not want to be seen, or only fleetingly. It is as if they were effaced by the grand movement of the lines: the mind is asked to find some other meaning for these things. So, by a higher law, both imitation and likeness are excluded. . . ."

"Ornament . . . the sign of the invention and the winning of each moment, or, if you wish, the sign of those movements of ideas which accompany research and which flower out of our sternest thoughts. . . ."

"It is the nature of style never to result from any rule."

Sculpture

"Pure thought is rare and momentary; not momentary because it is timeless; but always assailed, like a promontory. . . ."

"The object of sculpture is rather to represent the really immobile, and finally, instead of giving the appearance of human movement to marble, to do the opposite and bring the human form to the immobility of marble."

Design

"The line of the drawing is not at all an imitation of the lines of the object, but rather the trace of a gesture which takes hold of and explains the form."

"A good writer never counts upon a single word."

"Only the linking of thought supports prose. . . . The proper field for prose is thus what is well named analysis."

"Poetry is subject to the law of time . . . so it should be heard rather than read. . . . True prose should be read by the eyes."

"Proofs are not in any sense reasons. . . ."

"The unified narrative resists analysis by its firm progress under the law of time."

"It is the relationship between the dream and action which defines the novel, with action making the dream consistent, instead of wiping it out" (as in reality).

"The theme of every novel is the conflict between one romantic person and the things and the men he finds before him as he moves forward."

"The paramount rule of prose, which is to act with judgment and not with words. . . ."

4th May

In the mental disturbance and effort of writing, what sustains you is the certainty that on every page there is something left unsaid.

25th May

It is not that the child lives in a world of imagination (as Cantoni says: *I Primitivi*, p. 256), but that the child within us survives and starts into life only at rare moments of recollection, which make us believe, and it is not true, that in their time they were imaginative.

27th May

Dear Vittorini,[1]

[1] Elio Vittorini, one of a group of young writers and critics, headed by Alberto Carocci, responsible for the literary review *Solaria*, published in Florence.

Vittorini reviewed Pavese's early poems very favorably in 1926, and the two men became friends. Like Pavese, Vittorini was interested in contemporary American literature, and his very significant work *Conversazione in Sicilia*, published shortly after Pavese's *Paesi Tuoi* in 1939 was followed by the anthology, *Americana* (1942) to which Pavese refers here.

(Cf. also Pavese's comment on 29th December, 1949). Ed.

I feel I owe you this letter because I think it will please you to feel that we are all firmly in agreement with you. . . . All the value and the significance of *L'Americana* depends on your notes.

During the ten years I have been studying that literature I have not yet come across a synthesis so accurate and so illuminating. I want to tell you this, because it is certain that when your notes become generally known in the world, in your *Short History of Poetical Culture in America,* someone is sure to jump up and say that they are highly original, yes, but fantastic. Now, it should be widely proclaimed that it is precisely because they form a narrative, a novel if you like, that they are so illuminating. I leave aside the justice of the individual criticisms, arrived at by so many intimate and most informative monographs, and I will speak of the play of your theme, the drama of corruption, purity, ferocity and innocence you have established in this history. It is neither by chance nor by choice that you begin with abstract ravings, since your *Conversation in Sicily* had the same (unspoken) conclusion. In this sense it is a great thing that you have conveyed the same tension, the same excited cries of discovery, in your poetical history. Consequently, this work is not concerned with chasing clouds but with a challenging comparison with world literature (that world literature which is implicit, in its entirety, in American literature, if I understand you clearly?). The result is that a century and a half of American literature is reduced to essential evidence of a legend that we have all lived through and which you now relate.

There are naturally a few minor details with which I disagree (e.g., that *The Scarlet Letter* is stronger than *The Brothers Karamazov;* certain generalizations on Whitman and Anderson, and so on), but they are not important. The fact remains that in fifty pages you have written a great book. I do not wish to flatter you, but for you I feel the same sense of appreciation that Dante must have had for *De Vulgari:* a literary history seen by a poet as a history of his own poetical feeling.

4th June

The *unitarian composition* I am seeking could be the platonic development of "a discourse within a discourse." In *Fedro*, in *Convito*, and so on, everything said, every situation, almost every gesture has a realism of its own that combines with the rest to form a structure, but also has a place and an importance in a spiritual construction that transcends the first. Every situation is there for more than one motive: to form a realistic picture, to develop a line of reasoning, to symbolize a mental state, to align blocks of spiritual realities that form another picture in their turn. The technique for fusing this superstructure with reality, and achieving *the atmosphere of significant miracle,* is constant allusion to the θεία mania and to Socratic ignorance, the insidious reference to the myths that represent in Plato's world of ideas what memories are to you, your roots in the past that give sap and life to the abstract sensations you are writing about in the present (for *memories* cf. 28th January and 10th February '42). By Platonic mania I also mean the dialectic insistence on exhaustive analyses that are the voice of that ignorance.

1st July   At Santo Stefano

When the moon   When the moon
is old: is new:

                          Sowing flowers
                          They come

Beautiful and   Sickly and
With thick stems   slim and elegant

                          Cutting down trees,
                          they will be

Healthy   Worm-eaten

                          Except the pine tree
                          which will be

Worm-eaten | Healthy

Washing the sheets
with ashes
will make them

Clean and good | dirty—the ashes
will filter through

Pruning the vine
and the buds
will be

Harmful | Fruitful

10th July

". . . order, composition, of whatever kind it may be, is an assessment of proportions, of analogies. Fantasy, on the other hand, is free of all calculation, of all laws, however circumspect or hidden, or pretends to free itself from them. For this reason composition is of no importance in the novels of Giraudoux. . . ." (D. Mornet, *Introduction a l'Etude des Ecrivains Francais d'aujourd'hui.*)

I, in fact, have stated the contrary (preface to *David Copperfield:* "fantasy, which is pure construction"). This man Mornet distinguishes and classifies as a French pedant would do. Fantasy is not the opposite of intelligence. Fantasy is intelligence brought to establishing relationships of analogy, of significant implication, of symbolism. I have said that only fantasy can construct, because only fantasy can escape the tyranny of a real slice of life, of a natural occurrence, and replace the laws of reality (which is absence of construction, so much so that it has no beginning and no end) with fairy tales, stories and myths, which are constructions of intelligence.

Mornet applies the term "fantasy" to "reverie," which —except for pathological cases—is also an instinctive effort of intellectual construction.

2nd August

The unspeakable boredom it gives you to read travel pages in journals! The new, exotic surroundings that have surprised the writer! It stems, without any doubt, from the lack of roots that these impressions have, that they have, as it were, come out of nothing, from the outside world, unburdened by a past. They appeal to the writer as something amazing, but real amazement comes from the memory, not from novelty.

7th August

From the beginning I have been accustomed to think of my poetry as an illusion, a psychological blockade, so true is it that my richest style is the synthetic voice of the leading character, and that my formula is "to see how such and such a person would extricate himself from a given situation." This not only in my prose but even in my verse. It is quite different for Vittorini, who, ignoring the leading character with all the calm dignity of a Dante, can make a symbol of him without any effort.

14th August

In the little train I was thinking that the fields I saw speeding past, the tree-curtains, the houses, the little out-of-the-way corners, the reminders of former days, all would have served to make a memory, a past. Though the hour was commonplace and, in truth, boring, to find it again one day would no longer have been boring.

17th August

It happens that a conversation overheard makes us pause, interests and touches us more deeply than words addressed to us.

20th August

They say that to create while actually writing is to reach out beyond whatever plan we have made; searching, listening to the deep truth within us. But often the profoundest truth we have is the plan we have created by slow, ruthless, weary effort and surrender.

212

22nd August (At Pavone)

The things I once saw for the first time, in a past that has gone forever. If seeing them for the first time was enough to content me (amazement, ecstasies of imagination) seeing them again should bring another significance. What?

25th August (At Pavone)

When you tell little anecdotes or events you always get tied up and cannot choose: you want to say *everything*. A lack of confidence in art, hoping that by accumulating every little detail you will succeed in finding the good one that will make the *point*.

Your worst enemy is your belief in a happy, prehistoric time, a Garden of Eden, a golden age; and a belief that everything essential has already been said by the first thinkers. The two things are one.

30th August (At Gressoney)

Love is desire for knowledge.

31st August (At Gressoney)

As a child one learns to know the world not—as it would seem—by immediate initial contact with things, but through signs of things: words, pictures, stories. If anything in the world inspires a moment of ecstatic emotion, we find that we are moved because we were previously moved by it; and we were moved because, on some day or other, it seemed to us transfigured, detached from everything else, by a word, a fable, a fancy that we connect with it. Naturally at that time the fancy strikes us as reality, as objective knowledge, not as an invention. (Since the idea that infancy is poetic is only an adult conception, cf. 25th May.)

4th September (At Gressoney)

We want to produce a work that from the start will amaze even ourselves.

6th September

There comes a day when, for someone who has persecuted us, we feel only indifference, a weariness at his stupidity. Then we forgive him.

10th September

It is only by following instinct, the initial, spontaneous way of living, that one can feel justified, at peace with oneself and with one's own standard. But what of the man whose instinct pulls him in two different directions, so that he is always at odds with himself?

12th September

A man alone in a hut, eating the grease and gravy from a cooking pot. Some days he scrapes it with an old knife, on other days with his nails; there was a time when the pot was full, the food good; now it is stale, and to get the taste of it the man gnaws his broken nails. He will do the same tomorrow and the next day.

Like me, searching for work in my heart.

17th September

The chapter on responsibility and personality in Cesare Luporini's *Situazione e libertà nell'esistenza* has sorted out your thoughts on "the moment of ecstasy" and "continuous unity" (the symbol and the natural state), cf. 27th August, '39; 22nd, 24th and 27th February, '40. The new thing, today, is that the *ecstatic moment* corresponds to the *symbol,* which should thus mean perfect liberty.

We live in a world of things, facts, deeds, which is the temporal world. Our ceaseless, unconscious effort is to reach out beyond time towards the ecstatic moment when our liberty will be realized. What happens is that things, facts, deeds, the passing of time, all promise us such moments, clothe them, make them alive. They become symbols of our liberty. Each of us has a wealth of things, facts and deeds that are the symbols of his happiness; not that they have value in themselves by their very nature, but that they invite us, appeal to us; they are symbols. Time enriches this world of signs amazingly, in that it creates a play of perspective that multiplies the more-than-temporal significance of these symbols.

Which is as good as saying that there are no such things as negative symbols, pessimistic or even merely commonplace: the symbol is always synonymous with a moment of ecstasy, affirmation, a focal point.

So now you can be happy! (As you understood on the 6th November, '43.)

26th September

The theme in Greek tragedy is: *what should be, must be.* Hence the wonderland of gods who bring about whatever they wish; the rules of magic, taboos, destiny that must be observed; the final catharsis which is the acceptance of what must be.

(Does not the same thing happen in the five acts of Shakespeare? And in O'Neill, what must be is ordained by the natural laws of life?) The poetry of the Greeks is that this destiny, these taboos, these rules seem arbitrary, contrived, magical—perhaps symbolic.

There is no such thing as "seeing a thing for the first time." What we remember, what we notice, is always a second time. (I said the same thing on 28th January; 22nd August is illusory; 31st August is conclusive.)

27th September

In Greek tragedy the characters never talk to one another, they talk to confidants, to the chorus, to strangers. It is a method of presentation in which each one states his own case to the public. The character never descends to a dialogue with others, but is as he is, statuesque, immutable.

Murders take place off the stage and we hear the shouts, the exhortations, the words. Then the messenger appears and tells us the facts; the event resolves itself into words, a speech, not a dialogue. The tragedy itself is not a dialogue but an explanation to an idealized public, the chorus, with whom the real dialogue takes place.

(Hence the poverty of classical tragedy [French, or in Alfieri] which preserves the style, the absence of action and the exposition in the Greek manner, but lacks the chorus, that is the second personage which is the sum of all the other characters.)

18th October

In Aeschylus, the protagonist is motionless, statuesque, facing the chorus, and all the episodes take place around him (*The Suppliants, Prometheus, Persians, Seven Against Thebes*) This is probably the basic situation. It reappears in Sophocles (*Oedipus Coloneus*) and in Euripides (*Troades, Hecuba*).

The hubris is knowing the decree of the oracle and taking no account of it. But the hubris itself is also fate (oracle): what must be will be, as the chorus proclaims. That is why the chorus is forever conversing with the protagonists.

31st October

All these farces, tricks, witty inventions, which, in tragedy, appear as ambushes, revenges, enterprises, are the form in which is manifested the real psychology of the characters, but they go beyond it, surround and sustain it by a stylization that is half social, half mythological. In short, wit is not psychology, it is style.

5th November

Confessions by Kierkegaard which describe the man of letters, the pure intellectual: "my interests are not all subordinate to a single interest, but are all co-ordinated," and "what I lacked was the fact of not having led a perfect human life, following as I did only the road of knowledge." These were thoughts that I had last night as I talked about G. with the Romano woman, and which I found again this morning in Przywara (*Das Geheimnis Kierkegaards,* pages 11 and 12). The usual coincidence.

Before Romanticism, the intellectual did not exist, because there was no line of demarcation between life and learning. (I have already noted this once.) To perceive that life is more important than thought, means being a learned man, an intellectual; it means that his own thought has not become life.

1943

3rd February

The trouble is not the harshness of Fate, for anything we want strongly enough we get. The trouble is rather that when we have it we grow sick of it, and then we should never blame Fate, only our own desire.

9th-10th February

Leon Chestov, *Kierkegaard et la philosophie existante* (*Vox Clamantis in deserto*). Les amis de Leon Chestov. 1936.

p. 37: "The origin of philosophy does not lie in astonishment, as Plato and Aristotle taught, but in despair."

p. 42: (Socrates) "The 'best' comes first. The 'best' ought to rule the world. But in this case, before admiring reason one must first make enquiries: does it really assure man of what is best?"

p. 102: "Only the knight of the faith is happy: he reigns over the finite, while the knight of resignation is only a passerby here, a stranger" (Kierkegaard).

p. 140: "Mysticism lives in peace with reason and human knowledge, and since the reward that it promises men supposes nothing else, it excludes any supernatural intervention. Everything happens naturally; one obtains everything with one's own strength."

p. 148: "It was not that Adam was ignorant of the difference between good and evil, *but that this difference did not exist.*"

p. 201: "God, like the apostles, possesses no power; he only possesses authority: He can only threaten, demand, or at most, melt the heart."

p. 207: (Dostoevsky) "I assert that the awareness of our powerlessness to help or to bring the slightest relief to suffering humanity, even though we are deeply convinced of this suffering, can in our hearts change love of humanity into hatred for humanity."

p. 217: "Jesus taught men, then, to raise themselves above the finite, exactly as the ancients taught and modern sages still teach."

p. 222: "Kierkegaard denied faith in order to acquire knowledge: he repeated the act already committed by our ancestor, and the result was what was to be expected least—impotence."

p. 228-229: The life of Christ is an unfortunate love affair, if Necessity rules. He could weep, and do no more.

p. 230: "The task before Christianity is to realize 'ethics' on earth."

Where, then, is it different from the wisdom of the ancient Greeks? In its "diabolical pride" (Pascal quoting Epictetus).

p. 240: "And he (Kierkegaard) was obliged to consider the healing of the sick man not a miraculous victory over impotence—impotence cannot be beaten—but only the love and mercifulness of the apostle."

p. 288: Kierkegaard allowed himself to believe that "the Creator of the earth and the sky was as depressed, as miserable as he, Kierkegaard. It was at this moment that existential philosophy came into being."

p. 307: "the reasonable consciousness can not tolerate what madness and death say to it."

p. 323: "For if a choice has to be made between good and evil, this means that freedom has already been lost: evil has entered the world and taken its place beside the divine *valde bonum.*" The infinitely greater and qualitatively different freedom enjoyed by man "consists not in choosing between god and evil, but in ridding the world of evil. Man can have no relationship with evil: while evil exists there is no liberty, and everything that men have so far called justice is nothing but falsehood and trickery. Freedom does not choose between good and evil: it destroys evil."

p. 325: "Ignorance is not something negative, an absence, a lack, just as freedom is not a want and a negation, but an affirmation of an immense value. Innocence does not seek knowledge, since it is above it (I again recall the "flight over consciousness" of Plotinus) just as the will of Him who created man in His image is above knowledge."

p. 328-9: "And in effect, if freedom is freedom to choose between good and evil, then this freedom ought also to be inherent in the Creator in as much as He is the free Being *par excellence.* Consequently, it would be quite possible to admit that, having this choice between good and evil, the Creator might have chosen evil. This problem was a real *crux interpretum* for the philosophical thought of the middle ages. The idea that freedom was freedom to choose between good and evil could not then be abandoned: the middle ages, enthralled by Greek speculative thought, never managed to distinguish between the religious and ethical points of view (and did not dare to make this distinction). On the other hand it could not be admitted that God 'had the right' to prefer evil to good."

(John Duns Scotus) "God is the arbitrary: He is dominated by no principle and no law. What He accepts is the good. What He rejects is evil." (Eutiphrones.)

p. 332: "Before God every necessity uncovers its real essence and reveals itself as a void lacking all content."

p. 342: "for in the last analysis truth has to resort to torture, to violence. God . . . restrains nobody."

p. 343: "Kierkegaard was forced to the monstrous conclusion that the love of God is dependant on His immutability, that God is tied and cannot move, that God, exactly like ourselves, has 'a thorn in his flesh'; in other words those torments with which truth crushes men are there for God also. All this had to be if Kierkegaard was to dare to oppose speculative philosophy with existential philosophy, for him to have courage enough to ask himself how it was that truth had managed to dominate God, and to perceive in this monstrous rational construction what it asserts in reality—the fall of man and original sin."

p. 345: "All theodicy, which means the 'justification of God,' is based on the fact that God can not be master of the truths which He did not create. So theodicy does not so much justify God as evil."

p. 356: "And salvation consists neither of the knowledge that everything that happens is inevitable, nor of the virtue which has seen what is inevitable and submits to it of its own accord; salvation is faith in God, to whom all things are possible, who created all things of his own free will and compared to whom everything uncreated is only a miserable empty Void. There lies the true meaning of the Absurd. . . ."

p. 359: "God means that everything is possible. God means that the learning for which our reason is so avid, *pulling us irresistably* towards it, does not exist. God means that evil does not exist either: only the original *fiat* and the paradisal *valde bonum* exist, and in the face of these all our truths based on the principle of non-contradiction, on the principle of sufficient reason, and many other laws, fade away and change into fantoms."

p. 362: (St. Peter Damiani. Tertullian) "God determines just as arbitrarily, without considering the laws of thought or of being, what is true."

p. 372: " 'Compulsion' is evidence not for, but against the truth of any judgement and all 'necessities' can and must be resolved in freedom."

p. 376: "It was by the divine will that man fell before temptation and lost his freedom. And this same divine will—in the face of which, petrified immutability collapsed when it tried to offer resistance—will give man back his freedom and has already done so. That is the sense of the Bible's revelation."

220

p. 379: "The promised land is wherever the man of faith has come; it offers its promise just because he is already there; *certum est quia impossibile.*"

19th February

Ideally, the theatre has to do, not with action, but with acting. I mean an impartial, well-balanced presentation, not "veracity." The Greeks, in fact, made everything happen off-stage, and the "action" became words on the lips of the messenger. Anything that happens on the stage is not "theatre" but histrionics. Look at the absence of scenery in the great days of the Greeks and Shakespeare. That is why one dislikes realistic presentations, why stage directions always seem absurd. The setting may please one as a pictorial effect, but that is "spectacle," not "theatre." It is a step towards the technique of the cinema, which concentrates on telling a story, not on dialogue.

2nd April (At Rome)

The words they shall speak will be stereotyped, their movements like a dance. The story must not proceed according to a naturalistic sequence of events, but through abrupt changes, platonically construed. Everything should be prepared in advance, like granite blocks previously cut and ready to be placed here and there at will, not built up to a climax and described in the style of a running commentary.

Whatever evil may occur, do we deserve any better? I am still happy to be alive.

Presumptuous language.

The various episodes are not introduced by natural accidents, as in a diary, but, so long as the inner continuity remains constant and breath-taking, they are mutations indicating a manifold reality, placed above and outside time.

25th April

Provincialism in art means only moral timidity.

When the "word-fable-fantasy" of 31st August, '42 links up with reality, a memory is created: *here is the symbol!*

29th April

When I arrive in a fresh place, a new locality with different natural surroundings, different customs, houses, faces, I notice many things that, if I had always lived there, would now be childhood memories. That is what gives me the feeling, as I walk about, that I am disturbing and intruding upon other men's dreams.

2nd May

Out of the depths of bitter humiliation men utter two cries: either "We shall see, O World!" or "Don't you know that I love you?"

13th May

To write badly means employing words and phrases that do not ring true. Balbo and Petitjean do not write badly, but disjointedly.

3rd June

A rustic composition, peopled not by country folk or peasants but by girls with a sunshade. The Roman ruins please you because the reeds and poppies, the dry hedges on the hills, somehow link them with your childhood; also because history (Ancient Rome) and pre-history (Vico: blood sprinkled on the hedgerow or in the furrow) are in harmony with this rusticity, making it a world in itself, consistent from birth to death.

Your classical knowledge stems from the *Georgics,* D'Annunzio and the hill of Pino. To that background you added America, because its language is rustic-universal (Anderson, *An Ohio Pagan*) and because it is the place (*The Field of Corn*) where town and country meet. Yours is a rustic-classicism that could easily become prehistoric ethnography.

15th June

Going back to what I wrote on 23rd August, 1942, I believe that infancy is not important as a natural phenomenon, but only as a time for christening things, a time which teaches us to be moved by the sight of the things we have christened. One can christen things at any age, provided one is innocent enough to believe that such a transfiguration is, in fact, objective knowledge. This is why only a child can usually do it. Herein lies the spontaneity not of a poem, which is only a little tale, but of the prepoetic stage, which provides the necessary material for the poem. This is the spontaneity of inspiration, which is a completely different thing from composing poetry (cf. 10th February, 1942.)

30th June

Among the roots of your classicism you must include your passion for the stars, which began as a love of beautiful names, inspired suddenly, marvelously, by your first classics lectures (on the *Georgics*) *"Ante tibi Atlantides abscondantur ..."* and by D'Annunzio (*Maja*).

This living voluptuously you talked about on 20th April, '36 has now moved out of the realm of emotional sincerity to that of professional research on memories. Stop it and act.

2nd July

After my dream of June 22[1] I had another typical dream last night. At the end of a performance given by myself alone in an enormous theatre, and greatly applauded, the maid brought to my dressing room a potted plant and a letter. Who had sent it? My mind was a blank, though I knew the handwriting. The tone of the letter was bittersweet.

This was a typical dream of total discovery, like the reading of a novel. My surprise was entirely genuine. If I did not know who had sent me the flowers and, in reading the note, felt both surprised and afraid, how could I be the same person who was imagining the plot of the dream?

And yet, the shape of the flowers in the pot, the tone

[1] There is no trace of this dream in the manuscript. Other previous dreams were described in penciled notes upon separate pieces of paper. Ed.

of the letter and the handwriting are events which have occurred in these last few days. The maid I remembered from an old film I had seen. Could it not be that, as the seconds passed, one memory superimposed itself on another and, in this case, I was receiving the flowers because I have read and seen innumerable times that flowers are brought to one's dressing room? But this cannot be explained: that at that moment I was a thousand miles away from Fern. And yet the letter came from her; as a matter of fact, she was in the theatre and I had not known it until that instant.

4th July

Not only for their lovely names. Above all else, the stars were rustic-mythological complex bodies that fostered your interest in the prehistoric. Even more than poetry (the *Iliad,* the *Divina Commedia, Leopardi*) you enjoyed geology and astronomy, studies which may sound dull but which inspired in you a taste for rustic mythology. This growing enthusiasm, nourished by certain all-too-rare but exciting and suggestive indications you found in poetry (*esperos o callistos en uranò istasi aster*) led you to literature, to an appreciation of words as a medium, acquired first by tedious cultural studies ("required reading"), then by your discovery of Baudelaire.

10th July

Between sixteen and nineteen you thought it extraordinary that reality (which to you meant such things as the little path from Reaglie by starlight, or the woods of strong ash trees for making boats), was the very thing Homer or D'Annunzio passed over in silence. At first there was the emotion inspired by the *signs* of things (poems, fables, legends), then you came to recognize the beauty and interest of the world of things themselves. Though you were still looking at literature from the outside, your love of astronomy and the effect of such moving experiences as Flammarion, and the film on Dante, confirmed your interest in some realities.

Turin—and the armistice; then—Serralunga.

11th September

The characteristic thing, I do not say of poetry but of fable, or the myth, is the consecration of individual places that are connected with a fact, an action, an event, isolating that particular spot and giving it an absolute significance. For every man, places he knew as a child come back to him consecrated in the same way; the things that took place there make them unique, mark them off from the rest of the world as being legendary, though not as yet poetic. This individuality, this *uniqueness* ascribed to a place is part of that broader, general assumption that an action or fact is unique, absolute and therefore symbolic, which is characteristic of a myth. (It is quite unrealistic to regard a place in that way simply because something happens there now and then, and seems significant because it recurs.) In reality no action, no place, is more important than another, but in a myth such matters have a hierarchy of their own. This is why many people shun natural realism and, instead, devise a myth, reverting to their childhood.

15th September

With any writer, one can apply the term "mythical" to that central image, quite unmistakable, which moves him most fiercely and to which he always turns. In Dostoievsky, it is a man sinking himself to the level of the madness; in Stendhal, the isolation of prison life, and so on. Such an image is mythical in so far as the writer turns to it as something unique that symbolizes all his experience.

I was on a train, desperate and watchful.[1]

17th September

A level stretch of green turf surrounded by hills and ranks of trees with broad glades between, seen on a September morning when wisps of haze cut it off from the world, appeals to you as the sort of place that in the past might have been

---

[1] The manuscript reads: sad but curious, desperate and watchful. Ed.

considered sacred. Imagine those glades strewn with flowers, the festivals, the sacrifices where mystery beckons and threatens from the wooded shadows. There, between the tree-trunks and the sky, the god of that place might appear. The *mythological* spot is not one particular unique place, a shrine or something similar (this is a correction of 11th September), but a universal common denominator, *a* glade, *a* wood, *a* grotto, *a* seashore, which by its very vagueness evokes all glades, all woods, all grottoes, all seashores. If they are still further enriched by personal memories they can become material for poetry, a very different thing from their original significance as a myth. In short, what makes them "unique" is their power of evoking transcendental images. Could these feelings be our religious emotions?

30th September

Milton, in his use of fantasy, is still Elizabethan in spirit; in his imagery he mingles the world of fables, memory and nature with reality in such a way as to transpose the whole to a different sphere; he even has a sense (cf. the importance music has for him in *L'Allegro, Il Penseroso* and *Comus*) of the first intangible indications foreshadowing romanticism, but he has lost all appreciation of idiom, of dialect, of lusty speech. That is why he "forgets himself to marble," instead of savoring flesh and blood, the sweat of life.

1st October

The pre-Shakespearians (Peele, Greene) had no conception of imagination (in the sense I discussed on 28th May, '40), but by constructing their plays upon a mixture of buffoonery and serious, imaginative speeches they prepared the way for imaginative drama.

When Lily, Marlowe, Shakespeare and the rest not only mingled boisterous wit with serious passages but gave an interpretation to the whole, then narrative imagery came to life. Wit, of course, is style, not psychology (cf. 31st October,

'42), which means that characters use wit not to express their own individuality (that is revealed by their actions and their thoughts) but because it is natural to their world. Wit is an air, a song, not a serious analysis; a game of fancy pervading all men's conversation and so must be regarded as imagination, not as truth.

4th October

We only admire those landscapes that we have already admired. Image by image we find our way back to a picture, an exclamation, a sign with which others chose them and pointed them out to us (See 10th February and 31st August, 1942). Of course a moment comes when, having become wise through habit, we too can choose our landscapes as if they bore the mark of someone else's approval. So the law is not violated.

To admire, in other words to enjoy as a visual form, is in fact to see as a sign. This is why the beginning of admiration is always focused upon a sign which cannot as yet have been created by us.

This is why our very own landscapes are few (10th February, 1942). It is difficult for us to add new ones to those revealed to us thanks to accidental signs during our infancy when our imaginations are being formed.

You do not understand the craze so many people have to break away from the bourgeois mentality. Talking of poetry, you already feel more or less on equal terms with the ordinary man in the street. Appearances and actions are to be judged by elementary indications, before culture comes into it.

5th October

The last hundred years have ended the betrayal of dialect by discovering it, and giving it a place beside literary language. So dialect has finally lost the *all-pervadingness* it once had, underlying all literary efforts in Italian; a quality it began to lose during the centuries ('600 and '700) of academic restraint. Great poetry grew from a field where literary language and dialect were mingled indiscriminately —the vulgar tongue. Certainly one reverts to the forcefulness of dialect when seeking "rhetorical dignity," but that in no way conflicts with the mother tongue. Italy and England have had great poets because there the first attempts at poetry were made before the language was definitely formed. In France, no, because, for various reasons, ambitious poets began writing after the language was clearly defined ('600). Here is the reason for the power of American writers now, and of the Russians in the nineteenth century. The first had the good fortune of a language enriched by a fresh effervescence, a new blossoming in a new society—a dialect; the second had their own reasons of conscience for ignoring literary language, and made do with the more popular tongue.

As in everything to do with poetry, there is in this, too, the question of a certain balance. Poets of the great periods did not, of course, write in dialect. They used the language of the people, uplifting it with all sorts of rhetorical devices and poetical turns of phrase. With them *the transition from dialect to literary language was made in the name of poetry,* directly due to the way they used and increased the vivacity of dialect. On the other hand, when a literary language already exists, men no longer feel the need for this lighter effect because it seems that this language has *dignity,* and then it's "Goodnight!".

But, after all, what's done is done. Nowadays dialect is distinct from language and we cannot go back to it unless we pose as lovers of folk-lore. The problem is to find a new vivacity (or *naturalness,* as Leopardi would say).

7th October

Henry VI is one of the richest and most full of narrative of all Shakespeare's works. The triple construction of it lessens the theatrical quality and increases the narrative. It is many-colored: the wars in France with incidental adventures (the Duchess of Auvergne, the *Pucelle*); the intrigues and

228

factions at home, the tumults (Cade); fierce fighting, high treason (and low), escapes (the Scottish forest). There are the three parts. Is it possible that this was his first play? It already has all Shakespeare's command of tragic language, with well-judged transitions from high-flown rhetoric to the salacious humor of the common people. Here wit is specially devised to cast an imaginative light upon the narration. There are innumerable extremely vivid descriptions of actions and events where this wit reigns supreme. It is worth noting that already Shakespeare excelled in the use of wit in repartee, as a fanciful embroidery to the dialogue. Here, descriptive, informative witticisms take the place of dialogue. His comedies of the same period are already pure theatre, while this chronicle is entirely a record of events.

Each of the three parts has its own hero: Talbot, a brave, simple soldier; York, the clever, persevering heir to the throne; and Warwick, soldier, hero and politician. But what matters most is the swarm of characters, their multiplicity and profusion; presenting not the psychological truth about individuals but the vital world around them, with all its atmosphere and imagination (the sea, men's occupations, nature, wild animals).

8th October

Love's Labor's Lost is the most delightful of his youthful comedies. Possibly his first? A wild medley of talk, blows, counter-blows, wit, flights of fancy, tirades and fresh starts. One cannot see how the characters even have time to laugh. It takes your breath away. It is conceived as a true, supreme display of wit.

When you dream, you are an author, but you do not know how it will end.

9th October

The other youthful comedies (*Two Gentlemen of Verona* and *The Comedy of Errors*) are full of serious passages. Shakespeare's prose has not yet reached his new comico-tragic language, *images conveyed by dialogue* as in his tragedies (*Henry VI, Richard III* and *Titus Andronicus*). He has not yet gone beyond conveying images by means of descriptions. It is only after progressive efforts with imaginative verse (*A Midsummer Night's Dream, The Merchant of Venice*), dialectic prose (*Much Ado About Nothing, As You Like It, Twelfth Night*), delicate, psychological narrative (*Romeo and Juliet, King John, Henry IV, Henry V, Timon of Athens*) that he reaches the comico-tragic language of his maturity, equally powerful in comedy and tragedy, truly theatrical, with images conveyed by dialogue, in place of descriptions. A typical imaginative dialogue:

> Perdita: . . . to make you garlands of; and my sweet
> friend, to strew him o'er and o'er!
> Florizel: What, like a corse?
> Perdita: No, like a bank for love to lie and play on;
> not like a corse; or if, not to be buried,
> but quick and in mine arms. . . . .
>
> (*The Winter's Tale*, Act IV, Sc. 4).

Without question, Shakespeare has, even in his earliest works, occasional passages of finished style and imaginative dialogue. But he has not yet fused this style with the situations; it triumphs in occasional scenic discoveries, almost always farcical or lyrical, but the whole conception of his work is not yet *ironical,* i.e., conscious of a double or treble reality to be expressed in two or three shades of meaning fused together—the imaginative (lyrical passages); dialectic (comic interludes) and the tragic (insight into the depths of the human soul). Fused together, that is the important thing, into one line or a single word. His *irony,* as is to be expected, reveals itself first in his comedies—*A Midsummer Night's Dream, As You Like It*—but with *Julius Caesar* it pervades even tragedy. In fact, in *Julius Caesar* his style is sure and strong.

10th October

If *The True Tragedy of Richard, Duke of York* is by Marlowe, Peele and Greene with a little of Shakespeare, as is probable, one understands where Shakespeare learned his first tragic style, as in *Henry VI*. Working with them, he inherited the construction and the tone of the play. By himself, in the third part of *Henry VI*, he introduced more fluency, gave more plausibility to the transitions, gave the whole more imaginative fullness. (The sections he added all clarify the transitions, enrich and bring to life the cold, stiff imagery, or give fresh animation to the settings, e.g. the hunters in the forest). He still lacks irony, but that he will invent for himself, deriving it from his comedy.

Marlowe got as far as making a character talk in dialect (Ithnamore in *The Jew;* the various clowns in *Faustus*), but not to the stage of introducing exchanges of wit. In fact, his dialogue has no irony.

Obviously Marlowe, except in *Tamerlane* and *Edward II*, was writing hurriedly, for the scene between Ithnamore, the courtesan and the ruffian in Act IV could have been worked up into a strong scene of scurrilous dialogue that would have anticipated Ben Jonson, and has, in any case, plenty of blasphemous witticisms. Here is where he falls short of Shakespeare, who would have interlarded the scene with flashes of wit, all unexpected and all carefully devised (cf. *Henry IV*, where the scene with Falstaff in The Boar's Head is studied from life).

Dialect and lyrical writing are never mixed by any pre-Shakespearian. Except Lily, who, however, has no irony. Apart from his dry, scholarly references to mythology, Marlowe has nothing imaginative. His stand-by is straightforward, passionate expression (cf. the lines declaimed over Gaveston), though occasionally his descriptions are vivid and true. His pagan desires for power, wealth and sex are stated with utter frankness; he is energy at full stretch, but he is not a poet.

His *Edward II* is not so much a "chronicle play" as the delicate drama of "a brain-aired king, wanton and frolicky," wretched in his misfortune. The lords have no epic grandeur, and—a strange thing—there are no battles.

12th October

Creative power of a dream. A radio and a woman, or a naked woman functioning as a radio, or what have you; young G. called her a "Radio-péliga." [Italian play of words centered on "pelo," which describes the hair of the body, not of the head.] I laughed, greatly enjoying the expression and the image of hair. The word struck me as a magnificent one for cunt. The mystery is, where did this conviction derive from? As my dream became lighter it seemed to fade away, and I found it progressively harder to remember the word, which I could only recall by thinking of pellex-pellicis.

Is it not strange, this philological analysis performed during one's sleep? And how odd this conviction of the great power of expression of one word, which I had never heard before. Could there be, I wonder, a lexicon of invention in the language of dreams, on the lines of *Finnegan*?

Those birds flying away along the corridors amidst the greenery—I know them so well.

That in narrating one should not describe beautiful landscapes is clear from what I wrote on October 4th, when I stated that the landscapes one enjoys are seen as signs. The normal character, therefore, not being a fashioner of signs, should not enjoy them, at least not until the writer has finished filtering the surroundings through the character. This is the only decent way of telling a story. But this treatment should not be used in the case of the character's own signs, learnt in his infancy, in the case of his own myth, of that inner life which he, too, can and should have (17th September, 1942, II).

But in this case as well one should present without describing: for instance, the character's beautiful girl, though she is one of his myths, must not be described as beautiful, but presented.

14th October

Titus Andronicus has much that is doubtful; some scenes lack imagination, but certain passages are wonderfully rich; the contrast, in Act II, between fresh, joyous nature and a hotbed of crime (this scene is pure Shakespeare); and Act III, despair and malediction. The second scene in Act IV, about the little Moorish prince, has a savage humor, but still lacks irony. The rest, Acts I and V, are colorless and the style is poor. Aaron is a villain who foreshadows Iago and the rest, but he is also reminiscent of Marlowe's Barrabas. When the play reaches any heights of style it equals the best in *Henry IV* and even surpasses it in its sense of the global scene.

16th October

Reading *Every Man in His Humor,* I observed that, while other Elizabethan dramatists draw their comic elements from events (farces, fisticuffs, buffoonery), Shakespeare derives his chiefly from words (witticisms, repartee, puns and so on).

19th October

Every Man Out of His Humor. Jonson has learned the lesson of witty, Shakespearian prose and employs it to the full in giving a fresh direction to his realistic conception of his characters. But his witty explosions are not purely the play of imagination, as in Shakespeare; they are utilitarian, used to define or amplify the character.

22nd October

His *Richard II* (which is Shakespeare's *Edward II:* the deposed king and his passion) displays all the characteristics of Shakespeare's youthful tragedies: declamatory passages, resounding, all-embracing adjectives. Here wit appears in a frequent play on (serious) words. It needs to filter through comic prose to become a true expression of irony. But this play is far better than Marlowe's *Edward,* which makes no attempt at imagination or wit or any play on words but rushes straight on, merely talking about passion.

30th October

Poetry consists of conveying on every page the same thrill that reality gives. One believes one can achieve it by following reality. (*Cascina* was a failure.)

(Cf. 4th October, para. 2.) But is it enough to free you from the bourgeois mentality, to reduce things to elementary indications short of culture? That is escape on the lowest terms. Could there not be an escape on a higher level?

2nd November

". . . the first fable . . . the greatest ever imagined from then onwards . . . so popular, perturbing, and instructive. . . ." (*Scienza Nuova Seconda,* II, 1st sect. Chap. 1.) [This is the book by Giambattista Vico to which Pavese constantly refers on 5th November.]

This is the definition of your would-be popular-perturbing-instructive-poetry.

Italian poets like great constructions made up of very short chapters, brief, savory passages, the fruit of the tree. (Dante's short cantos; Boccaccio's short stories; Machiavelli's brief chapters in his great works; Voci's aphorisms in *Scienza Nuova;* Leopardi: the thoughts of Zibaldone; not to mention the sonnet.) That is why it seldom concerns itself with narrative (which requires a long, extended outpouring of effort as in Russian or French novels), but is, instead, intellectual and argumentative. It is the negation of naturalism, which in fact began with the casual development of English narrative prose by Defoe.

5th November

Vico is the only Italian writer with any feeling for the country way of life, outside Arcadia. The rough simplicity of his style heightens the atmosphere of genuine rusticity. The very fact that he only mentions it in passing, and then with a definite purpose, confirms his sincerity.

5th November

Book II[1]

p. 234: "Just as nowadays when our peasants want to say that a sick man lives they say he still eats."

p. 239: "Even as we daily observe in our stubborn peasants, who yield to every reasonable argument that is put to them, but, because their powers of reflection are weak, as soon as the argument which has moved them has left their minds, return at once to their original purpose."

p. 241: "The fire that the heroes must have kindled with flints and set to the thorny underbrush on the mountain tops, dried out by the hot suns of summer";

p. 249: ". . . Grain (the sole or at least the chief thing for which the peasants labored all year)."

p. 253: ". . . As a frog is born of a summer shower."

p. 227: "These people . . . would beat (their sons) within an inch of their lives in the Temple of Diana, so that they often fell dead in agonies of pain beneath their fathers' blows."

p. 200: "Similar payments in labor or goods are still customary in the transactions of peasants."

p. 191: ". . . eternal property expressed in the saying that servants are the paid enemies of their masters."

p. 180: "And finally many are charged with rakes, which are clearly agricultural implements."

p. 171: "And in the country districts of our most remote provinces . . . they give bread made from grain to the sick, and they say the sick man is eating grain bread when they mean he is at the point of death."

p. 162: ". . . Perennial springs, which for the most part

---

[1] These quotations taken from *Scienza Nuova* are given in the English version by Bergin and Fisch (*The New Science of Giambattista Vico,* New York, Cornell University Press, 1948).

rise in the mountains. Near such springs the birds of prey make their nests, and consequently in their vicinity hunters set their snares."

p. 116: "The farmers of Latium used to say the fields were thirsty."

And always the "peasant-heroes," the "farmers," the "daily hands," etc.

6th November

Today you made a discovery. The reflection that every man is in a rut he has made for himself troubled you very much at one period (cf. 4th April, '41), then it seemed a price to be paid gladly for being alive at all, and from then on you stopped moaning about it, devoting your energies instead to investigating how one begins to hollow out those ruts in childhood ('42 and '43). You started that research even before re-reading Thomas Mann's *Jacob* in December, '42. You ended (September, '43) with the discovery of myth-unity, which resolved your former mental fury and merged it with your most lively creative mythological interests.

And this proves that, for you, the need to create is born of this law of a return to first causes. Bravo! It also proves that the purpose of your life cannot be anything but creation. How is it that, without knowing it, you directed everything towards this central focal point? Inner logic, providence, vital instinct?

All is repetition, a second journey, a return. Indeed, even the first time is a "second time." (26th September, 1942, II.)

10th November

For women, history does not exist. Murasaki, Sappho and Madame Lafayette might be their own contemporaries. Yet *fashion* exists for them. Is it a trick they have, or some great talent, that enables them to appear at any moment exactly as fashion decrees?

236

11th November

Narrating incredible things as though they were real—the old system; narrating realities as though they were incredible—the new.

12th November

The pleasure of walking on the hilltops where the little trees are, among all the casual, accidental features of the landscape that will always be your own personal horizon! Walking there, you may come to the edge of that horizon, feel detached from it, look at it from the other side. It is one of those places that are *unique*.

14th November

In Murasaki, nature is symbolic. A branch of blossom, a bud, a conventional view, all assume that special quality. But they grow monotonous, like all symbols: their significance is always the same.

17th November

There is a risk that your idea of ambivalence (avarice-prodigality, laziness-activity, love-hate) may become a rule in all your life; the *same* energy that produces an effect is corrected by the opposite effect.

18th November

(On Shakespeare's style, cf. 9th October, '43.) The fool, full of dialectic wit, is later replaced by a leading character who is either mad or driven beyond endurance (Hamlet, Cleopatra, Lear, Macbeth), and then the witty speeches can become tragic without losing their pithiness. That is irony.

19th November

Shakespeare reveals the landscape by his art of weaving it into the dialogue (cf. Act II of *Titus Andronicus*); *"the moon . . . that tips with silver all these fruit treetops"* in Act III, scene 5. It is a simple device that dramatizes even nature.

He shows us many other things in *Romeo and Juliet;* the flights of fancy describing Queen Mab (Shakespeare's *own* poetry) in Act I, sc. 4; the well-devised secondary theme with Mercutio; the piteous ending with its tragic judgment on the world; the two contrapuntal strains, passionate love and the mockery of love, with Romeo and Mercutio; the comic and most convincing (pre-Dickensian) eccentric character, the Nurse.

1944

14th January

Dialogue, *conversation,* is our natural custom. We prefer to avoid long, informative accounts of events (*narration*), or, rather, we change even these into conversation by putting them into the first person and coloring them according to the personality of the speaker. In short, what we look for in a narrative is drama, not a scenic effect. Is this due to the influence of the cinema, which has taught us to distinguish between visual presentation and the spoken word —the basic art of the theatre? What happens now is that the cinema tells a story visually and the novel presents it verbally; we no longer want to bother with the theatre. Even great plays of the past we would rather read than see acted.

29th January

We humble ourselves to ask a favor, and so discover the sweet, inward balm of the Kingdom of God. We almost forget what we wanted to ask, longing only to enjoy forever this outpouring of divinity. That, beyond all doubt, would be *my* way of finding religious belief, my way of being faithful to it, renouncing all else, letting myself sink into a sea of love, faint with rapture at the first glimpse of such a possibility. Perhaps everything lies in this trembling thought: "If it were true!" If it were really true. . . .

1st February

We feel this same glow of divinity when suffering has brought us to our knees, so much so that the first pang can give us a sense of joy, gratitude, anticipation. . . . We reach the point of wanting pain.

This rich, symbolic reality, heralding another even more true and sublime, what is it but Christianity? To accept it means, quite literally, entering into the world of the supernatural.

We must not, however, confuse it with the little hoard of symbols that each of us makes for himself in life. In them there is nothing supernatural, though there may be a psychological urge, an effort of will, to transform moments of experience into moments of the Absolute. That is Protestantism without God.

2nd February

A certain pattern of daily life (with fixed hours, confined spaces, always the same people, religious rites and places) induces thoughts of the supernatural. Break away from that pattern, and those thoughts vanish. We are wholly creatures of habit.

3rd February

The place where you are really yourself is that avenue in Turin, noble yet unpretentious, broad, calm and serene, where it is always spring or summer and where your poetry was made. The material came from many sources, but that is where it took shape. That avenue, with its humble little café was your study, your window on the world.

When poetic inspiration comes to you, that is the sort

of place you try to find; when you are writing a story, no. Is this only because story writing is less contemplative? Yet you wrote *Memorie di due stagioni* in that café and most of *Paesi tuoi*. Then. . . .

The fact is that you have lost your taste for observing, feeling, gathering new experiences, and now you are eating out your heart.

6th February

A cypress and a house on the crest of the hill, dark against the crimson sky—the place that evokes your passion for this land of yours. Ethnology sprinkles such familiar places with blood, shed irrationally, mythically. That is why.

7th February

Blood is always shed irrationally. Every single thing is a miracle, but one is more acutely aware of that in the case of blood, because beyond it lies mystery.

To weep is irrational; to suffer is irrational (cf. "suffering serves no purpose," in '38). Your problem, then, is to evaluate the irrational. Your poetical problem is to evaluate it without taking away its mythical quality.

When we bleed, or weep, the amazing thing is that it is we, ourselves, who perform an act that raises us to kinship with the Universe, the Everything, the Myth.

8th February

Why does something irrational raise us to such a height? A romantic idea, but is that any reason for tossing it aside? Beyond all doubt, the irrational is the vast reservoir of the spirit, as legends are for nations. Your own creations are drawn out of what is nebulous, irrational, and the problem is how to convey them into the realm of consciousness. So true that it seems banal.

Amazement is the mainspring of every discovery. It is,

in fact, the emotion to which we are moved when faced with the irrational. Your *modernity* lies wholly in your sense of the irrational.

12th February

"Sacrament" also means "symbol." Here is a way to the conception of a symbol which is potent by combining the gifts of the Holy Spirit with magic. Here is the common root of poetry and religion, given that a symbol is also an image. Ritual was originally the same thing, the cause producing the effect; later, it became symbolic (pagan baptism and the baptism of John). (Cf. L. Allevi, *Hellenism and Christianity;* "Life and thought"; 1934, p. 117.)

13th February

The richness of life lies in memories we have forgotten.

15th February

Admiration, before being aesthetic, is religious. From Shintoism (and the polytheism of the Greeks) is derived the love of nature shown by the Japanese and the Greeks.

24th February

There are people who view politics not as something universal, but only as a legitimate defense.

The things we do not write about are more than those of which we do. Just as men in the mass move in the circle of their own preoccupations and come, safe and sound, through their various problems, so you, sick of literature though you are, write of nothing but literary questions. As far as everything else is concerned, you move among your own preoccupations, dealing with them soundly and conscientiously. So one can brush aside the stupid controversy against writers and maintain that they, too, are men. At least as much as illiterates, or those who do not write.

3rd March

I had the news on 1st March.[1] Do others exist for us? I could wish that were not so; it would be less terrible. I am living in a sort of fog, thinking of him all the time, but vaguely. I shall end by making a habit of this state, always postponing real grief until tomorrow; so one forgets, and has *not* suffered.

8th March

This impression of solitary waiting in front of the hills Comes back to me for the second time.

17th March

In *The Maid's Tragedy*, what is lacking is simply imagination, and in the most unfortunate way. It seems impossible that this play (1609) gave rise to a new style. All sense of wit is lost. All the fire and fantasy of Shakespearian imagery (and that of Webster, too) has sunk into a dead, stilted language in which the emotion is either mere sentiment or a stage trick. Psychology has disappeared as well. All that is left, especially in the first acts, is a strong, obsessive sense of sex (tragic and comic), as in modern, contemporary plays. Evadne is alive as long as she stands for sexual aspirations; then she is redeemed and becomes of no account. The language is lifeless. Ben Jonson at least knew how to talk in dialect.

22nd March

Philaster (1608) is very different. In comic or tragic vein, the language is rich, lively, full of meaning, reminiscent of Shakespeare. It has a fine, colorful group of characters and an air of good theatre, for which, I should say, the credit is due to Beaumont. It lacks Shakespeare's ironic, significant construction; the plot is sentimental and melodramatic

---

[1] On 1st March, Pavese learned that Leone Ginzburg, his close friend and fellow-student at the University, who became the leader of the resistance movement in Turin, had died under torture in the prison of Regina Coeli on February 5th. Ed.

(though it has points of similarity with *Cymbeline* and *The Winter's Tale*); and that is due to Fletcher.

24th March

Bonduca makes the whole thing plain. It is by Fletcher only, and has no rich, coherent imagination. In the comic scenes there is buffoonery, but no fanciful witticism; in the tragic, characters declaim but have no depth of thought. Caratach, Petillius, Penius are lay figures with no life of their own. In Shakespeare, all the imaginative sequences are apparently polished with equal skill, and this gives his characters a rich general humanity against which their individual traits stand out clearly. As in life, where men seem all alike. Fletcher's characterization, on the contrary, is abstract.

30th March

On R. Guardini's *Lo spirito della liturgia*.

p. 185: "If one examines the question more closely one can easily perceive that the formula 'priority of Logos over Ethos' need not be final and supreme. Perhaps one might say, rather: in the general sphere of our life definite priority should be given to *being* rather than to *acting*. In fact this does not concern action so much as becoming: the supreme value is not what we do, but what *is* and *unfolds*. The roots and the conclusion of everything are not to be found in time, but in eternity, in the eternal present. The ultimate value lies not in the moral conception but in the metaphysical one, not in the judgment of worth, but of essence, not in effort but in adoration."

p. 187: ". . . priority of truth, but in the realm of love. . . ." In liturgy this position shall triumph: placid, calm, contemplative, indifferent, non-authoritative, non-educative, play.

31st March

Peter Wust, *Uncertainty and risk*.

p. 196: "Truly the primeval unconscious and objective instinct of human nature in its quest for happiness is aimed above all at that full realization of oneself by which one attains personal perfection and eternal salvation through the achievement of one's natural ends. The tendency to 'endemonia' agitating the depths of man is therefore primarily the quest for the substantial perfection of his form, and only in a lesser sense is it a search for a subjective moment of happiness, of repose, of definite harmony of the soul, in connection with the objective moment of 'endemonia.' "

4th April

"There are many dawns which have not yet shone: give us that we may see them, O Varuna!" (*Rig-Veda*, II, 28. Translation by Darmester from the translation by M. Muller. *Origine et développement de la Religion étudiés à la lumière des religions de l'Inde.*)

12th April

How can God want prolonged humiliations in prayer, endless repetitions of rites and ceremonies? Wouldn't you, yourself, instinctively prefer a swift thought of acknowledgment, a glance of concord from someone you have helped, and abhor all those mournful thanksgivings? You are not God, but still. . . .

True Georgic poetic feeling in Italian, and the only study of nature that accords with our temperament, is to be found in prose works on agriculture by such men as Pier dei Crescenzi, Davanzati and Soderini. The description is completely sincere and (the reason why it continues to live) utilitarian. Here and there a phrase is often, and truly, a whole poem, which cannot be said for the verses produced during the same period.

16th April

The classical poets have no need for descriptions of nature because in their works gods and sacred places conjure up multiple visions of natural surroundings. (On reading *Hippolytus.*)

When we are tormented by a noise, a smell, an unpleasant sensation, our discomfort can be sudden, brutal and most painful. But we also feel half-hopeful that the culprit will repeat the offense and so give us cause to rush out at him in fury.

18th April

Concrete evidence:

(a) The Pharisees do not doubt the resurrection of Christ. (Barravalle.)

(b) The promises made by God to Eve and Abraham do not mention the chosen people, but the whole human race.

The same applies to Jacob's promise to Judas. (Bossuet.)

The same applies to Zachariah, Haggai and Malachi.

20th April

In the Helena by Euripides the chorus recapitulates the events or recalls known facts. This confirms the Greek tragedy's character of a judgment which takes place before a chorus-audience. It is not a story.

The tragic motive is nearly always a hidden thing emerging with some difficulty (Hippolytus-Ion)—it is, therefore, a debate. This hidden thing is often a crime committed by the gods and which, by coming to light, produces either death-purification or a happy ending. The divine crime is the "what should be must be," which you discovered in 1942.

24th April

Those races who possess a rich mythological background are those who thereafter become the most dogged philosophers: the Indians, the Greeks and the Germans.

29th April

Concrete evidence:

Samaritans and Hebrews have the same Pentateuch. It follows that the Pentateuch preceded the separation, in other words it existed before Jeroboam and Rehoboam and for that reason, "a fortiori," before Ezra. (Bossuet.)

15th May

Have you ever pondered on the fact that those who originated the Italian novel—seeking in despair for fluent narrative prose—are primarily lyric writers—Alfieri, Leopardi, Foscolo? The *Vita, I Frammenti di Diario* and *Il Viaggio Sentimentale* are the sediment of imaginative minds entirely given up to illuminating flashes of lyrical eloquence. And the first successful novel, *I Promessi Sposi*, is the maturity of a great lyric writer. This must have left traces upon our narrative standard.

On the other hand, think of English or French novels of the eighteenth century and Spanish works in the seventeenth: there, the prose of the novel was born without a spark of imagination, as in nineteenth-century Russia.

22nd May

Your conviction that what one was as a child he will be as an adult, and never will the "span of his bridge" become shorter or longer has now lost all its dreariness and has moved into the realm of the search for the fantastic roots of the "instant-eternity."

27th May

The idea, which you considered a whim, of "modifying your own past" (Spring, 1939?) is now clearly in line with your present way of thinking: the rediscovery of infancy, carried out, of course, by modifying its meaning, which means discovering it.

Who knows how many things have happened to me: what a very good question on which to base your "summa." It simply means: who knows in how many different lights I shall again see my past, and this implies that I shall discover in it many new developments.

It is difficult to transform oneself into a Dantesque

"I," a symbolic Ego, when one's own problems are the product of such an individual experience as the "city-countryside" and when all figurations lead only to personal and psychological meanings. (The vine, the sky behind it, the seascape, the fruit-bearing trees, canes, hay-stacks, etc., can at their best become only an absolute of toilsome usefulness. The fact that you are lost is proven by your search for an outlet through the magic power of such symbols or in the artichoke richness of their many strata. If nobody else thinks of these things, you are going to be all right.)

8th June

. . . and the man who did that is a Christian. If he had not been a Christian he would have done worse.

13th June

Memory is the absence of imagination (Rousseau, *Emile*, I, II): "in things that we see every day, it is no longer imagination working, but memory"—"habit kills imagination." Yet the memory of far-off things brings objects back to us renewed, no longer habitual, but broken into new facets by time and forgetfulness and so made into something that spurs our imagination, all the more so because things remembered are new, yet mysteriously our own.

14th June

In 1824 Leopardi's letters became dry, consisting only of facts and figures, devoid of thoughtful effusions and of all self-pity. He was writing the *Operette Morali*. In 1825-26 he did not complain much, he was almost healthy and appeared to enjoy life. He lived in Milan and Bologna and was a senator.

17th June

Nations achieving supreme power are generally quite unaware that they are in process of creating an empire. Dedicated to a series of minor tasks, they find, by dint of conquest after conquest, they have brought about a great historical design. Those that ride forth with a blare of trumpets to become "the great nation," break their legs at the first fence, as normally happens in this world. Then all the other nations who have been alarmed at their program, hasten to hamstring them. In short, even in this, what they receive is not what they were seeking. Always.

26th June

Pierre Corneille, *Da la tragédie, et des moyens de la traiter selon la vraisemblance ou le nécessaire.* He says of Aristotle: ". . . theatres in his time when it was not customary to save the good people by the downfall of the bad ones, unless they, too, were defiled by crimes. . . ." As regards the four tragic actions which "take place among close relations": (a) one knows and kills the victim; (b) the victim's identity is discovered only after the killing; (c) one does not know the victim's identity and one discovers it in time to abstain from murder; (d) the victim's identity is known, but the killing is prevented at the last moment. In Aristotle's belief the last case is the worst one. Corneille draws a distinction: if the would-be killer abstains through a change of heart, fine, but the best tragedy is that in which the abstention is due to a great event, because this presupposes the "conflict between passion and nature, or duty and love." Chimène does her best to destroy the Cid. Either this contrast or the punishment of the evil ones: such is modern tragedy, such is Christian psychology.

You have written once that for the ancients it was the isolated hero who counted, the man who spoke a soliloquy, the man who faced the chorus. These contrasts do not exist. The bad ones, not being seen in terms of contrast, are not bad. They simply *are,* just like the good.

P.S. Let us remember that Aristotle condemns (a) and (d) and approves of (b) and (c). He condemns, in fact, the cases which might reflect a possible inner conflict and approves the coup de scène, in which there is no moral life.

2nd July

Corneille, "Epitre" from the *Suite du Menteur:* ". . . I, who agree with Aristotle and Horace that our art should only aim to please . . . as long as they please, they have fulfilled their obligation to their art; and if they sin, it is not against it but against accepted social behavior and their public. . . ."

"Reward for good deeds and punishment for bad ones . . . that imaginary law is completely opposed to ancient tradition: without citing examples among the Greeks, Seneca . . . Plautus and Terence. . . ."

7th July

Herodotus is for Jünger what Homer is for Vico.

9th July

Rousseau's enormous success is explained by the fact that he made more profound, and interpreted, a cultural world already known and accepted for centuries, Arcadia. The reasons why his innovations evoked such enthusiasm is that they contain flattering, intriguing new ideas while still allowing readers to cherish what they know and love.

11th July

Hath not our mother Nature, for her store
And great increase, said it is good and just,
And willed that every living creature must
Beget his like?

(*The Faithful Shepherd*, Act V, sc. 4).

All woodland fables have this thought, this appeal to nature. Rousseauism in embryo. But not only that. They all have a "forest hermit," who generally collects herbs and studies the more or less magical qualities of potions. Strange that Rousseau knew nothing of magic. But German philosophers of nature made up for that.

Long ago I noted that all pastoral fables are based

on the chastity of Diana, which must be preserved by various caprices and is at last yielded in a love affair. When it is not so yielded, the hermits are simply hermits.

13th July

In *War and Peace* there is everything unendurable that the nineteenth century produced. One of the good things is missing, demonism.

Nature becomes savagery when some forbidden thing happens; bloodshed or sex. That may seem an illusion, based on the impression you have formed of primitive culture—ceremonial rites of sex or bloodshed. From them it is plain that a savage is not living naturally, but in a state of violent superstition. Nature is impassive. If a man falls from a fig-tree in a vineyard and lies prone on the ground in his own blood, that does not seem to you "savage," as it would had he been stabbed or sacrificed.

Any man who gives way to brute passion is super-stitious.

14th July

In fact a man in love or one consumed with hatred creates symbols for himself, as a superstitious man does, from a passion for conferring uniqueness on things or persons. A man who knows nothing of symbols is one of Dante's slug-gards. This is why art mirrors itself in primitive rites or strong passions, seeking for symbols, revolving round the primitive taste for savagery, for what is irrational (blood and sex).

17th July

The plague of descriptions of nature, complacent ap-peals to things or to the world in general, in works of art arises from a misconception: the work, seeking to be a natural object like any other, thinks to succeed by reproducing as many of them as possible, as in a mirror. But the *nature* of a mirror does not lie in the reflections that flit across its surface; they are only its *utility*.

When we say that poetry is original thought expressed in rhythm, we simply mean to define its nature. Our own poetry strives always to eliminate objects, to become its own object, the *substance* of words. Verbal sensuality, generally decadent as in D'Annunzio's work, confuses this substance with the mere flesh of things, a universal imitation of sounds. In our work the expression is pure, disembodied, finding its rhythm in something far deeper than the voice of things: as though unaware of itself, reluctant to say all it might. Herein lies our anxiety, distrusting words though they are our only reality; seeking the substance of something about which we are still unsure; hesitating, suffering.

Even my *Lavorare stanca* has this about it, under the surface; seeking its object below the sound and shape of the words, striving for a rhythm that should be neither a song nor verbal sensuality. For this reason it avoids musical verse and uses neutral words. Its one mistake was to indulge in phrases colored by the spoken word, which is another way of holding a mirror up to nature. But, little by little, it freed itself, disciplined by the rhythm. Then, in the prose passages, it relapsed into the spoken word. Why? Because it lacked the support of the rhythm. Now the problem is how to penetrate to the essential substance while taking this support for granted.

The life of the subconscious. The work we achieve is always something other than we intended. So one goes on, and one's deep inner ego is always intact; if it seems exhausted, it is only shaken and confused by fatigue, like water clouded with mud, but then it grows clear again, as full of purpose as before. There is no way of bringing that purpose to the surface; the surface is never anything more than a play of reflections of *other things*.

18th July

Love is a feverish attack that leaves behind an aversion. Every day of our lives, however, we are aware of gay young bodies all around us: it is natural that most of our experience lies with them.

20th July

The support which prose enjoys from rhythm, others have found in cadenced repetition (Stein, Vittorini, etc.).

25th July

The foamy smell of maceration, which is the briny of the countryside.

30th July

"Listening to pure and agreeable sounds, it seems we are ready to penetrate the secret of the Creator and seize the mystery of life." (*Corinne.*) This happens whenever one *feels* any natural event, such as the smell of a flower, the ripple of water, the luscious taste of grapes. Music is the most material of the arts (cf. Lamartine, *Histoire des Girondins,* "music, the least intellectual and the most sensual of the arts") because only thought is immaterial and there are no conscious elements in music. Music strives to dress up the form of its sensations as symbols, but the comparison is too wide and never seems fit. In effect music has exactly the function I have described on July 17th, in that it offers something in place of nature, so much so that nothing in nature is equivalent to music.

8th August

It is nice and consoling to think that not even a married man has solved the problem of his sexual life. He thought that now he could lead a peaceful and virtuous life, but what happens is that after a while one becomes disgusted with the woman. The very sight of her is enough to make you gasp for air, as you do when you are with a prostitute. (Cf. Tolstoi and . . .) One then realizes that life with a woman is uncomfortable, even if one has not yet come upon the question of "having a baby each time," which compels us to abstain or to seek other precautions. In both cases, it would appear, one has lost that beautiful sincerity.

10th August

In Greek tragedy everything is sacred, preordained, the will of God.

19th August

What is so charming about Vico is his constant wandering between what is savage and what is rustic, each trespassing in the other's field. The whole of history is reduced to this germ.

20th August

A *heraldic sense* may be the best description for this faculty of seeing symbols everywhere.

Though all his interpretations are wrong and absurd, Vico brought to history a feeling for interpretation, a taste for examining documents against the light of day. With this end in view he created for himself a psychology which broadened his heraldic sense into a necessary faculty of the human mind.

Facts in themselves are not so interesting as the fact that they are hidden and can be discovered. A similar experience was undergone by the artists of this century who concentrated more on telling the tale than on the tale itself. The human spirit counts inasmuch as it expresses itself. To contemplate a symbol is to contemplate an expression. Monomania of technicism.

23rd August

To fall from a fig tree and lie stretched in a pool of blood (cf. 13th July) is not an unnatural event, not "savage," but becomes so if it is regarded as a law of life. If, in one way or another, blood gushes forth in torrents on the ground and beasts *naturally* swallow it, while the fallen man has no rights of appeal, that is savage because our feelings would prohibit such a thing; a mere event, not a law. Here one's natural feeling is to blame nature, which, by its very lack of feeling, seems to be performing a rite and to be, itself, superstitious.

Every inadequate theodicy is superstitious. When any vindication of the justice of God is superseded, it becomes superstition. Justice, as long as it is just, is natural.

26th August

Impassive nature celebrates a rite; man, whether impassive or wrought to a pitch of excitement, celebrates his even more terrifying rites; such things are superstitious only if they strike us as unjust, forbidden by conscience, savage. Then savagery is overruled by conscience. As long as we believe in superstition we are not superstitious. To be superstitious is essentially retrospective, in the realm of memory, an apt subject for poetry; like evil, which is always in the realm of past remorse; while activity, in the realm of the present, is good. But how is it that the exercise of memory is a pleasure, a good thing?

Again. To celebrate a rite is to justify oneself. Nature, then, is not superstitious because she celebrates a rite (of blood), but because that rite does nothing to justify her. To us it seems merely chance (though it may be regulated by a law). Like savage rites that no longer appear to us sufficient to justify the one who performs them.

Perhaps to exercise one's memory is a pleasure, and a good thing, because it is a thing of the present. (Cfr. 10th September.)

Alexandrine des Echerolles (history of the siege of Lyons).

Jeanne de La Force (history of the religious wars of 1622).

Madame de la Rochejaquelein (Vendée).

Madame Roland—*Memoires.*

27th August

The great task of life is to justify oneself, and to justify oneself is to celebrate a rite. Always.

29th August

Only uniqueness justifies . . . the absolute value which puts us above all contingencies (*Of myths of Symbols etc.*).

1st September

Impassive nature is perhaps simply a collection of rites that we have surmounted, the most ancient of the superstitions by which the universe tried to justify itself. It was so by instinct, founded on laws of its own and drawing out of them a reason for life. Then, with the advent of the spirit, nature became *arbitrary,* the divine will, and rites shaped themselves accordingly. Now it has reverted to a law a mechanism—that is why instinct is emerging again and the true ritual of rationalistic epochs is art (the ritual of the instinctive subconscious).

From 23rd August it results that outside our moral conscience there is no criterion of certainty except superstition. The truth of the universe is modeled on our moral sense. Religion is the meeting of truth and justice. Every crisis can be reduced to a lack of balance between these vital necessities.

2nd September

Any explanation of the universe that thinks to blend truth and justice but no longer succeeds in doing so, is superstition. Outside religion there is only suspended judgment— as far as that is possible.

The savage is not picturesque, but tragic.

You have dealt up till now with two kinds of savage. In *Nudismo* you have touched upon what is savage to the adult, the virgin countryside, that which has not yet been spoilt by the human hand (and here it is implicit that any work, any rite, can justify nature). In *Storia segreta* you have described the savage that is in a boy, something that is remote and evasive, even if, and in fact more so, others succeed or have succeeded in seizing it. (In both cases this is what we are missing, "that which we do not know.")

Poetry, *now*, is the effort to grasp superstition—the savage, the unspeakable—and give it a name, understand it, make it harmless. Hence true art is tragic—it is an effort. Poetry participates in everything that conscience forbids—intoxication, passionate love, sin—but redeems itself by its need for contemplation, that is, for knowledge.

3rd September

Smoking is something entirely rustic and natural. This transformation of a dry herb into a cloud of fragrant, lively, fertilizing smoke is not without significance. In other days it would quickly have become a symbol (like the pipe of Gitche Manito in Longfellow).

4th September

Important writers are swept away by the passing of their generation, not because of criticism, a new evaluation, but simply because their soundness is denied *en bloc*. Men condemn anything that precedes their own work.

5th September

Of the seven instances in which Herodotus, in describing Egypt, states that he is reluctant to touch upon the mysteries, three are cases of animal gods, two of phallic rites, and the other two deal with self-inflicted wounds and sacred enlightenment. Why is Pan depicted with caprine head and legs (XLVI); why is pork flesh considered obscene during the rest of the year and eaten only on the feast of Bacchus (XLVII)? Why are animals generally sacred (LXV)? At this point Herodotus feels threatened by a taboo and is afraid to speak. Why do the phallic figures in the feast of Bacchus have an articulated phallus moved by wires (XLVIII), and why do the Athenians carve phallic statues (LI)? Herodotus knows very well that the phallus and the god coincide, but does not dare to say it. In whose name do they fight during the feast of Isis (LXI), and why do they have a feast of

256

lamps at Sais (LXII)? Behind these customs too there is probably some mischief or other which Herodotus' worldly and respectful curiosity dares not confront.

This exemplifies the Greek way of dealing with the savage: one acknowledges with tolerant respect its sacred nature and that is all. This respect implies the rational knowledge that the *whole* world of what is sacred and divine conceals such chasms, and it is therefore necessary to leave well alone.

Once people sacrificed to the gods without naming them (LII). Only a short time before Homer and Hesiod had described the gods and told stories about them (LIII)— Herodotus sounds almost reproachful about this.

7th September

The mysterious passages in Herodotus' Book II are these: LXI, LXXXI, LXXXVI, CXXXII, CLXX, CLXXI. In each of these one finds covert references to Osiris, who however remains unmentioned. Why? At other times Herodotus mentions the name, but adds that is a version of Bacchus (CXLIV).

8th September

Prophecy by oracle is no more than the imaginative expression of destiny. Things happened, and the ancients gave them the stamp of uniqueness by making them foreseen by the god.

A *beautiful* country girl, a *beautiful* prostitute, a *beautiful* young mother, all these women for whom beauty is not the artificial occupation of their whole life, are firmly impervious to mockery.

10th September

The exercise of memory is a pleasure and a benefit (cf. 26th August) because it involves knowledge. To re-evoke a superstition is not to practice it but to learn about it.

30th September

The arches and columns of loggias create conventional landscapes by serving as frames for them. Obviously the impression is increased by the memory of so many fourteenth-century craftsmen whose paintings are divided up by columns and arches in just the same way. The man who invented loggias knew nothing of this effect, which came about when this new style of architecture appeared in paintings.

1st October

There comes a time when we take into account the fact that everything we do will become a memory in due course. That is maturity. To reach it, one must already have memories.

3rd October

Boiardo is an honest poet-narrator. His adjectives are epithets, in other words small lyrical blocks visible under the narration's stream as objects, not as impressions. His speeches, his exclamations are well-defined melodic windows, one could almost call them pre-existing modulations, and they too form a block, as objects, in the stream. After one has read an episode one remembers the gestures and the actions, not the feelings.

7th October

"If a man be fair he will do fair things, or else, by doing them, he will become fair" (*Council of Trent,* Barbera edition, vol. II, p. 77). The scholastic opinion that one may be just "in abstracto" is not without reflections in the practice of medieval allegory: abstractions become part of man independently of his objective or psychological activities.

20th October

To be fearless and to be right: the two opposite poles of history. And of life. The one generally contradicts the other.

3rd November

A dream always leaves an impression of something grandiose and absolute. That comes from the fact that in a dream there are no commonplace details, but, as in a work of art, everything is devised for its effect.

7th November

Horace, *Letter to Augustus:*
... *vestigia ruris* ... (line 160).

In this letter the concept of "rus" is opposed to that of "ars" and it is used to recall the primitive lack of culture. This is *your* savage. Not even if one wants to condemn it can one renounce the countryside. See Vico. He is a perfect humanist, opposed to the contemporary scientific habit of considering barbarism as a previous stage to rusticity. Locke is incontrovertible, but abstract (husbanding peoples, hunting peoples). Vico, too, recognized that form of barbarism, but relegated to pre-divine chaos.

The hick, the rustic, the boor, as opposed to the citizen. But humanism blended what is rustic with what is mythical, and thus had its savage (cf. Vico). Now it would appear that the savage pre-existed the rustic, divested of myth.

26th November

Dreams are symbols of reality. You dreamed that someone had wrongfully sold your books and you were overcome with grief and anxiety. Your real sorrow was that they are slowly deteriorating in the cellar. Passion in a dream is never untrue. It creates for itself a fact (a symbol) which makes its expression possible.

2nd December

It seems impossible that even a single spark of goodness, hope or love, though encased in a whole crust of iniquity or indifference, should flicker out and stand for nothing in an eternity of suffering. Once more I know the feeling that one longs for pain so as to draw nearer to God.

28th December

(Eratry: *Commentary on St. Matthew's gospel.*)

The very suggestion that the subconscious may be God, that God lives and speaks in our subconscious mind, has exalted you. If, with this idea of God, you review all the thoughts of the subconscious scattered here and there in this work—don't you see?—you are changing all your past and discovering many things. Above all, your toilsome research for the symbol is illumined by its infinite significance.

1945

9th January

A strange, rich year that began and ended with God, with much deep thought on the primitive and the savage, and which has seen some notable creative work. It could be the most important year of your life so far. If you persevere with God, it certainly will be. (It must not be forgotten that *God* means also a technical cataclysm—symbolism built up through years of following the gleam.)

16th January

The peoples who practiced the most frequent, most atrocious human sacrifices were those who lived by agriculture (matriarchal civilizations). Shepherds, hunters, artisans were never cruel like tillers of the soil.

26th January

You wanted an excuse not to move. Here it is. Who should be thanked? You hoped for a miracle and it happened. For now, be humble. You shall judge it by its fruits.

28th January

A tropical garden amid the snow. Magnolias, firs, yew trees, cypresses, lemon groves—dark green, bronzed and metallic against the azure sky. But what uplifts you most is the red brick wall of the farm stables. There, are all the most intense natural colors: green, blue, red, white. Is it the unfamiliarity of it all that strikes you, or is there some secret virtue in these pure qualities?

It is easy for colors to become symbols. They are the most visible quality of an object, but not the object itself. Remembering you once said that legend lives in epithets, colors would be the epithets of things. Pure creation. All sensations—that of music, for instance, are symbols that tend to take the place of nature.

30th January

The man who cannot live with charity, sharing other men's pain, is punished by feeling his own with intolerable anguish. Pain is rendered acceptable only by raising it to the level of our common destiny and sympathizing with other sufferers. The penalty of the egoist is that he realizes this only when he himself is under the lash; then he vainly strives to learn charity, out of self-interest.

4th February

Blondel, *L'Action*. "Man always endows his acts, however obscurely he knows it, with this quality of transcendance. What he does is never done simply for the sake of doing it" (p. 353). "Even among those who say they are free of all superstition, one should notice this need for ritual and this counterfeiting of a true liturgical cult, the all too visible poverty of quite naked action" (p. 312). (Cf. 27th August, '44.)

13th February

The "unique event" which you find so exciting can only have its full value if it has never taken place. It must remain a myth, engulfed in tradition and past; it must be, in other words, a thing of your memory. In fact spiritism, miracles, etc., can only bore you. Inasmuch as such things "happen" they are no longer unique, but become normal events even though they take place outside all natural laws (in so far as they happen, they come under a law, though an occult one).

All that one may discuss about such events is their authenticity, their pros and cons, but they are a negation of imaginative uniqueness.[1]

18th February

The "return of events" in Thomas Mann, and especially the chapter "Ruben goes to the well" express substantially an evolutionist concept. Events try to happen, and each time they are more satisfactory, more perfect. The "mythical imprints" are like the "forms of the genus." What appears to detach this concept from naturalistic determinism is that it's factors are not sexual choice or the struggle for existence, but a constant act of volition by God that a certain program may be transformed in reality. After all Mann's enunciation seems to imply that what decides, moment by moment, the course of events is the human spirit which, according to its own laws, perceives them and "makes them happen" each time substantially similar but also richer. If one were to describe this conception in a unitary sense one could call it a Kantian formalism applied to mythological material. Behind all this there is Vico.

2nd March

L. Todesco, *Corso di Storia della Chiesa* (Marietti, 1925), vol. III, p. 539:

". . . The main instruments of torture were: the brazier with lighted charcoal to which the accused person's feet were brought; the rope (the accused being lifted up with

[1] In the manuscript this appears as uniqueness absolute. Ed.

it and then let down); and finally the rack: therefore, mainly, gymnastics."

12th March

In the long run, grief grows detached from the anxiety, the recollection, the suspicion that caused it, and lives on alone in the spirit. Tonight you were suffering, and then the moment came when you sought within yourself for the forgotten or not yet remembered cause of your pain.

15th March

The first breaking-forth of tiny leaves is an outburst of little green flames, jewels appearing among the dead branches that clothe themselves in green and bedeck themselves.

25th March

To express admiration one says that a thing is like something else: a confirmation of the fact that we never see a thing the first time but only the second—when it has changed into something else. Confirmation and explanation: in so far as we admire it, the first thing *is* the second, that is we see it the second time under another aspect.

5th April

To live in any environment is fine when one's spirit is elsewhere: in the city when we dream of the country, in the country when we dream of the town, anywhere else when we dream of the sea. This may seem sentimentalism, but is not. On the contrary, it proves the *all-pervadingness* of the imagination. We assess the value of one reality only by filtering it through another, only when it changes into another. That is why the child discovers the world through literary or legendary transfigurations, all of them formalized. That is why the essence of poetry is imagination.

From that we can deduce that the world, life in gen-

eral, acquires value only when one's mind is turned to another reality, outside this world. We might even say, when
one's spirit is turned to God. Is it possible?

6th April

So you affirm the existence of God in so far as you
postulate the *value* of the world and of life. But it is precisely
this value that is now made plain. This value exists. You feel
it, and it has a value beyond what one feels. What would
be the point of an objective value that one did not feel?

18th April

The petals of the apple and pear blossom are flying in
the wind and the ground is strewn with them. They look like
butterflies.

23rd April

In the III book of the *Aeneid,* one meets simultaneously with a sequence of portentous events and the names
of famous mythological landmarks. The portents are mythical
and the mythical names are portentous. This is religious
poetry.

The religion of Herodotus. So many countries, so many
portents. This is not only the book of the "grande route," but
also the book of the breathless quest for a fatherland, for
the footprints left by the ancestors.

This is what was "sacred" in the ancient world, and
what the ancients were seeking in life and in art. Not the
beautiful.

25th April

To roam the streets and find marvels, that is the great
incentive, yours especially.

2nd July

Sex, blood and alcohol: the three Dionysian moments
of human life. No one can escape from one or the other.

28th August (Then Rome)

When a word, a deed, a suspicion has caused us a strong outburst of passion, there comes a moment when, on thinking it over, we no longer recall what that word, deed or suspicion was, but our passion grows ever more intense.

6th September

There is nothing fine about being a child: it is fine, when we are old, to look back to when we were children.

13th October

People made gods of animals because animals were "the other thing," outside humanity; and because the animal did not seem an individual. It was a beast in general, not in particular.

14th October

(The moon was trembling.)

15th October

What would you say if, one day, all natural things—springs, woods, vineyards, the countryside—vanish from the earth, absorbed by the cities, remembered only in phrases from bygone times? They will have the same effect as the gods, nymphs and sacred groves we find in certain Greek poetry. Then the simple phrase: "There was a spring of water" will be deeply moving.

18th November

I am your lover, and therefore your enemy.

22nd November

We do not free ourselves from something by avoiding it, but only by living through it.

23rd November

When we drive away a beggar we say to him: "You will find all you want at the next farm." To him that hath, to him shall be given.

26th November

How can there be, between a man and a woman, anything more important than love? That would mean that it is possible to regard a woman as one does oneself; agreeing with her every gesture and movement as though they were our own, feeling pleased that she should enjoy her own pleasures as we enjoy our own, not feeling deprived if she does with others what we do with others, which means loving our neighbor as ourselves. That sort of love is called charity. But if she disappears? Can we love a vanished part of ourselves? We should have to believe that no one ever disappears, that there is no such thing as death.

She will die and you will be lonely as a dog. What remedy is there?

Very well, then. But if you can accept death for yourself, how can you refuse anyone else the right to accept it? That, too, is charity. You can arrive at nothingness, but not resentment or hate. Always remember that nothing is owed to you. In fact, what do you deserve? Had you any claim on life when you were born?

27th November

It came to you for the third time, today. It is dawn, a dawn of scattered cloud, pale mauve. The Tiber has the same color. Sad, but not overbearingly so, ready to be cheered by the sun. Houses and trees are still sleeping. I watched the dawn just now, from the side windows. There was haze, stillness, and a human warmth. Astarte-Aphrodite-Melita is still sleeping. She will wake in a bad humor. For the third time, my day has come. The keenest pang of my grief is to know that grief will pass. Now it is easy to feel humiliated, but what next? (I was rejected) on 13th August, '37 in the after-noon; on 25th September, '40 in the evening; and on 26th November, '45 at night. Exactly the opposite of what we were taught. When young we mourn for *one* woman, as a grown man, for women in general.

What a great thought it is that truly *nothing is due to us*. Has anyone ever promised us anything? Then why should we expect anything?

Yet it is quite simple. When we no longer exist we die, and that is that.

Aphrodite has "come from the sea."

This terrible feeling that what you do is all awry, so is what you think, what you are! Nothing can save you be-cause, no matter what decision you take, you know you are distorted and so will your decision be.

28th November

How can you have confidence in a woman who will *not* risk entrusting her whole life to you, day and night?

2nd December

The woman who jilts another man to come to you, will jilt you for someone else. All those little things she does to charm you, she will do to charm another in your place. But you know that such things are like a myth—they have value only in being unique. And then. . . ?

7th December

T. told you only that your poems were enough for you, and she loved them very much.

F. without discussing their practical application, had read them with patient curiosity.

B. says that they are all you will have, and, viewing them critically, she quite likes them.

This makes twice in the last few days that you have put T., F. and B. side by side, showing how the myth recurs.

What has been, will be. There is no remission. You were thirty-seven and all the conditions were favorable. You are *looking for* trouble!

The body blow that . . . . dealt you, you still feel it in your blood. You have done your utmost to accept it, have even forgotten it, but that does not mean you can escape the consequences of it. You know you are alone? That you are nothing, and that is why she left you? Is it any good to talk about it, own up to it? You have found it does no good at all.

9th December

But all fools, rogues, criminals were once children, played like you and believed that something fine lay ahead for them. When we were all three years old, or seven, before anything had happened to us, when everything lay dormant in our nerves, and in our hearts.

1946

1st January

That year, too, is finished. The hills, Turin, Rome. You have gone through four women, published a book, written some fine poems and discovered a new form that weaves together many different threads (the dialogue of Circe). Are you happy? Yes, you are happy. You have power, you have genius, you have something to do. You are alone.

Twice this year you have toyed with the idea of suicide. Everyone admires you, compliments you, dances around you. Well, then?

You have never had to fight. Remember that. You never will fight. Do you count for anything with anyone?

6th January

Gods, for you, are *the others,* individuals who are self-sufficient, supreme, seen from the outside.

12th January

In Greek tragedy there are no wicked characters. It is not a matter of allocating responsibility but of stating a fact— a destiny.

26th January

To be hardened—that means keeping your own work ever more clearly before you, watching it reach fulfilment, knowing that little spurts of effort are enough to keep it going, and letting other people—in the feminine—play round you with their temptations and their wiles. You know how it would be—the disturbance, the ferment, the sudden shock when it ends—and so you let them rave, without being captured or dominated by them. You have something else to do. That is "being hardened."

"Being a god" in these little mythological dialogues, is the same thing as "being hardened." Their formulae—fate, a god, a mortal, a name, a smile—contain a rich reality, but only within the bounds of that world. The atmosphere, the tone, the background are all coherent in the myth, but would not mean what they do mean if they were reduced to present-day sophistication.

8th February

Twelve months ago, you did not know how much life would bring you in the course of the year. But was it really life? Perhaps your sorrowful, introspective walk to Crea taught you, symbolically, more than all the women, the passions, the things you experienced in those months. Certainly, the myth is a discovery you owe to Crea, to the summer and two winters you spent there. The whole mountain is imbued with it.

Today, the woman who lives with . . . . came into my study as she often does, said good-day then quietly sat down and watched me. Every man has a woman, a human body, peace. But have you? And the husband of the woman who lives with . . . , who is he? Has he still got a wife?

If a man has not always had a woman, he will never have one.

Certainly, to have a woman who waits at home for you, who will sleep with you, gives a warm feeling like having something you must say; it makes you glow, keeps you company, helps you to live.

You are alone. Having a woman to talk to is nothing. All that counts is the press of body against body. Why, why are you without that? "You will never have it." Everything has its price.

And the man who has a woman, looks for another. . . . That's how it goes. As long as you want to be alone, they come looking for you, but if you hold out your hand, they ignore it; that, too, is how it goes.

13th February

You remember people's voices better than their faces. There is something indicative, spontaneous, about a voice. Given the face, you do not think of the voice; given the voice—by no means negligible—you try to envisage the person and look forward to seeing the face.

16th February

Things and people belong to us, that is, they count with us, only for what they cost us, not what they give us. To keep a woman tied to us we must exploit her, not devote ourselves to her.

20th February

(Preface to the *Dialoghetti*[1]). Had it been possible, we would gladly have done without so much mythology. But we are convinced that myths are a language, a means of expression; not arbitrary, but pregnant with symbols that, like all languages, have a special significance which can be expressed in no other way. When we introduce a proper name, an action, some legendary marvel, we are expressing, between the lines and in a syllable or two, something comprehensive,

[1] *Dialoghi con Leuco,* written in 1946. Ed.

all-embracing; the pith and marrow of a reality that will vitalize and nourish a whole living structure of passion, a complex conception of human existence. And if this name, this deed, this marvel is something we have known from childhood, from our school days, so much the better. Our concern is more real, more incisive, when it is centered on something familiar. Here we have contented ourselves with Greek myths, in view of the present, very understandable, popular vogue for them and their immediate, traditional acceptability. We detest anything vague and formless, anomalous, incidental, and we try, even with material things, to confine ourselves within certain limits, as if in a frame, and insist on an atmosphere of concentration. We are convinced that a great revelation can come only from persistently pressing on through something difficult, simply because it is difficult. We have nothing in common with those who flit from one thing to another, experimenting, seeking adventure. We know that the surest, quickest way to find amazement is to fix the mind firmly upon the same object all the time. The moment will come when that object will seem, miraculously, as though we had never seen it before.

Such happiness without adventure probably arises from the fact that it leaves you open to all adventures. You see them all around you, but you do nothing to induce them or let them effect you. What do you do? Simply observe them, indulge your fancy, and learn. Would it change anything to find yourself mixed up in them?

Works of poetry come about in just the same way as that happiness does. An amazing counterpoise of truths, all on the verge of being expressed, all rich with infinite possibilities, imminent, inexhaustible. The art of not trying to enjoy, that is the real art. Poetry is not a sense, but a state; not understanding, but being.

22nd February

You have started spending your evenings alone again, sitting in a corner of the little cinema, smoking, savoring life and the end of the day, watching the film like a child, for the adventure, the brief pleasure of beauty or an awakened memory. And you enjoy it, you enjoy it immensely. It will be the same at seventy, if you live that long.

23rd February

Something is coming to an end. When you relax and sit smoking, you find you are troubled and anxious. Are you afraid of the practical things of life? No. What you fear is the vacuum within you. This town holds no memories.

24th February

Alone again. For you, home means the office, the cinema and your own clenched jaws. In the story of a passion, the sign that it is over should be the urge to go home again and be alone.

26th February

With the others—even with the only one who stands out—you must always live as though things were beginning at that moment and would finish in the next.

1st March

She has always followed her caprices and her own convenience—making demands, refusing you, holding herself aloof—but she has been friendly, and now she is gone. You gave her almost everything, lost your sleep, wasted your time and trouble, thought of death—all because of your great need —and what else can you do but blame yourself?

They are fools, those ethnologists who think that all they need do is to bring together the masses of various races (no matter what their past and present culture) to ensure that they will become used to one another, learn understanding and tolerance, grow out of racialism, nationalism and prejudice. Collective passions are roused by inevitable self-interests that are wrapped up in racial or national myths. And self-interest can never be erased.

272

3rd March

Revenge yourself on someone! Act as though you forgave him, leave him to the vengeances of life. The passing of time, by itself, without any help from the victim, invariably inflicts terrible sufferings on everyone. And not only time. Other men will do the same, the very men who led your enemy to offend and injure you. Let them be, all of them. They will avenge you. All the more if your enemy loves them. Just let them live, all of them. What revenge would there be if they were not all there?

4th March

The women you love feel about you just as you feel about one of those women who leave you flat.

There is no finer revenge than that which *others* inflict on your enemy. Moreover, it has the advantage of leaving you the role of a generous man.

9th March

The gods have no feelings. They know what should happen, and ensure that it does. They are utilitarian.

14th March

Men do not complain of suffering, but of the overruling power that grips them and makes them suffer.

28th March

When you wash your hands under a tap, you feel an impulse to urinate. A good example of sympathetic magic. One can understand why savages believed that rain-making rites must include the emission of water or sperm.

29th March

Never have I felt so aware of being cornered, finished, as during these afternoons and evenings. The vacuum within me is still unlit by a single spark of vitality. Well do I know that I shall go no further, that all I have to say is already said. The worst of it is that I have already achieved some success, and so cannot resign myself to total failure. I know that I shall rise above it and produce more work, but the break is there, plain to see. *Hell!*

31st March

The wisdom of fate is, fundamentally, our own wisdom, because it gives us a never-ending awareness of what, when we get to the root of things, it is permissible for us to do. Whatever temptations we may have, we make no mistake about that, ever. We act always with a sense of destiny. The two things are one.

A man who makes that mistake does not yet understand his own destiny. That is, he does not understand the consequences of his own past which determine his future. But whether he understands it or not, the indication is there, just the same. Every life is what it has to be.

3rd April

One of them is dark and vibrant, the other icy and blonde. They make an amazing pair. Anyone would call me very lucky. One has a lovely figure, the other a keen and lively mind, but to make anything of them those things should be changed around. The dark one ought to have the intelligence, and the blonde should have the figure. Instead, it is not that way, and so much the better.

4th April

Every morning, like a stuffy, damp, warm mold of ourselves, like an astral body, we leave behind our weariness in our bed.

April 8

If you are you, I am myself—which means that I do not care for it.

10th April

Those intellectuals who have broken away from the P.C.[1] over the question of liberty ought to ask themselves what they would do with this liberty that they are so concerned about. Then they would see that—leaving aside apathy, indolence and the hidden self-interests every man has (a life of leisure, vague thinking and elegant forms of sadism), there does not exist a single instance to which their own answer would be any different from the collective one of the P.C.

16th April

This sense of power, of being equal to anything, does it come from your earnings or from maturity? If, in fear and trembling at your vocation, you managed to achieve your present result, of what things should you now be capable! You should be ashamed of yourself.

17th April

What you find distasteful about psychoanalysis is its evident tendency to transform faults into illnesses. You could understand it changing them into virtues, by means of an access of energy, but no. It discovers that the trouble was caused, for instance, by being afraid of frogs and then it expects to cure it. What rot!

Let us be clear about it: I have nothing against the formulae of psychoanalysis—our inner life is all the richer for them. My quarrel is with those brazen-faced rascals who use them to excuse their own stupid negligence, who think that when homosexuals corrupt little boys it is the result of some past experience they had with corkscrews, and therefore excusable. But no! There is no excuse for upping little boys.

[1] The *Partito Comunista Italiano*. The Italian Communist Party was originally strongly anti-fascist and composed mainly of intellectuals. Its motto was *"Giustizia e Libertà,"* but the party was split by differences of opinion as to the meaning of "Justice" and "Liberty." Ed.

25th April

Every evening, after you have finished at the office, had your visit to the local, and your companions have all gone home, there comes that fierce joy, the warm glow of being alone again. It is the one really good thing that happens every day.

You discover that every little corner of nature has an order of its own, its own range of contacts. For instance, the flowers of a particular region all have colors of the same tone. Ter. suggests that this may be due to a special quality of light and humidity in that place. True. Nothing can interfere with providence. The interplay of natural laws suffices.

Ter. is the usual *aftermath* of your bouts of passion. They rage high, she is little; they are stern and hard, she is sweet and gay; they are very involved and difficult, she is frank and friendly; they are your enemies, she is a good companion. When passion has left her exhausted, her recovery is natural, *wistful*. Like all her predecessors. Will she end like them?

4th May

Writing is a fine thing, because it combines the two pleasures of talking to yourself and talking to a crowd.

If you were able to write without making any alteration, without revising, without repolishing, would your pleasure be increased? The ideal method is to polish yourself; calmly and quietly to set about making yourself into a crystal.

5th May

What can life be like for such people? A little gaiety, a little laughter, a foolish medley of clothes and chatter. Is yours any better?

8th May

I had already discovered Rome and realized its significance in my life during June and July, '43. Note the close connection between the lectures (on ethnology) I had attended for more than a year, and the fact of Rome. Why did I come here, and was it by chance?

And now, with the whole mythical-ethnological world matured in my mind, I come back to Rome, invent a new style for the *Dialoghi* and write them.

23rd May

I have met a really exceptional woman—S.A.[1] I was not in the least embarrassed. I understand her perfectly. I am better off than she is, not only because I am younger, but in all essentials. I know what form is, she does not. Yet she was the flower of Turin, 1900-'10. She moves me like a souvenir. In her I see Thovez, Cena, Gozzano, Gobetti; she is Nietzsche, Ibsen, lyric poetry. There are the hesitations, the muddled thinking of my adolescence (How long ago!). There is the confusion of art and life that *is* adolescence, error. D'Annunzionism; now all vanquished and in the past.

24th May

You cannot bear any sudden, unexpected alteration in your day, an extra guest for lunch,[2] an unforeseen journey, etc. Doesn't that bear out your craze for making a whole scheme for a novel depend on some discovery you have made, as in *Mari del Sud, Le Streghe,* etc?

31st May

On my way from Rome to Piedmont I noticed many things. The trees of this part of the country and their grouping (alders, oak trees, ash and willow, great rows of vines, rising from the level ground like the wings bordering a stage), are those of Virgil and other classical writers I studied at college. I saw that in Piedmont it is not so much the individual tree that strikes one's eye as the all-over greenness, the sea of vege-

[1] Sibilla Aleramo, with whom Pavese corresponded on literary subjects for several months. Ed.
[2] At this time, Pavese was living with his sister Maria, her husband and two children. Ed.

tation. Strange, for the trees of the classics were certainly those of Rome, while I, instead, have seen them in Piedmont and nowhere else. That may be because I was reading in Piedmont.

I noted the abstract shapes of the long, high city streets; smelt, this morning, the fragrance of the red wine of Piedmont that perfumes everything. Here there is nothing of the dryness or the sharply defined colors of Rome.

3rd June

The charm of traveling is enjoying innumerable glorious scenes, knowing that we could make any one of them our own, and passing on to the next like some great lord.

18th June

It is ridiculous to look for altruism in a passion composed wholly of pride and voluptuousness.

19th June

I begin to write poetry when the game is lost, but a poem has never been known to change things.

23rd June

I am in the state of atrophy that usually follows the end of a passion—out of sorts, exhausted, temperamental. But this time it was not passion, and I see all the more plainly how indolent-voluptuous was my abandonment to it. The clear law of my myth. As a conclusion to my life in Rome I could not imagine anything more appropriate.

When I have to leave a city, that city begins to stink. I am lucky.

24th June

All the amorous satisfaction he gets is the smirk of mockery that every woman gives him, the only sort of smile that comes his way.

278

27th June

To have written something that leaves you emptied of your vital powers, still quivering and hot like a gun that has just been fired; to have poured out not only all you knew was in you, but all that you suspected and imagined, the turmoil, the shadowy visions, the subconscious; to have achieved that with long weariness and tension, learning caution through days of hesitation, sudden discoveries and lapses, concentrating all your life and energy on that one point; and then to realize that all this is as nothing unless it is welcomed by some sign, some word of human appreciation. To lack that warming response is to die of cold, to be speaking in the wilderness, to be alone, night and day, like a dead man.

2nd July

All you need do is to tell lies, exaggerate, embroider the facts a little, and the results are surprising. You can see the girl hesitate and grow submissive. What more can you ask? The carnal game cannot avoid lies and evasions.

5th July

Having regained their liberty, the liberals no longer know what to do with it.

7th July

Dissolute and worried, therefore grave and stern, "Mino" says. . . . He does not know how right he is. Why does his wife rub against me and then go off with him? Obvious, isn't it?

Why does T. look at me with clouded, unseeing eyes? She is afraid that I may close them. Was any parting ever as sad, as well-deserved?

(The end of Rome).

13th July (Milan and Serralunga)

What moves you when you gaze down upon an extensive view—for example, a broad plain with its hillocks and dells, seen from a height—is the realization that those stretches of farm land, all the same dull color, those little clouds, those distant, hazy patches, even the blue horizon, are so many real objects in a definite, individual countryside. How rich it is, this prospect stretching away into the distance, composed of things that are real and perfect!

19th July

Your conviction that this girl is sensual in the extreme and thinks of nothing but love—provided at present by her Lesbian friend who knows it all—does it not suddenly fill your heart with regret, disappointment, a sense of failure? She had you in her arms and did not want you. Or was it that you did not take her? The old story.

21st July

(Rereading Fraser.) What did you find in this book in 1933? That the grape, the corn, the harvest and the sheaf were full of drama and to speak of them in words was to verge upon profound significances that involve our blood, the animal world, the eternal past, the unconscious mind. The beast that strayed into the corn was the spirit. For you it merged ancestry and childhood, your recollections of things that puzzled and alarmed you in the country took on a sense of uniqueness, of something unfathomable.

3rd August

A mythical event that happened once and for all may express a recurring cosmic truth—the Rape of Proserpine, for example. In the same way one can express in art an oft-repeated experience of a countryside, an action, an event. How many times had you seen the hill of Quarti and Coniolo before you expressed it?

18th August

Lessons are not given, they are taken.

19th August

Whenever you are seized by the thrill of mythology, you have in mind the tree trunks, the river, the hill with the moon behind it, the highroad, the scent of field and meadow of your own homeland. Why?

21st August

The ancients liked to locate a god in exotic, far-off places, to give them titles that denoted his presence, or call him by a name that linked him with those distant places; which is as good as saying that the ancients were literary men, too.

9th September

Think the worst. You will not be wrong. Women are an enemy race, like the Germans.

We have pity for all the world, except for those who are bored. Yet boredom is considered a maximum penalty provided by law—prison.

15th September

Waiting is still an occupation. It is having nothing to wait for that is terrible.

16th September

There is only one pleasure—that of being alive. All the rest is misery.

27th September

For a man who knows how to write, a new style is always irresistible. He runs the risk of talking nonsense and saying it badly, but he cannot resist the style, the tempting form waiting to be imbued with his own words. (I mean, for instance, the style of my little mythical dialogues.)

29th September (At Turin)

Realism in art is Greek; allegory is Hebraic.

281

5th October

It can be taken as true that war restores the world by creating it afresh, which stems from the fact that in time of war one learns to live hoping for the morrow and enjoying the present, not storing up days like a miser. We live, that is, like children, and that, in general, is the cure for every ill.

In a thickly planted vineyard the serried ranks of vegetation—green, russet, yellow, are like the waves of an ocean, containing in their depths all the richness of the sea—freshness, amazement, hidden treasures.

26th October

I am well into a novel. Piv. was married this morning. I have a cold. Good.

27th October

What happens once, happens repeatedly. Unless some outside influence intervenes. But then the effect will be to produce a negative.

> (A certain man will always act in a particular way.
> If he becomes paralyzed, he can no longer do so.
> But he will not act in a different way; he will do nothing.)

I know by now that these entries in my diary are not important for any specific discovery made in them, but for the insight they give into the way I unconsciously live. What I say may not be true, but the fact that I say it betrays my inner being.

31st October

In the *Dialoghetti,* the mortals sigh for divine attributes, and the gods for human qualities. The multiplicity of gods does not affect the issue. The work is a conversation between divinity and humanity.

282

5th November

Allegory is any symbol viewed through the intelligence.

16th November

Last spring, Pintor's uncle came to Rome, and showed me a few lines about me he had copied from Gaime's[1] diary: "July, '42: P. is the best young fellow in Turin, quiet and sincere." . . . "The gentlemen there are rather ladylike."

Why have conferences? Newspapers and books are accessible to all, even to the outcast. Inside conference halls, a man has plenty of opportunity to play to the gallery or pose as a live wire, which "go-getters" find very pleasing. As for the fact that conferences provide a convenient method for distributing the bread of science, the answer is that nothing of any cultural value ever comes out of a conference; all that one hears there, if it is to bear fruit, must still be sought in books. And then? All that remains is that they are a school for superficiality and personal success. A fellow who is not disposed to raise his hat to culture, to undertake a lot of hard work, to act as though he were entering a shrine (for so it seems at first, later it gets into your very blood), remains unnoticed. He deserves it.

If it is true that religion and magic, by rendering objective such subconscious complexes as demons, spirits and the dead, liberated primitive man and left a free field for the ego to develop, the same thing will happen with all experience. Anything with which we experiment—love, adventure, risk—becomes objective and so leaves us free.

26th November

When a woman smells of sperm and it is not mine, I don't like it.

[1] Gaime Pintor, a young contemporary writer, was a close friend of Pavese, sharing his admiration for books and for freedom of thought. Pintor became a leader of the Resistance movement and was killed while fighting with the guerillas in [?] 1943. Ed.

17th December

In Crete, the cypress was sacred to Artemis; Taygetus and Erymanthus to Artemis, Cyllene to Hermes.

27th December

A woman, with other men, is either in earnest or fooling. If she is in earnest, she belongs to that other man, and that is that. If she is fooling, she is a cow, and that, too, is that.

1947

1st January

At the end of '38 I was hard-pressed and working at full stretch; when '46 began, I was contemptuous, rich and rather bitter. This time it is different—I am hard-pressed and rich (*Dialoghi con Leucò, Compagno*), but I feel a driving power that throbs louder than the voice of my work and predicts, not fresh works, but sordid realities. (Written in the Café Rampone, the skyscraper in the Via Viotti, where in 1932 I had the idea for *Ciao Masino*.)

26th January

There are only two attitudes to life, the Christian's and the Stoic's. Probably the Communist's is a fusion of both. He has charity and a sense of stern reality; he knows the world is hard, yet he does good.

3rd February

You talk and talk and talk. It is because you have been silent for so long. Does it dismay you to think that one day no one will still listen to you? No.

We only forget what was already forgotten when it

284

happened. You don't remember anything except your closed inner worlds.

A man, a woman, a boy.

For me the hill-mountain is the Taygetus, which I discovered at fifteen in Catullus, and the Erymanthus, the Cyllene, the Pelion, discovered in Virgil etc., as I stood looking at the hills of Reaglie and remembering the fiery hills of S. Stefano, Moncucco, Camo, S. Maurizio, Luassolo.

24th February

Cronus was a monstrous figure, but he reigned in the Golden Ages. He was defeated and Hades was born, together with the Blessed Isle and Olympus, unhappiness and happiness, opposed and institutional.

The monstrous and golden era of Titans was the age of undifferentiated men-monster-gods. You have always considered reality as a titanic idea, or rather as a human-divine Chaos (= monstrous), which is the perennial form of life. You present the gods, who were Olympian, superior, happy and remote beings as the spoil-sports of humanity, to which the Olympians granted favors under the spur of their titanic nostalgia, of their pity rooted in time. (For the Dialogues.)

4th March

To me, a friend no longer means fellowship, a way of living, but a pastime, an alternative to the cinema. Why? I no longer believe that work can be shared. I work alone and then I seek distraction. In the days when I believed in friends, I did no work.

5th March

It is night, as usual, and you are glad that in a moment you will go to bed, disappear. Then, an instant later, it will be morning and you will again begin discovering amazing things. It is fine to go to sleep, because you will wake up. It is the quickest way to make the morning come.

9th March

On the Salino road: Today you saw that great hill with its hollows, its clump of trees, the brown, the blue, the houses, and you said: "It is as it is, as it should be. That is enough for you. It is a place that never changes. Why look for any other? Dwell among these things, let them enfold you, live on them, like air, like a trail of clouds. No one knows that everything is here."

It is logical for unbelievers to want a secular government. To them it is a conquest, a step forward. For Christians, it is absurd. Priests, prelates, the Pope *must* concern themselves with politics. Dante could separate the spheres of pope and emperor because it was understood that the emperor's politics would be Christian.

10th March

You had almost forgotten the tranquil moon above the empty streets. Every year, the beauties of nature reveal themselves anew, and the emotion they evoke is always: "You had almost forgotten. . . ."

The difficulty of art is to present things you know well in such a way that they are surprising. If you did not know them well, you would not be sufficiently interested in them to treat them in a way that makes them surprising.

The delight of art: perceiving that one's own way of life can determine a method of expression.

12th March

One thing is to say that Olympus was patterned upon the Greek civic institutions, and another that the institutions were fashioned along the lines of Olympus.

14th March

Hemingway is the Stendhal of our time.

15th March

Things I write here are what I shall no longer talk about; they are the shavings thrown off by the plane as it shapes the day's work. Here, so to speak, is a quick way of cutting through the preliminaries, the framework, the incidental odds and ends; clearing the ground so that the main construction to come can be plainly seen.

You have maintained that the form, the style, the page itself, are realities in their own right, distinct from the reality you have lived through and wish to express. That is a commonplace. But they are a new dimension. This is not to say that you express nothing, by writing, but that you create another reality, the written word.

All Jews, all such men, act as though nothing had happened. They talk of their troubles, problems and the world itself in a tone that makes light of them. I should like to see them proclaim that they amount to something, that they matter as much as anyone else, that they have a word to say in things. They have, and they do not say it.

17th March

When a work is finished one seeks to improve its form, not its substance; the style, not the sentiments; the symbol, not the thing symbolized. Where fatigue shows is in the style, the form, the symbol. As for the sentiments it contains, one always has those in abundance, from the very fact of being alive.

19th March

Stendhal-Hemingway. Their stories are not about society, the world in general; they do not give the impression of portraying a vast reality and interpreting it in their own way, as Balzac does, and Tolstoi, among others. They have a constant pattern of human tension being resolved in situations created by blending sensations with environment, expressed with absolute directness. They would not know how to present other subjects, as the following writers would, but upon that constant pattern they have built a whole ideology, which is, after all, their function as storytellers: forceful, clear and non-literary.

Flaubert chose a certain setting; they do not.

Dostoievsky constructed a dialectic world; they do not.

Faulkner stylizes atmospheres, deals in legends; they do not.

Lawrence sought out a cosmic sphere and interpreted it; they do not. They are typical storytellers in the first person.

22nd March

The character is a theatrical conception, not specifically narrative. Characters are not essential in a story. The greatest Greek story-teller is Herodotus, not Homer—who is, rather, a pre-literary dramatist.

The nineteenth century aspired to create drama, but did not achieve it. Instead, it created the great novel which, because of its characters, was theatrical. Nowadays we tend to interest ourselves afresh in pure narration. We do not even bother to create characters—that is a commonplace job, anyone can do it. What we seek lies in the sense of rhythm, the feeling that reality itself is disturbed—as in Herodotus. Currently we are more concerned with creating symbols; we are intellectualists. Not the *Iliad,* but Herodotus.

The epic is drama as yet unaware of the technical means, the theatre, the stage.

This is why *Moby Dick* is a revelation of our epoch; it is not a tale of characters, it is pure rhythm. The man who tells it now is not the one who "knew human nature," and discovered profoundly significant psychological truths, but one who deals with reality *en bloc,* whose harsh experiences give rhythm, cadences, embellishments to his story. Hemingway has violent death; Levi, prison; Conrad, the mysteries of the Southern Seas; Joyce, the stereoscope of word-sensations; Proust, the impossibility of seizing fleeting moments;

Kafka, the cipher of absurdity; Mann, the *mythical* reassessment of facts. (I apologize for having included Levi.)[1]

28th March

Here is a confirmation of 17th March. I have a wealth of sentiments as starting points for the *Dialoghetti,* but I am blocked because I lack a satisfactory method of introducing them. I want a new pair of speakers, different from the usual hackneyed ones.

2nd April

The gods know and see, thanks to their magic-rational nature, and with detachment. Men act, not magically, with pain. They give names, that is to say that they solve their problems in creative terms.

5th April

While resistance was undercover, all was hope: now all is a prospective of disaster.

12th April

To have the impression that every good thing that happens to you is a fortunate mistake, a stroke of luck, an undeserved favor, is not due to a noble mind, humility and detachment. It is born of long servitude, of the acceptance of oppression and dictatorship. You have the soul of a slave, not a saint.

When you were twenty and your first friends left you, you felt you were suffering nobly. That was an illusion. What pained you was having to break pleasant habits. And you do just the same now.

You are alone, and you know it. You were born to live under the wings of someone who would sustain and justify you, someone kind enough to let you play the fool and imagine yourself capable of remaking the world singlehanded.

[1] Carlo Levi, Pavese's friend and contemporary, who became a colleague of his on the editorial staff of the Casa Einaudi. Ed.

You never found anyone who could endure so much; hence your suffering when friends depart, not because of any tenderness for them; hence your resentment towards the one who has gone; hence your facility for finding a new ally—not out of cordiality. You are a woman, and like a woman you are obstinate. But alone you are not enough, and you know it.

12th May

The greatest benefit that a writer brings to poetry, to literature, is that part of his life which, while living it, seemed to him the furthest removed from literature. His days, his habits, incidents that seemed to him not only a waste of time but a vice, a sin, a downfall. Such things enriched his life. Look at the childhood period in every biography.

13th May

The innocent, honest citizen, the man who "had nothing to do with it" but yet was the victim of a tragic mistake during the civil war, becomes less and less interesting, almost comic. In our day, no one, in reality, "has nothing to do with it."

27th May

The entrance to Hades. A road encased in volcanic rock, and covered by alder trees and elms; the road is green, transparent and dark, and it emerges in the sun at the gate of Sovana. The Etruscan world is beyond Hades, its *chthonic*. Standing here one suddenly knows what is meant by the word "underground"; it means dug into the volcanic rock.

One also finds out what they meant when they said that Hesperia was the land of the dead. The two faces of a country before history passed over it and afterward resemble each other. They are nature. "Nature" is the kingdom of the dead.

If you find someone objectionable, put up with him. In a little while—without fail—something out of the ordinary, some truth, will emerge. Even if you are bored by his banality, his insincerity. Indeed, all the more because of that.

This woman with a mustache, who says such "sufficient" things ("Sampierdarena which now is part of Genoa," "Don't speak to me about Naples," "I cannot tell you, you know, what effect asparagus have on me" etc.) is now explaining that asparagus should be cooked with the tips sticking out of the water, so as to steam them and preserve their flavor. She says that Cinotti (in the Via XX Settembre) is the best restaurant in Genoa. She has eaten fish soup in Naples on a barge. She is despicable, but full of things.

("I had a girl friend who now plays an instrument.")

("During the war I did not suffer. Oh no, I didn't suffer. I would have a salad, perhaps, but under the salad there was a steak." "At Ranieri's in Via delle Carrozze, I found a waiter whom I had met in Chianciano. He looked after me.")

2nd June

The crowd, when viewed as a human hotbed producing what you live on, restores your serenity and gives you fresh heart.

There are holy men, energetic priests, who have a childlike assumption of their own power. But not all that childlike: they know how to use and exploit it.

The intolerance shown by the male writer in his letters and diaries, in his gestures, and his need to listen anonymously to his own work, derive from his necessity to find something that is absolute, a point of comparison, an operative reality. These are the premises of his classicality.

4th June

However keen may be the pleasure of being with friends, or with anyone, a greater pleasure is going away afterwards and being alone. Life and death.

After all, he is a fine fellow, G. . . . He really does like company. He has the tremendous handicap of old-fashioned tastes and does not realize it. But are you sure that your grudge against him is not merely because he let you pick up the check? "This will ruin me," he said, "I'm no good. Lord, let me put off paying as long as possible."

23rd June (Turin)

A meeting of the Party has all the characteristics of a religious rite. We listen to be assured of what we already think, to be exalted by our common faith and confession.

1st July

What is the real reason why we want to be big, to be creative geniuses? For posterity? No. To be pointed out when we stroll in crowded places? No. To carry on with our daily toil under the conviction that whatever we do is worth the trouble, is something unique. For the day, not for eternity.

10th July

Today you looked for a long time at the hill beyond the Po, and noted that it is all parks, villas, streets you have walked through again and again. Why that sense of something *savage* about it, which even now fills you with awe? What was savage has now been reduced to a familiar, civilized place. "Savage," as such, has no basic reality. It is that things *were* so, in that they were inhuman. But things, in so far as they interest you, *are* human.

Note that *Paesi tuoi* and *Dialoghi con Leucò* are the fruit of your yearning for "savage" things—the country, the titans. In this vein, can one hope to go further than *The Call of the Forest,* which, in any case you find rather boring?

All the art of the nineteenth century is a harping on "the savage." First as a subject (Kipling, D'Annunzio and so on), then as form (Joyce, Picasso). Leopardi, in the poetic illusions of his youth, was fascinated by "the savage" from a psychological angle. Anderson, in his own way, touched upon it in the natural surroundings of life in the Middle West. Everything that struck you, creatively, in your reading, had this same atmosphere. (Nietzsche and his Dionysius. . . .)

Having discovered ethnology, you reached the stage of relating "the savage" to history. The city-country of your first books has become Olympus and the Titans in your latest. You sigh for the country, for "the savage," but you appreciate the good sense, the moderation, the clear understanding of people like Berto, Pablo, the man in the street. "The savage" appeals to you as something mysterious, not as historical brutality. Tales of partisans or terrorists do not please you. They are too explicit. "Savage" means mysterious, open to any possibility.

Your idea (23rd-26th August, '44) that "savage" means "superstitious," something no longer acceptable morally, while a simple mischance is natural (even the cruelty of nature seems acceptable), is still the burden of your song, with the "savage," the titans, the brutal and reactionary, replaced by the citizen, the Olympian, the progressive. (Cf. *Paesi tuoi, Dialoghi con Leucò, Compagno.*) You preach order by describing disorder.

21st July

We like to have work to do, so as to have the right to rest.

26th July

From Nilsson, *The Minoan Mycenean* etc.

p. 279: "Earth is on the one hand the resting place of the dead who are buried in its entrails, on the other the provider of fertility. The Hyksos divinities appear in the double aspect of masters of death and of fertility.

"I have often expressed my doubts about the general validity of this hypothetical system, especially when it is further developed to the extent of opposing the Hyksos divinities to the Olympian gods."

28th July

Ditto, p. 413: "In ancient times the reason for building a temple on a particular site was that the site itself was already sacred. Its sacred character was inherent in the place, and it derived especially from cult."

Apollo is the sender of all evils. Cf. "Fiore e Cavallo" where he appears in such a guise and only in such a guise.

The *Dialoghetti* preserve the elements, the gestures, the attributes, the knots of myth, but they abolish its cultural reality which springs from a long tale of graftings, copying, derivations etc. (which makes them understandable). The social background (which made them acceptable to the ancient) is also abolished. What remains is the problem, and this your fantasy is solving.

4th August

From Harrison, *Prolegomena* etc. p. 650.

The Olympians are equally indifferent to Before and Afterwards; they are neither the source nor the end of life. Furthermore, and within the strictest limitations, they are "human." They are not at one with the lives of animals, streams and woods, and men. Eros, "whose feet rest upon flowers," who "sleeps in the folds," belongs to life as a whole; he is Dionysus, he is Pan. Under the influence of Athens, Eros becomes enveloped into a purely human form, but the "Fanes"(?) of Orpheus was polymorphous, a mysterious beast-god."

(Without being conscious of it, you have applied this idea to the *Dialoghetti,* where you argue against the Olympian world and take sides with the world of Titans and beasts.)

6th August

The surrealist idea (Herb. Read) that images and inspirations are perhaps captured telepathic messages—and all the theory of dream-poetry, and of automatism—tends to uproot writing from the rich, well-planted natural and social soil where it has meaning for all of existence and to throw it into an exclusive heaven of illuminations and discovery that, by themselves, are only games—as a case of telepathy is a theatrical act and not a human issue.

The interest of a work for the man who has written it—and for the man who understands it—is to see it shaping itself amid opposing tendencies, clarifying them, merging them, giving them form and meaning. The greatest conflict is between the unconscious and the conscious (social or ethical requirements, the need for communication). A work produced wholly unconsciously, automatically, is uninspiring, or a mere joke.

10th August (Forte dei Marmi)

The problems that agitate one generation are extinguished for the next, not because they have been solved but because the general lack of interest sweeps them away.

These mountains should be Greek. From the sea you view the first of them, dark, wooded, russet-green. Behind them, far away against the sky, you see the airy, spectral outlines of those that are all rock, pale and light. Their supernatural whiteness comes from veins of marble. They look wild and "savage," but full of form and rhythm, harsh, austere, mythical: Greek.

16th August (At Forte dei Marmi)

Autumn, this most mild, peaceful and tender of seasons, takes over from the previous one and then establishes itself with fearful quakings, tremendous storms, darkness at morning, whirlwinds and a massacre of leaves. All this violence is the price of maturity.

18th August

A work settles nothing, just as the labor of a whole generation settles nothing. Sons, and the morrow, always start afresh, light-heartedly ignoring their fathers and what has already been done. Even hatred, a revolt against the past, is more tolerable than this bland indifference. The virtue of the ancients lay in their constitution, which always looked back to the past. This is the secret of their inexhaustible completeness. Because the richness of a work—of a generation—is always determined by how much of the past it contains.

25th August

The first great manifestation of literature and also the examples that founded it are linked with the myth of the Golden Age, of an ivory tower (in Virgil's Arcadia).

26th August

To say that the same things always happen to each one of us is not to make a deterministic statement. On the contrary, if these things happen it means that the subject, far from being determined by a natural necessity, brings to every encounter his own constancy, his nature, his personality, his essence etc., and these are the elements which chose the encounters and made them all resemble one another. The human Ego plays a part in them, but the encounters are free.

7th November

The *Compagno* and *Leucò* are published, the works of '46, your thirty-eighth year. More than ever, you want to write. Less badly.

This tranquil love affair, without complications, is your biggest problem. It is in your very blood, more than the others. Is that true? Who knows?

8th November

I hold that to give oneself up, absolutely, trustfully, to humility, to grace, to God, has the defect of being an act of presumption, conceit, unjustified hope. A convenient hypothesis.

They reply: every man is like that. He falls in the

street and stretches out his hand for help; he feels he is dying and trusts himself to anyone. Genuine experience drives him to total surrender and to hope. When we are lost, we hope.

I answer: that is no proof that the thing hoped for is real, actual.

They reply that I must accept my instinctive gesture. I cannot be mistaken. There can no longer be any question of a mistake, for in that way everything is vouchsafed to me, even faith.

I answer that in that case . . . they reply . . . I answer. . . .

11th November

If the woman you are awaiting does not turn up, never seeks you out again, stays away, her bravado would have the pointless effect of making you miss her and regret her absence. You, who are so fond of making others miss you, learn how futile this can be.

The *Casa in collina* may be the experience that has culminated in *Ritorno all'uomo*.

21st November

To know that someone is waiting for you, someone who may ask you to account for your actions, your thoughts, follow you with their eyes, hoping for a word from you—all that depresses you, embarrasses you, offends you.

The believer's idea is sound, even in carnal matters. He knows that someone is awaiting him—his God. You are a bachelor—you do not believe in God.

7th December

So many alarming things have been said and written about our life, our world, our culture, that to see the sun, the clouds, to go out into the street and find grass, dogs, pebbles, moves you like some great boon, like a gift from God, like a dream. But a real dream that endures, that actually exists.

11th December

The Latins said "mothers," referring to Bacchantes. Is that not strange. Not if you realize that a Bacchic orgy was an initiation rite of a matriarchal period.

". . . the hunting, the fighting, or what not, the thing done, is never religious; the thing redone with heightened emotion is on the way to become so. The element of action redone, imitated . . . is, I think, essential. . . . Not the attempt to deceive, but a desire to relive, to re-present" (Harrison, *Themis*, p. 43).

Does not that correspond with your view of myths, your "seeing for the second time?" This simulation is the secret of poetry. To re-present "the thing done," the hunt, the battle, is not that narration? To represent it before it happens, to make it happen (magic), what is that but prophecy? Here is poetry, magic and ritual, religion.

The charm of Greek myths stems from the fact that viewpoints which were originally magic, totemistic, matri-archal, inaugural, were, by the active elaboration of conscious thought that developed during the tenth to the eighth centuries B.C., reinterpreted, distorted, corrupted, merged by the light of reason, and so they came down to us enriched by all this lucidity and tension of the spirit, but still bearing the marks of their ancient, savage symbolism.

20th December

That ritual always precedes myth and dogma is the great law of spiritual things. If for "ritual" we say "life," and for "myth and dogma," "poetry and philosophy," it becomes clear. The rite of the love feast and the eucharist preceded the gospels and determined their form.

28th December

The Greek myth teaches that we are always fighting against a part of ourselves, the part we have outstripped, Zeus against Typhon, Apollo against the Python. Conversely, what we are fighting is still part of ourselves, our former selves. Above all, we fight in order *not* to be something, to free ourselves. The man who feels no great repugnance, does not fight.

1948

1st January

A romantic morning, with sunshine over land and water, sparkling, vibrant, full of warmth. Such a New Year's Day has never been seen. Will the coming year be one to dread?

At three o'clock, an operation that will bring me peace again. In '47 I have written nothing (a dialogue or so and the start of a novel). Nothing achieved. Two books have been published. I have been in Rome and at the sea, always active, always on edge. Fear or irritation?

But what a day, today! It does not seem like Turin. It is a winter even stranger than that of '43-'44. When you came off the train this morning it seemed like a new town to walk around in, look at, live in. A seaside town, with the sun shining on the upper stories of houses and palaces, and on the open hills.

10th January

Your need to ensure to your words their spoken linearity, their legitimacy of expression, their materiality, is caused by your conviction that art is an exploitation of one's material means (sounds, marble, colors etc.), in order to extract an expression from them without violating their materiality. Language is subject to a syntax, to a grammatical coherence, in sum to a tradition—just like sounds are governed by mathematical rules, stones by the law of gravity and colors by chromatic relationships. That is why you instinctively rejected the free verse of futurism.

The unconscious as an end to itself, obscurity of form and the use of allusions in order to create sudden enlightenment, in what do these differ from the old rules of art conceived as an imitation of Nature? Here conscience is made to conform to the object. . . .

(On reading L. Rusu, *Essai sur la creation artistique,* Alcan 1935, p. 307.)

12th January

If a little operation makes one suffer so. . . .

Why is it that when you are able to write about God and the desperate joy of that December evening in Treviso, you feel surprised and happy like a person who has just come to a new town? (Today, a page of Chapter XV of the *Collina*.)

16th January

The Greeks *recitation,* the Romans, *literature* (cf. Bérard and Snell). See, too, your note on 22nd March, '47. The Greeks were narrators only in their historians (Herodotus, Thucydides) and even Herodotus composed his works to be read aloud. Homer was declaimed, the lyrics were sung, the tragedies performed, the speeches delivered, the philosophy discussed. Always voice and gesture.

Narration, which is a matter of spreading oneself over the page, mixed up with things and events, was invented by the Romans with poems, romances, histories, although with them, too, the conception of oratory persisted—in history, for instance. The celebrated naturalness of the Greeks stemmed from their use of a *spoken* language, in the true sense of the word. One cannot *speak* in an unnatural way; anything that jarred would be perceived at once with an actor, a flesh-and-blood speaker. Literary language, a composition, is created only after the matter has been filtered, dehumanized, depersonalized, on the written page.

The present day tendency to tell a story in the first person is an unconscious impulse towards naturalism, while still wishing one's self to remain on the page; an account, not a portrayal in action. It is a way of reverting to unsophistication, the only approved method now that the theatre, with us, is too academic in tone.

19th January

Not a good day. Wasted. Met various dull people, exhausting, useless. Serious situations not mentioned, stupid. Nothing invented, nothing done. Yet I saw plenty of people: Natalia, Balbo, Maria Livia, Piero, the existential novelist, Simone and others. The evening papers are threatening. That's all, or so it seems. Bought a new pen.

Like certain days in '46. Thinking of them again, you find them good. Reading over what you wrote then, you realize how down-to-earth you were. In retrospect you particularly enjoy the periods that, while you were living them, seemed intolerable. Nothing is lost. All the difficulties, the reservations and aversions, the anguish, gain a richness when remembered. Life is greater, fuller, than we knew.

20th January

Today, acclamation. They implore me to write, beg for my autograph. If you had known this when you were twenty! Does it mean anything to you now? I am sad, useless, like a god.

21st January

Young . . . , with his hard-set, intense face, is not a pleasant specimen. Rather alarming. He says nothing about the things he has done, but allows them to be discussed while he puts on an air of supreme importance. He is obstinate, wrapped up in himself, observant and fanatical. One cannot chat with him; even his jokes are serious, with unexpected undercurrents. "He has a superiority complex," says Calvino, and he is right, for there is in him, too, a stiffness, an air of boredom. An unpleasant man.

25th January

It is not that things happen to each of us according to his fate, but that he interprets what has happened, if he has the power to do so, according to his sense of his own destiny.

There are, in Turin, streets and avenues where people whom the war has beaten down and destroyed, live and stroll about. Contented, intelligent people, who once counted for something, whom you hardly recognize. A whole society of them. What good has their existence achieved?

30th January

A night of stars, rare and clear-cut. Seen through the branches of the trees they look like precious stones, buds, the first of the year.

(12th October, '43—25th July, '44—15th March, '45 —18th April, '45: what can one do with these five fragments? Nothing. Could each one of them be perfect? Yes. The effect produced by what is rare.)

4th February

On Monday the 2nd I stopped, just for fun. It does not seem difficult.

Falqui is a good fighter. His column "Laboratorio" in *Fiera Letteraria* is always written with great intelligence. His idea of comparing Didimo's prose with Leopardi's, and then contrasting it with the style of the romantics who wrote in dialect is an excellent one.

5th February

My growing dislike of N. comes from the fact that she takes for granted, with a spontaneity that, itself, is "granted," too many things of nature and life. She always carries her heart in her hand—her muscular heart—talking of childbirth, her periods, her coming old age. Since B. discovered that she is open-hearted and primitive, there's no living with her.

In religion, one looks not to life but to death, because the things of life gain their value by being viewed in relation to eternity, above and beyond death.

10th February

Tuesday. A feverish cold. Two days ago I started smoking again, and felt the same terrible, unbearable irritation. Stop it! Stop it! The same game as when I was twenty, when a cigarette stifled me and I had to put it aside. Shall I find any way round it?

13th February

"A philosophy cleansed of all speculative aroma and reduced to pure history, or historicity, or pure humanism" (philosophy of Praxis, Gramsci). Does this not resemble the poetic of pure poetry, cleansed of all content and reduced to pure form, to pure song?

1st March

When the sad evening comes and your heart is broken, for no reason, your consolation still lies in your usual thought that not even a gay, intoxicated, exalted evening has any particular reason, except perhaps a pre-arranged meeting, an idea that flashed across your mind that day, a trifle that might never have happened. That is, you console yourself with the thought that nothing has a reason, everything is casual. Strange. It presupposes an enormous optimism, a confidence in the mere event. As long as things simply happen and there is nothing behind them, you are quite happy. Epicurean renunciation! The serene life! Is it possible?

2nd March

This need to be alone, not to feel that people ask anything of you or carry you along with them . . .; this dread lest they should have the least right over you, and make you feel it; this obvious tactlessness by others who expect something, take you for granted in any way.

Instantly you become incapable, extinguished, stiff, rebellious. Not one good word can you produce. You break off, leave it.

Your fierce resentment for the one who has so disrupted your work and whom, out of pity or self-sacrifice, you must still treat kindly!

The inner well-being that comes from the profession of moral politics, contact with the masses, is no different from what we derive from any work, any activity to which we devote ourselves. When you write something, immerse yourself in it, you are serene, poised, happy.

And if everything is only a question of well-being, health, living efficiently? What will you say at the point of death?

5th March

The Roman school—that meeting place of journalists, adventurers, writers, painters—has invented a reflexed art of the type associated with Alexandria, a taste for remodeling a given style, technique, world, exercising their intelligence without becoming involved. Longanesi and *Omnibus,* Cecchi and Praz, Cardarelli and Bacchelli, Moravia and Morante. Outside of Rome, Landolfi and Piovene. This substantially was fascist art; what was alive and true—and cynical—in the fascist period. Only the two extremes stayed free of it, Sicily and Piedmont, which were not fascist, and discovered "barbarian" culture across the sea—Vittorini and Pavese. For them, you need another formula.

Fundamentally, humanistic intelligence—the fine arts and letters—did not suffer under fascism; they managed to follow their own bent, cynically accepting the game as it was. Where fascism exercised vigilance was in preventing intercourse between the intelligentsia and the people, keeping the people uninformed. Now the problem is to shed the privileges we enjoy at the moment—servitude—and not to "approach the people" but to *be* the people, to live by a culture that has its roots in the people and not in the cynicism of the "free Romans."

(Balbo says you are a pagan. No, a stoic.)

9th March

The four greatest men—complex, inexhaustible worlds in themselves, modern, but beyond our comprehension—are Plato, Dante, Shakespeare and Dostoievsky. Each nation has but one. If a nation is a complex mass of communal memories, customs, habits and legends, it is natural that only once can there occur a moment when the whole is perfectly balanced, alive in the true sense.

23rd March

Why eternity? We cannot understand what it may be. To the objection that whatever boundary one puts to existence, our thought would immediately leap beyond it, one may answer: this does not prove that "beyond" there is a true reality; a small spore, endowed with the power of thought and placed upon a sphere would always leap beyond it; this does not detract from the fact that—for it—the sphere is limited. We are so fashioned that our mind is always leaping beyond—that is all—but it is not proven that time really exists, therefore the problem of our caducity would disappear.

How is it, though, that if time does not exist we are built along the lines of a temporal scheme? If reality is always unchangeable and motionless, why are we always changeable and mobile?

27th March

I and, I believe, many others, are seeking not for what "is real" in an absolute sense, but for what "we are." In these thoughts that you are jotting down, you nonchalantly tend to let your real personality emerge, your fundamental tastes, your mythical realities. You would not know what to do with a reality that had no roots inside your subconscious self.

Deep down what you dislike about God is his greatest quality—the fact that he is detached, different to you, the same for everybody, and still a supreme being.

But why, then, do you accept "yourself"—that whatever self that you happen to be? In a sense, is not God's self an object, just like yours? I don't think this is due to ambition. Could it, perhaps, be laziness? Or the conviction that it is useless to lean on someone, cultivating qualities which you do not possess, write about things that you do not feel etc. Perhaps the fault lies with your poetic education, which has accustomed you to believe only in your real nature.

28th March

This evening, a star between the branches of a tree luminous as a yellow plum. Today, a fire beyond the hill—a cloud of smoke in the clear sky—the first atomic bomb.

This spring is like that of '46 in Rome. There is a vague sadness, the absence of occupation after a work is finished.

30th March

The scent of the first evening shower, under a clear sky. The open season returning. In life, there is no return. As the seasons come around, the passing years color the same theme in ever-different ways. The beauty of our own discordant rhythm—moderation and invention, stability and discovery—is that age is an accumulation of equally important things, growing richer and deeper all the time.

31st March

One cannot understand how, in the days when the only explanation of the world was that given by Christianity—the Middle Ages—any man dared to be wicked, to die impenitent.

1st May

I have now clearly understood this question of the Chinese, and not without smiling. I explained to M.L., in front of the beautiful hill, that I was angry at not being able to do anything about it. I could only admire it. That was all.

I could not even express the idea of wanting to possess it, to drink its secret, to make it part of my flesh. I used the parallel of the fruit: one eats the fruit and one assimilates it; the same is true of the hill. But, and then what? I said; in the meanwhile the fruit has disappeared.

I admitted that the problem was only a literary one; I explained to M.L. the reasons for the Chinese naturalistic poetry—four thousand years of identical poetry—and I explained the magical structure of Chinese thought and society, the correspondence between power and identification with territory, the continuous reality of mountains, woods, swamps, rivers, animals, etc. which goes to form the substance of human reality. The Chinese—I said—have already done all this. And as a result? They have described landscapes. That is all.

The West has always preferred man to nature. Narrative poetry with heroes. The West discovered the landscape through Romanticism, through (a magical) identification with nature (Schelling etc.).

11th May

This affair (from 13th September, '47) is over. I expected not to mind so much. It troubles me. She is more sincere, being more passionate.

13th May

Begin: This was the first time that C. left a woman without feeling the urge to slam the door.

Collect all your typical situations (you were born for this):

Violence and blood in the fields
merry-making on the hills
a walk around the summit
the sea from the shore. . . .

Luckily, these situations are many.

26 Nov. '49

Is this not the theme of *The Moon and the Bonfires?*

27th May

A man who describes the country, the colors and shapes of things, their delicate variations, the sensations they evoke, does not see why he cannot in the same way describe a woman's body—coloring, firmness, downy hollows, curves, sex. The attitude is the same.

15th June

"A pre-Christian pagan can save himself provided that he follows the road of natural goodness."

Then what is the use of Christ's revelation?

a) If he who hears it and observes gains more merit than he who does not—then it's an injustice.

b) If he who does not hear it but follows natural goodness gains the same merit—then it's useless.

26th June

The more a person is intolerant of chains and needs freedom, the more that person is a slave of habit. Evasiveness is mean.

The memory of a hilltop you climbed long ago—the field of daisies that, to your childish mind, was the whole of nature—moves you deeply, even now, because it stands out as the symbol of a great experience, the infinite number of possible experiences that dawned upon you on that hill-top. That is what "symbol" means. It brings before you, objectively, a vast countryside, as if seen through the wrong end of a telescope, presenting it as something wholly your own, implying infinite possibilities.

This applies to primitive fantastic creations, which are simple, humble, infinitely less complex than the life we lead nowadays, and yet fascinate us as much as a genuine top-level experience.

3rd July

Our trouble is that we no longer believe in the distinction between things sacred and profane. (Sacred things

should be those imbued with power, unique, mythical.)
Consequently, things are either wholly profane (materialistic,
mechanical) or wholly sacred (reformed Christianity, of the
spirit and not of the letter).

Taking it on a higher level, which means detaching
oneself from profane things in order to come closer to sacred
things, changes the viewpoint. One must detach oneself from
everything, to draw near to *everything;* enjoy *every single
thing* profanely but with a sacred detachment. With a pure
heart.

24th July

How humiliating is a woman who gives you to understand that she has her own way of life, has ideas, forms her
own opinion about you and other men, can do without you!
All you can do is ignore her, treat her as she treats you.
Lovely company—a cry in the night.

3rd September

She talked and talked, told you the finest things. You
had work to do and she bored you. She said that werewolves
are the offspring of mad dogs; she said that dogs and vipers
have the same spine and the same smell; that the skin of a
viper infuriates a dog. She said that beasts know the hour of
Pan, that the werewolf howls at the moon, since it is a mad
dog. She said that she passed her time searching for the links
and relationships between things, etc. She talked of *Paesi tuoi,*
which she has summarized.

3rd October

To Hemingway: Did you ever see the hills of Piedmont? They are brown, yellow and dusty, sometimes "green."
. . . You'd like them. Yours, C.P.

7th October

On 4th October, *Diavolo in collina* was finished. It
has the air of something big. It is a new language; dialectic,
written with an atmosphere of culture and introducing

"student discussions." For the first time you have really set up symbols. You have revitalized *La Spiaggia,* putting into it young men who make discoveries, the liveliness of debates, mythical reality.

8th October

(...................)

Strange. The women tolerated and hated in *Paura* have names beginning with E; the desired and intangible ones have names beginning with C: Elena, Elvira; Concia, Cate.

I opened *Compagno* at random and reread some of it. It was like touching a live wire. Its tension is well above average, due to the smooth cadence of the phrases; a surging forward against constant frustration, a breathless excitement.

10th October

The reputation with which they are saddling you of a man who is solid, hard, wilful and successful, implies that they intend to lean upon you, to push their roots into your strength, to deflect it to their own advantage. In sum they wish to destroy you. They do not seem to know that your solidity was built with one end in view, which was not to support them.

An old dream. To live in the country with a beautiful woman—Greer Garson or Lana Turner—and lead a simple, perverse life. This was a thing of the past. You don't think about it any more.

14th October

". . . I don't give a damn what's in it . . ." says Nat.[1] She wants "real life," tales about wretched women.

15th October

Before the cock crows.

---

[1] Natalia Ginsburg, widow of Pavese's great friend, Leone Ginsburg. Ed.

16th October

Since you are an egoist, they all fawn upon you to serve their own ends.

24th October

"It is an honor for us" the person said . . . then. In the spring of '45. These things only happen once. What is it that matters? As long as the world is in a crisis, you can play this game, but afterward?

Are you ready to die in obscurity? It must happen one day. To consider death as an incident—whereas it is something tremendous.

31st October

You discovered that V. does not *feel* embarrassing situations. Strange in one who aspires to be a man of the world. When one gives him an evasive reply he insists and insists. Why? Out of affection or self-interest (trying to seem in the social swim)? Sheer boorishness? In any case, it pleased you to observe this.

11th November

Another discovery: the pleasure of going into a suburban café you have never seen before, watching the gamblers and the few customers, savoring the life of a world that you have always felt outside of, that yet seems to hold so much of your own past and the hopes you had then. A modern café, almost empty. Soon after, a red-headed, rather uncouth girl came in with a man who was no stranger, and you went away happy.

For some time now, general impressions and thoughts have seemed less important. You notice the moments.

19th November

Knowing what one wants from the day, working seriously, that is, also gives us a way of summing up situations and men. B. gets involved in painful situations, floundering about in them with a great loss of time and energy, because he does not work seriously. Then he fails to notice other situations which can only be clarified by applying intensive effort and technical skill to that end. A fresh proof that to know something one must do it, to *know* the world one must *construct* it. Take care not to think that to construct means to overthrow, to change at all costs. The science of reality is the science of the possible, the progressive, not of violent agitation to no purpose.

That he who does not strive towards an end does not understand reality, in other words cannot perceive a rational order in reality, seems to mean many things. It means that rationality is only an instrument for action (Bergson), or else that our nature is rational whereas action tends towards truth (St. Thomas and Marx)?

Before and after do not count. We "exist in a rational sphere." This is inescapable; it's the logic of the irreversibility of culture, of progress, of knowledge. Leopardi complains that one cannot escape real bitterness. Why bitterness? Because all departure from habit is uncomfortable. Nothing else. The new generation arrives and thrives on it. The older one might as well have made the effort.

27th November

A situation with little white curtains of lace on windows overlooking the Valentino Park; a warm room in the morning (it's winter outside); the dream has come true—during the night, suddenly and in the dark, woman and love had entered.

3rd December

It is a pleasure—one of the most authentic—to realize that everyone is compelled to choose, that he cannot have two things at once. It is an appeal to the tragic in life, the fact that one value runs counter to another. You have renounced so many things to have just one, and it pleases you that this same rule bears heavily on every man.

People who take something for granted annoy you, in

that they are trying to escape this element of tragedy. The same applies to people who enjoy things like pagans, in that their avidity does not recognize the uncertainty of the occasion. Aspiring to obtain something, laying claim to it, is in itself annoying, in that it seeks to obviate the irony of life.

We hate others, because we hate ourselves.

Yet you take things for granted when you should not. Which raises the point of purity of heart, humility, acceptance of God's world.

5th December

A place that pleases you (Turin with its red clouds in winter, the countryside, parks and so on) is not to be described enthusiastically as you did when you were young. Rather, it should be presented in a plain, clear-cut fashion, as life is to a man who lives there. That is its true expression, as in Dostoievsky, for instance. In that way, indirectly, such places will remain in the imagination of the reader. One obtains what one does not strive for.

8th December

The Greek spirit originates from the encounter between a "quality" and a pre-existing culture (Achaeans-Pelasgians). Hence the critical effort to adapt and to understand. Hence "criticism" (Homer, Hesiod—the Ionians etc., the Trage-dians). The other (Eastern) people did not make this effort —they either succumbed, or destroyed, or vegetated together.

From that effort came detachment, irony, plasticity, rationality, individual freedom. The other people never emerged from their maternal magma (autochtony, satrapy, universal slavery. In art: the fable and hieratic decorations).

Ionic culture was already a Renaissance (in that it involved the discovery of another culture, the encounter and the acquisition). The other culture was the Minoan.

11th December

The Hebrews who, in their day, exalted morality and justice, calling them the Holy Spirit, Wisdom, ended, without realizing it, by exalting intelligence, which is also called the spirit. (Cf. recent history.)

18th December

R. Bene says: "Neither the proletarians nor the bourgeois will like it."

20th December

The girl who is working and watching herself in a mirror. The man who sees her, sees her and talks to her. They go out together.

The girl praying by the cash register. She prays and prays for her customers. She goes to the Valentino Park with one of them, who knocks her down and rapes her.

The girl is ugly and sees herself in the mirror. All day long. The man tells her that he is laughing and she seeks comfort in the mirror.

21st December

The man thinks her flat and cold. She is tremendous and orgiastic. She loses all control. The man is afraid.

(Reading Lucas.)

The art of the nineteenth century was centered on the development of situations (historic cycles, careers, etc.); the art of the twentieth on static essentials. In the first, the hero was not the same at the beginning of the story as he was at the end; now he remains unchanged. Childhood as a preparation for manhood (nineteenth century); childhood viewed only as such (twentieth).

25th December

The man who renounces things systematically and with conviction, has built his life upon the very things he has renounced. They are all that he sees.

Strange, this craze for wanting a duplicate of everything: of the body, the spirit; of the past, the memory; of

314

the work of art, a critical evaluation; of oneself, a child. . . .
Otherwise the first theme would seem wasted, vain. And then,
what of the second? Is it because everything is imperfect?
Or because "things are seen only for the second time?"

"I came to Turin at carnival time, as students and
mountebanks used to, in olden days."

30th December

Latin epithets are impressionistic, lyrical and fairy
tale, exquisite inventions; the Greek ones are a residue of
antiquity, hieratical, obscure clots.

The first consequence of the concept poetry = terra
incognita is that the poet works and discovers when he is
alone. All the advice that he receives is centered upon known
themes (= literature).

31st December

A most important year, my work definitive and assured, my technical and material position established. Two
novels. Another in preparation. As an editor, a dictator.
Recognized by all as a great man, a good man: By all? I do
not know.

You will find it difficult to go further. Not that you
think much of all that. You did not hope for it in the past and
it amazes you. You reached it while seeking only to work
hard, with a good will. Go on, prepared to find that the fruits
may burn to ashes by tomorrow. That should not matter to
you. Only so will you expiate your good fortune and show
yourself worthy of it.

1949

3rd January

Another stroke of luck. *Poesia è libertà,* read and
much enjoyed.

8th January

I have heard of . . .'s stubborn conviction that his book (. . .) is important. He and his wife refer to it as "our" book. A . . . appears to have liked it and he also says that I am a hermetic, difficult writer. . . . He would have written for the people, for everybody. His poetical theories are in agreement with those of Socialism. (You could say what R had to say on 18th December about *The devil in the hills*: neither the proletarians nor the bourgeois will like it.)

The discovery you made in '38 that the message of the Americans is the sense of a mysterious reality underlying the words (cf. the preface to *Alice Toklas*) is true, but must be extended to cover the period of Emerson, Hawthorne, Melville and Whitman. At that time you attributed it to Anderson, Stein and so on. This shows how authentic was the revival of 1916, taking up again the great national theme. A new sense of American democracy considered as a means of enlightenment. The man who is free discovers cosmic reality—a harmony between things and the spirit, a play of symbols transfiguring the things of daily life and giving them a value, a significance, without which the world would be reduced to a skeleton.

11th January

The blockhead you listened to this evening ("we all seek our own advantage, the partisans are just the same, idealists are fools, what matters most is dying, and tomorrow all will be well") is like you yourself in your moments of prudence. If you had refuted that in the past (i.e., taken action), perhaps you would not be here now (Leone). Tragedy. Yet in a hundred years will anyone believe in you? No. Then, everyone will believe in conforming.

13th January

To live amid people is to feel like a leaf in the wind. There comes the need to isolate oneself, to get away from the determinism of all those billiard balls.

19th January

A review by Cecchi; review by De Robertis; review by Cajumi. You are acclaimed by the great masters of ceremonies. They tell you: "you are forty years old and have made your name; you are the best of your generation and will go down in history; you are exceptional, authentic. . . ." Did you dream of anything else, at twenty?

Well? I shall not say: "Is that all, and now what?" I knew what I wanted, and I know what it is worth now that I have it. I wanted to go on, take it further, absorb another generation, become everlasting, like a hill. Hence, no delusion. Only a confirmation. Tomorrow (always supposing my health stays good) go on fearlessly. I will not say "begin again" because no one ever begins. There is always a past, a previous time, even in this. Tomorrow I shall be back at work, as I was yesterday.

Yet, what sound insight I had, what a coincidence of will and destiny! What if the value lies in this and not in the works?

28th January

The state of vagueness, of indefinite seeking, still persists. The problem I have previously often touched upon presents itself again: you are unaware of living, because you are looking for a fresh theme; you pass through days and things as in a dream. When you have begun to write again you will think only of writing. In other words, when *do* you live? Plumb the depths? You are always carried away by your work. You could be on the point of death without noticing it.

That is why infancy and childhood are a never-ending source of inspiration: then you had no work and looked at life dispassionately. Hence the healing power of love, grief, adventures: then you put aside your work, become a boy again and discover life.

A writer should never have to live by his writing, for then he has to produce work to order. He no longer has freedom of choice. At any moment he should be able to say: "No. I won't write this." That is, he should have some other means of livelihood. What is more risky than to support a family on one's novels, or in a general way by one's pen?

8th February (At S. Stefano Belbo)

For glory to bring us pleasure, the dead would have to rise, the old grow young again, absent friends return. We have dreamed of it in a tiny setting, among familiar faces that for us were all the world, and we want, now we are grown up, to see the reflection of our deeds and words upon those faces, in that little place. They have vanished, scattered, died. They will never come back. Then we despairingly look around, trying to re-create the little world that left us alone but wished us well, and now should be amazed at us. But it no longer exists.

13th February

Strange, the moment when (at thirteen or twelve) you left your country home, had your first glimpse of the world, and set out, buoyed up by fancies (adventures, cities, names, strong rhythms, the unknown). You did not know you were starting a long journey that, through those cities, adventures, names, delights and unknown worlds, would lead you to discover how rich in all that future was your moment of departure, the moment when, with more of the country in you than the world, you gave your backward glance. The world, the future, is now within you as your past, as experience, skill in technique, and the rich, everlasting mystery is found to be the childish you that, at the time, you made no effort to possess.

Everything is in one's infancy, even the fascination of what the future will be, which only then is felt as a shock of wonderment. (Cf. 26th June, '48.)

27th February

A limpid night, clean and crisp. At one time, it used to excite my senses. Not now. I have to remember, tell myself "it's the way it was then," to feel it. Nor does that urge to talk, to impose my personality, still come over me. Is this because of my never-ending anxiety, my state of nerves over what has already happened or because of some imminent disaster? Is it due to age, to the glory and security I have more or less acquired?

In reality, the one thing that touches me, moves and inspires me, is the magic of nature, a glance fixed upon the hill. When that theme is not in mind, when instead I have a human subject, a game of city life and morality, that is when my imagination flags.

1st March

A laugh—casting doubt upon your motives, voicing the suspicion that you have maneuvered things shrewdly to achieve a given purpose (publishing your book) without seeming to do so. May it not be that the laugh conceals spite at hearing you talked about, aims (falsely) at discrediting you, hinting that you are a crafty schemer—attributing to you, that is, the very incentives of the man who laughed?

7th March

She says: "the way a man interests himself, or not, in a woman, all women, reveals his manner of living." You say: "I can do without them," and so you avoid every entanglement of life that might hinder you in your work. Another man says: "I must not lose my chastity, lest sanctity should be barred to me," and so, in his doubt, he would like to consider the matter closed. Another takes things as they come, enjoys himself, and so lives in close touch with daily life. A man who likes to analyze and vilify everything to do with sex, does the same with life and in the way he lives; he cheapens things because he views them as material organisms. Vulgar stupidity.

11th March

The thing is not to analyze, but to *represent*—in a vivid way, with analysis implied; present *another* reality on which new analyses can be based, new standards, a new ideology.

It is easy to talk about new analyses and so on; difficult to bring them forth as a rhythm, a coherent, complex grasp of that reality.

The dialect ideal is the same in every period. Dialect underlies the story. One must, however, run the risk of writing standard speech, that is, of entering into history, choosing a way of expression, a style of literary language, a danger. In dialect one does not choose—it is spontaneous, unpremeditated, spoken instinctively. In literary language, one creates. Of course, dialect used in fiction is a way of telling the story; it is then a choice, a style, etc.

27th March, '48 is important. We always confuse what we are with the truth. This is the historical error—idealistic relativism. We can try to justify it attributing importance to what *we must be* according to the iron law of historic necessity. This is called dialectic materialism. If nothing else it obliges us to know thoroughly the necessity that governs us. But is that all there is to reality? In that way, the tendency is to place the absolute in the future, in revolution. Yet do we not also deeply enjoy the present—hic et nunc? *Lavorare stanca?*

13th March

The boy: what I do not get at once, I no longer want.

The men of the sixteenth century acted as men of the sixteenth century. They represent the first case of a culture consciously and critically rooted in another one; theirs was a culture of adaptation, of pose. Not even the Hellenized Romans were so "reflected," because in fact they did not have a sufficient culture to make an impact on the one they had acquired.

23rd March

Without seeming to, I have begun my new novel: *Tra donne sole*. A clear-cut, assured work that presupposes a sound construction, inspiration that has become habit. (It takes up again the theme of *La Spaggia, La Tenda* and several poems about women.) It should bring out something new.

3rd April

Before Christ and the Greek Logos, life was a constant close contact with nature, a continual exchange of magic between men and nature; whence came power, determination, destiny. One turned to nature, and was regenerated.

After Christ and after Logos, nature was no longer taken as the mystical spring of strength and life (which now comes from the Spirit). The ground is prepared for modern science, which states and classifies the material world, indifference to nature.

5th April

All passions fade and die away except the oldest, those of infancy. The ambitious or libidinous dreams of childhood are insatiable, because maturity—the only age that could satisfy them, has lost the opportunities, the fresh sensitiveness, the means, the true setting in which those passions originally come to the surface.

10th April

Your sound position, the esteem in which you are now held, came about just as you imagined they would when you were a boy. This amazes you—that maturity should be exactly what you expected when you were without any experience. Unless you have forgotten the wild dreams of those days, and little by little have transformed yourself into what you now think you sighed to be then? In any case, you made no mistake about one thing, and it was believing that you would feel satisfied with your beginnings and your hopes.

Many people—perhaps all—reveal faults, cracks in their make-up. Natalia, Balbo, even the new ones (D'Amico) —no one charms you any more. If you had no faith in what you are doing, in your work, the material you are creating, the pages you write, what a horror, what a desert, what a void

life would be! The dead escape this fate. They keep themselves intact. Leone, Pintor, even Berto. Fundamentally, you
write to be as dead, to speak outside of time, to make yourself remembered by all. This for others, but what for yourself?
Will a memory, many memories of yourself, suffice you? Remembering that you are *Paesi tuoi, Lavorare stanca, il Compagno, I Dialoghi, il Gallo?*

12th April

A newspaper black with headlines like a storm.

14th April

"She proceeds and returns without a pause
Because her task is eternal,
Because her icy breath puts out a light
which shines once more, and gloriously."

I wrote these lines when I was fifteen, in reply to a
sonnet by St. in which Death was described ascending a hill.

17th April

Discovered today that *Tra donne sole* is a great novel;
that the experience of being engulfed in the false, tragic world
of high society is broad and congruous, and blends well with
Clelia's wistful memories. Starting from her search for a childish, *wistful* world that no longer exists, she discovers the gro-
tesque, sordid tragedy of those women, of Turin as it is, of
her own realized dreams. Her discovery of herself, and the
emptiness of her own world, which saves her ("I've got
everything I wanted").

20th April

We all educate ourselves in our own fashion. He who
appears to be committing a mistake, is actually "doing" something. (You and M.)

26th April

They do not aim at creating works. They theorize
about poetry that is to be the exact reflection of the present

moment (the atomic bomb, world communications, nuclear physics, etc.)—and then—why write the work? By the time it was done it would already be out of date, a compromise with reality, with traditions; it would be objective history, and so, instead, they are disturbed because they have studied history or heard about it (things *done,* styles created); they grow impatient, they want *the style of the period,* not works; they lose touch and are concerned only to make no mistake about corresponding precisely with the present moment. Never anyone who says: "Anyway, I have a style and I like it. It must be some use for something. . . ."

28th April

The Americans are not realists. I discovered this while watching an American film remade from an old French film. What had been *real* atmosphere, a genuine setting, was now a shabby backcloth. Their vaunted realism 1920-1940 was a particular kind of romanticism about "living reality." The fanciful idea that everything is realism (Dos Passos). The point of view is not tragic, but "voluntaristic." Tragedy is a clash with reality; "voluntarism" is to make a comfort of it, a way of escape from true reality.

29th April

It is extraordinary, the idea that all your awkwardness, every uncertainty, every fit of rage—in short, every negative thing—may always reveal tomorrow, when seen from a different, wiser point of view, a new value, a quality, a *positive treasure.*

But the converse is also true. Every boast of yours may fail, may collapse under you. What does it matter?

7th May

In any other business or profession one can live according to the *clichés* of that particular job, "playing the part." Writers and artists, no. They would be *bohemians,* blockheads, intolerable bores. Why? Because painting or writ-

ing is not a business or profession. At least, not in these days.
(Cf. 28th January.)

26th May

Today, *Tra donne sole* is finished. Each of the concluding chapters written in a day. It came with extraordinary,
questionable, facility. Yet it clarified itself little by little, and
the great discoveries (journey through a world dreamed of
since she was a little girl, and now vile, hellish) came to me
after about a month, in early April. I tackled it with a good
heart. But I wonder whether I was playing with lay figures,
miniatures, lacking the grace of a stylized creation. But the
basic idea, was it not tragic?

22nd June

Now the itch to write is over, the vacuum in my
brain begins again. My novel finished, I feel twinges of rheu-
matism or arthritis. Is it that you can feel only one thing at
a time, or do you imagine them?

What a lot of things you have done in this last month.
Your brain is empty; S. Stefano (a week), then sun and
water, outline sketches, an idea for a new book. Probably
this is your most intensive period, and it is getting past its
best. That is so true that you notice it yourself. What new
thing shall we discover, how shall we live so that we can
watch it when it begins to stink? The end will come. And
then?

There are people who have never known this maturity,
this efficiency, this measure of richness. What do they know
of life? Life is nothing but this. And then? The happiness of
a peach, a grape. Who would ask for more? I am alive, and
that's enough.

We all like or are interested in a different scene. The
R.'s like Via Calandra, the R.'s like Ivrea; Nat. likes the
foulard. It's a good sign.

G. and the woman resemble each other. They only
talk about themselves. Theirs is the narrowness of the high life,
the problem of the viveurs who run around in their cages

like squirrels. The others, the ones without a care in the world, are not like that. But these viveurs are cheating at their own game. They have no manners. This is the lowest form of a mentality created by D'Annunzio.

25th June

Old Mentina, at the Cabianca, what does she see in life? What does she know of the vast accumulation of thoughts, of the facts of the world? She has never changed the sense, the rhythm, that the far-off days of childhood had for you. And now that you see her again, in her seventies, ready to die, not even thinking she could change this static way of life, what has she less than you? What is all your multiple experience, compared with this? For 70 years she has lived as you did when a child. It is a thing to make you shudder. It means ignoring history.

1st July

A serious and real person, who lacks the "Spirit" is bound to become stubborn in life, because the letter by itself, without the Spirit, kills. That person shall adhere to the letter of things, of thoughts, of feelings, as if trying to give them a consistency, a reality which they would not have otherwise.

This evening, when I dined at Pavarolo with the three G.'s and with E. N. and M., I was aware for the first time—in an objective sense—of a physical decline, of my incapacity to make an effort, a leap, an "exploit." I felt ill and distorted the whole evening. To save myself, I hated the world, man, the whole company. It's an old story. Fil. came today. She knows Fed., who knows Mar. She said that she begrudges me the fact that I am famous and that Mar. is always mentioning me. This is an easy, common trait— barefaced innocence. There's nothing in it.

27th July

The word that describes (echoes) a rite (a magic action), or a forgotten, mysterious fact (evocation), is the only art that interests me. To portray life directly—if it were possible—would be useless, because man interests himself only in a rite or an occult reality.

30th July

Going through the rough copies of *Lavorare stanca*, I have found in the pages of August-September, '32 ("Fumatori di Carta") the following lines, which had been crossed out.

. . . . I have seen once again the August moon
among the alder trees and the cane fields,
on the gravel by the banks of the Belbo,
and each thread in that stream was filled with silver.
But the silent companion who was sitting
by me on a tree trunk could not see that sky,
nor feel the plants. I knew that all around, all around me,
great hills were rising. . . .

18th August

Literature is not in conflict with the sense of what is practical, but with a sense of reality. The fact that the things described really exist gives them a significance and strength outside literature. If they do not exist, literature is enough for us; if they do, we want poetry and myth.

22nd August

From rejections (failures '41-'47) this beginning (of 15th November, '39):

2) Cinina was not thinking about the fog, and still she walked as if she were alone in the road. The feeling that nobody was near or around her was sweet, and Sunday-like.

1) Cinina was walking in unforeseen directions, vaguely following the patches of fog which the morning was clearing away. She stopped when she came to a square. . . .

(preparation for the *Curtain*
or *The beautiful summer*.

23rd August

In art one must not start with a complication but work up to it; not begin with the symbolic fable of Ulysses, to astound the reader, but with a simple, ordinary man and, little by little, give him the significance of a Ulysses.

2nd September

All Christian explanations of history (see them in Lowith, *Meaning of History,* p. 188)—that Palestine is the dramatic center of the world, etc.—sound like fabrications.

Nature is not a breath of wind, a dream, an enigma destined to vanish away—it is something solid and substantial.

Inherited resourcefulness is simply this: *to do a thing well because that is how it should be done.* (On reading *Piedmonte* by A. Monti in *Il Ponte*[1]).

12th September

The really absorbing residual-mythical constructions are in books that employ a system of analytical research: Propp, Philippson, Toynbee. Probably also in scientific works. Here is the true, authentic prose of research (a story—seeing how someone, or something, reacts to a given situation), similar to the construction of a detective novel. We can believe in such works because they are the only ones that *keep us in suspense,* make us want to see what the end will be. (And the story has no characters, no psychology; it is not a chronicle of events but a series of proofs, each leading to the next and carrying us on to a final elucidation that includes all the preceding ones.)

30th September

You no longer have an inner life. Rather, your inner life is objective and is the work—galleys, letters, chapters, consultations—that you do. That is dreadful. You no longer

[1] Italian Literary Review. Ed.

have hesitations, fears, the sense that life is amazing. You are drying up.

Where are the moments of anguish, the outcries, the loves of those years between eighteen and thirty? All that you are now expressing was acquired then. What now? What can you do?

This is where fate must come in and show what you are. Everything is implicit in yourself. Even your intolerance of this state of affairs and its consequent disorder and chaos. Vico's solutions.

16th October

Does anyone exist besides yourself? You talk of nothing but yourself and your work. You have reverted to that state of childhood *before you discovered the world,* when life consisted of you and the game you were playing, and nothing else. Something in you is coming to an end. And then?

La luna e i falò: That is the title I have had in mind ever since the time of *Dio caprone.* Sixteen years. I must put everything into it.

How many times in these last entries have you written "and then"? Aren't you getting into a *rut*?

I am too happy. Polycrates and Amasias.

17th November

On 9th November I finished *La luna e i falò.* From 18th September is less than two months. Almost always a chapter a day. It is certainly my greatest *exploit* so far. If it succeeds, I have reached my goal.

I have completed the historical cycle of my own times: *Carcere* (anti-fascism behind bars); *Compagno* (anti-fascism under cover); *Casa in collina* (resistance); *La luna e i falò* (post-resistance). Side issues—the war of '15-'18, the war in Spain, the war in Libya. The saga is complete. Two young men (*Carcere* and *Compagno*); two forty-year-olds (*Casa in collina* and *La luna e i falò*); two workmen (*Compagno* and

La luna e i falò); two intellectuals (*Carcere* and *Casa in collina*).

20th November

> G. has fallen. Do you care?
> Love as you have always desired it. Do you care?
> A solitary celebrity. Do you care?
> One could continue.

Thoughts spring to life—precise, fresh, well-phrased, efficient. Maturity. If you had known this at the time you were mad for it ('36-'39)! Now you rave because it is coming to an end. First you panted to have it, now you dread losing it.

You also have the gift of fertility. You are master of yourself, of your fate. You are as famous as any man can be who does not seek to be so. Yet all that will come to an end.

This profound joy of yours, this glow of super-abundance, is made of things you did not take into account. *It was given to you.* By whom? Whom should you thank? Whom will you curse when it all disappears?

24th November

"One must be reasonably honest" says . . . . . I have never said so, but I have always done so, unconsciously. For fear of complications. To live without disturbance. Why do I not spend money, pick up women, stay at a big hotel? Simply to save myself the trouble of overcoming the boredom that would follow such efforts. I have no aptitude for living in style—it troubles me. A question of upbringing. But nor do I feel any special need for the things I have always been used to—modest well-being, careful dressing, good repute—the things that show. What I must have is something more fundamental: undisturbed peace of mind about the morrow. Therefore my honesty is due to self-interest. What point would it have otherwise?

Today, the first copy of *Estate*. Lovely. Virginal. Respectful congratulations from my colleagues. The status of a man who has arrived. Gave some advice (from the height of my advanced years) to young Calvino: I apologized for working so well; I, too, at his age, was always behindhand and in difficulties. Did anyone ever talk to me like that when I was twenty-five? No. I grew in a wilderness with nothing to help me but a proud determination to build my own atoll in this unknown land, burst out of it one day and (when other people had noticed it) be already an important man. It seems that I am succeeding. That is my strength (and that is why I will not read or describe a book of mine to others, before it is finished).

D. has remarked that my women are whores. She is amazed by it. My amazement is that it should be so. I have never thought of it.

26th November

(Cf. 28th January, '42.) Levi has been saying that "memories" are the moments when we feel face to face with things, with other people, when we are most conscious of our individuality. This is the reason why memories bring such delight: in them we find our moments of awakening, our knowledge of the world.

Lavorare stanca

1930 1933 1936 1938 1940	Words and sensations

Carcere, Paesi tuoi	1938, 1939	Naturalism
Bella Estate, Spaggia	1940, 1941	

Feria d'agosto	1941, 1942	Prose poems and an
	1943, 1944	understanding of myths

La terra e la morte	1945	the extremes:
Dialoghi con Leucò	1945	naturalism and detached
Compagno	1946	symbolism

La casa in collina	1947-48	
Il diavolo sulle colline	1948	Symbolic reality
Tra donne sole	1949	
La luna e i falò	1949	

28th November

Night comes, when I begin to feel drowsy. Every noise —the creaking of wood, a disturbance in the street, an unexpected far-off cry—stirs up a kind of whirlpool in my brain, a sudden, swirling whirlpool, in which my mind and the whole world are swept to ruin. In an instant I anticipate an earthquake, the end of the world. Is this a relic of the war, the air raids? Is it an acquired awareness of the possible end of the universe? It leaves me exhausted—that is the word—but what does it mean? It is not unpleasant—a light buoyant feeling, as though I had been drinking, and when I recover, my teeth are clenched. But what if, one day, I do not recover?

1st December

Walking on the banks of the Po, in front of the Monte dei Cappuccini. It is growing dark and foggy, the villas sink into obscurity, all I can see is the dark, shaggy outline of the hills, wild and shadowed. What use is all this beauty? What, at least, does it mean? There come to mind my thoughts on the superstitious-savage (the summer of '44), on the unreality of what is savage (10th July, '47), on the magic of the countryside, and I reach the conclusion that "savage" is nothing but a magical conception of the world, with no possibility of influencing us in ways that are irrational, not to be measured or foreseen. What does it amount to, this disturbing sense of what is "savage," this somber, obscure beauty, this emotion, if it affects us only as something beautiful, impressive? Is not all this a refinement of civilization? What is savage, to exist at all, must have a vital effect even upon someone illiterate, on a peasant, on a practical man; it must be power, not beauty.

I discovered the other evening how much I have been influenced by reading *Sun* and *The Woman Who Rode Away* by Lawrence ('36-'37).

3rd December

Graves' idea (in *The Common Asphodel*) of broadening a telegraphic poem by Cummings into a rhetorical-descriptive sonnet, to show how right Cummings was in writing in that impressionistic and boneless fashion, thus avoiding the meditated and thought-out cliché of the full sonnet, proves only this: that neither the sonnet nor the futuristic poem should ever have been written. Cummings' poetry in fact is no more than a sensorial display of sensations and images (as shown by the paraphrase) which tells us nothing but a cliché. Poetry must "say" something, and therefore it is pointless to make it violate the rules of logic and syntax, and the universal manner of saying things. All the rest is literature.

General condemnation of the whole of "avant garde" art.

I must find: W.H.I. Bleek and L.C. Lloyd, *Specimens of Bushman Folklore,* London, 1911. It contains stories about mothers and the moon—the magic world of hunters, of real things and animals—in the time of Aurignac.

5th December

Fundamentally, the pleasure of screwing is no more than that of eating. If there were embargoes on eating, as there are on screwing, a whole ideology would come into existence, a *passion* for eating, with standards of chivalry. This ecstasy they talk about—the vision, the dreams evoked by a screwing—is no more than the pleasure of biting into a medlar or a grape fresh from the vine. One can do without it.

That snug feeling of December, '44, with everyone gathered together into one room, between the smell of the kitchen and the window misted over by the snow-covered hills, the way we looked forward to coming back from those hills in summer weather—will it all come back again? And our thoughts about quiet, spiritual reading, the hope of supreme peace (like that of the kitchen)—we need those, too.

6th December

What is intolerable is not that there should be a formal, elementary culture of an average type imposed on us, a *righteous* type stuffed into us as birds feed their young, but that this should be the only type; that it should no longer be possible to go beyond it and see it from the outside, in the world where discoveries are made.

My thought on 1st December makes it clear how fascism is born. The irrational culture of the nineteenth century had to emerge from contemplation and become power, economic security. It had to stop being of use only to the educated classes, and also begin to serve the illiterate. The origins of our present barbarisms.

15th December

The fact is that I have become that strange creature: a made man, a name that means something, a "big man." Where is the little boy who wondered how to talk, the adolescent who fretted and grew pale on thinking of Homer or Shakespeare, the youth of twenty who wanted to kill himself because he felt good for nothing, the deluded wretch who clenched his fists, doubtful whether he would ever be able to confound his girl with his greatness? Obviously, it is only your experiences as a young man that enter into your stories, the only fundamental, unselfish experiences you have ever had. As for the "big man," you will write of him when you are old.

Your two adult experiences—success and importance, bewilderment and nothingness—('45-'49 and '43-'44) you have already treated in *Tra donne sole* and *Casa in collina*. You will have to express them more fully.

17th December

Who would have guessed that Spagnoletti (Pintor's strange Spagnoletti!) would have discovered your *Terra e la Morte*? That little poem was an explosion of creative energies which had been pent up for years ('41-'45) and were never fully released by the short stories in *Feria d'Agosto*, but indeed were excited by the discoveries made in writing this diary and by the tension of the war years (Create!) in which you found a new passional virginity—through religion, detachment, virility—and finally there were the mixed opportunities deriving from women, Rome, politics and the book on Leuco, swelling inside you.

Generally speaking you must remember that in the years between 1943 and 1945 you were reborn in isolation and meditation (in fact during "that" period you theorized and lived your infancy). This explains your open season of '46—'47, with *Leucò, The Comrade, Before the Cock Crows, The Beautiful Summer, The Moon and the Bonfires,* etc.

Grandeur is not forbidden. What is forbidden is grandeur without the sanction of the powers that be.

18th December

There was a warm wind last night, and I read the myths and legends of Africa. Now it is morning, a fresh, blue morning, with yellow sunshine. These legends are the story of something happening for the first time; they have that simplicity, that sense of surprise. Even if what they say is not *ab origine,* they have that atmosphere; simple statements, never descriptions, no adjectives; a rhythmic structure that constitutes drama, suspense.

23rd December

It is starting. . . . Gigli: "Triptych by Pavese."[1]

[1] The first review of *La bella estate*. Ed.

334

29th December

A visit to Milan, a trip to Rome. Am I beginning to enjoy moving around again, traveling? Coming back from Milan, after twenty-four hours absence, I rediscovered Turin. May this always be the finest thing about traveling, rediscovering one's own place?

I really am excited. Tomorrow I go to Rome. Will it be as it was in July, '45?

The fame Vittorini has won in America, has it made you jealous? No. I am in no hurry. I shall beat him in the long run. Vittorini has been the voice (in anticipation—that is what is so grand about it) of the clandestine resistance period, naked, vital love, abstract ragings that bring it all to life in an heroic mission. He has sensed the epoch and given it his own legendary quality. Just as D'Annunzio presented the "imperial" epoch and the "literary civilization" of the nineteen-twenties. Both of them are mouthpieces. They create a style of life, of talking, feeling, *doing*. You aim at a style of *being*.

R. has told you (talking of *Diavolo sulle colline*) that your work gives the impression of a young man, and is rather alarming because of that; you are handling a material that may fly to bits. I did not quite understand this. But was it entirely complimentary?

30th December-6th January

My trip to Rome.

1950

1st January

Rome is a crowd of young men waiting to have their shoes polished.

A morning walk. Bright sunshine. But where are the

impressions of '45-'46? After some effort I found what inspired me then, but nothing new. Rome is silent. Neither the stones nor the trees tell me anything more. This amazing winter; under the clear, cold sky, the berries of *Leucò*. The usual story. Even grief and suicide were part of life, shock, tension.

At great periods you have always felt, deep within you, the temptation to commit suicide. *You gave yourself to it,* breached your own defenses. You were a child.

The idea of suicide was a protest against life; by dying, you would escape this longing for death.

2nd January

Came back through Uffici del Vicaro. Old faces (the girls, the men, myself). We realize things are happening when they have already happened. You know now how full your life was in '45-'46. Then, you lived it.

It is the same with history. A taste for the past, for conservation. Destiny is giving yourself to life, living it to the full. Only later does it clarify itself and become coherent, constructive. Destiny is what we do without knowing it, surrendering ourselves to it. In one sense, everything is destiny: we never know what we are doing. There is a slight, rational consciousness that pricks us superficially, and that we ought to cultivate as deeply as we can. What remains outside our consciousness (posterity will understand it—in this sense it is not irrational), is destiny. Historical example: the true significance of Robespierre's work, which he himself believed was the political edification of virtue, is now understood as a scientific, historical development, but for him it was his destiny. Later generations, of course, will see an even deeper meaning in the work of Robespierre, and then the historical interpretation, too, will be part of his destiny, it *will have been* his destiny (a result of which he was unaware).

The connection between destiny and superstition: the former is an instinctive action, not yet understood or foreseen, the latter is an instinctive action after its meaning is understood. The first is a way of being alive, the second of being dead.

3rd January

The directions that destiny can take are not subject to variation. We may affirm that a certain undertaking (sometimes? always?) is good, that it welds together all our days in a planned development—but it was, initially, a bud that had to take its own course and come into existence.

4th January

Now I see, I realize, what is so wrong with Rome. Easy friendliness, taking life as it comes, money earned and spent without a thought, yet everyone's standards, tastes, desires are wholly subjugated to money-making.

Even your thirties are beginning to seem to you like infancy, adolescence. Now the culture you acquired then can be used in your novels. Virility becomes a matter of intuition ("fiction-writing") when it seems part of your adolescence.

When one has absorbed an experience and can view it with detachment, it takes on a childlike ingenuousness. Great poetry is ironic.

7th January

In Rome, you explained to "Uncle Sandro" that everything of value must be preserved—all hopes, all that gives savor to life, the humanities, liberalism, good education and so on. It is a question of finding the historical-political canon that will permit this. Now, would his way of thinking save the things that you yourself feel must be saved? Apparently not.

9th January

Your inordinate passion for natural magic, for what is "savage," for the truth about spirits dwelling in plants, stretches of water, rocks and country places, is a sign of timidity, of your urge to escape the duties and obligations of the human world.

While you are so absorbed by this mythical need to grasp the reality of things, it takes courage to look with the same eyes at men and their passions. It is difficult, uncongenial—men lack the immutability of nature, her vast scope for interpretation, her silence. Men come up against us, imposing themselves upon us with their agitations and self-expression. You have tried in various ways to petrify them—isolating them in their most natural moments, immersing them in nature, reducing them to their destiny. Yet your men talk and talk—in them the spirit expresses itself, comes into bloom. This is your tension. But you suffer in creating it, you would never wish to find it in real life. You long for the immobility of nature, silence, death. Of them you make myths with infinitely varied meanings, eternal, intangible, yet throwing a charm upon historical reality, giving it significance and value.

10th January

You have had the fruitful idea that destiny is myth, the savage (the emotion of La Vigna) and that for this reason —once it has been explained—if destiny were to remain as a concept in its archaic form, it would become superstition. Destiny is what is mythical in a whole existence, in a drama. It is what happens before one knows that it has happened. It is what looks like freedom but later reveals itself as dictated by the iron rules of a pre-established pattern. Destiny is the historian before he is understood in terms of his associations and of his necessity-freedom. Poetry, when dealing with men, always looks at destinies—moves along its lines and perhaps understands destinies, makes them clear, transforms them into stories.

But you (9th January) start from the men who are understandable and, in order to make them poetic, reduce them to their destinies. Your process seems to be the reverse of art, which transforms myth into "logos." Or else one works at establishing this transition. One debates it, striving towards form, towards a fable, a self-sufficient organization, and then one rebuilds, on a basis of rational understanding, the figure of myth-destiny. Wishing to "recreate life" one goes back to natural forms, plunging once again into the mythical vortex, into the forms that will surprise, just as nature and life are endlessly surprising.

14th January

I am filled with distaste for what I have done, for all my works. A sense of failing health, of physical decadence. The downward curve of the arc. And your life, your loves, where are they? I retain a certain optimism: I do not accuse life, I find that the world is beautiful and worthwhile. But I am slipping. What I have done I have done. Is it possible? Desire, longing, the urge to take, to do, to get my teeth into something new. Can I still do it? (All that because of a flood of unfavorable reviews of *Diavolo sulle colline*.)

Thinking again of the sisters D.,[1] I know that I have lost a great opportunity of playing the fool. Rome grows more colorful as I look back.

17th January

Relationship between "destiny" and "superstition." After the "Poetic interpretation of destiny" one finds that destiny is the real mythical aspect of human life; superstition is the known mythical aspect of life, and therefore a false one. A life is "fatal" when it has a mythical cadence, a pre-established rhythm which, however, should not be dissolved into a rational awareness, as this would destroy it; a life becomes superstitious when one insists in regarding it as a mythical scheme, knowing full well that it is not, and understanding it rationally. A life whose rhythm, whose rotations, are deliberate and willed.

[1] Constance and Doris Dowling, two young Americans in Rome with a film unit. Ed.

We are in this world to transform destiny into freedom (and nature into causality).

(Corrected on 30th January).

Continued from II para of 10th January.

Poetry is repetition. Calvino has cheerfully arrived to tell me this. He was thinking of popular art, of children, etc. For me poetry is repetition in as much as it is the celebration of a mythical scheme. Herein lies the truth of nature's inspiration, of art being fashioned along the lines of natural forms and sequences, for these are indeed repetitive (the patterns of single parts—leaves, organs, mineral veins—and the fact that each part is repeated ad infinitum). Therefore one overcomes nature (mechanicism) by imitating it in a mythical fashion (rhythms, returns, destinies). But each generation must take into account what it knows about nature, and overcome it by means of mythical schemes which may not be separated from such knowledge. (This evolutional method was unknown to ancient art which had therefore an easier task because its rational notions were fixed and consequentially it applied old and familiar mythical schemes.)

30th January

A superstitious man is one who still believes in a myth that has already been eclipsed by history, that we now have the means to dispel. Correct 17th January. The man who parades a myth he no longer believes in is a hypocrite, a reactionary. The superstitious man may be a fanatic, the reactionary, a cynic. A skeptic is one who does not believe in any myth. A fatalist is one who realizes within himself an authentic myth that he believes; such a man is not free.

To create a completely free character is impossible. The ups and downs of his own life (which cannot be eliminated) will be his destiny.

Shall we be able to go further one day and consider even liberty a myth? That is, view it from a point at which it reveals itself as destiny?

340

1st February

Intuition produces myth-religion.
Will power produces history-poetry or theory.

Errors:

Wanting to make history out of intuition.
Wanting to make myth out of will power.

Will power can be applied to myth in order to transform it into history. Destinies which become freedom.

9th February

Corollary. The theme of a work of art cannot be a truth, a concept, a document etc, but only, once again, a myth. From myth directly into poetry, without passing through theory or action.

15th February

"Pavese is not a good communist"[1]. . . . Tales of intrigue everywhere. Shady counterplots, that could then be the talk of those who are nearest your heart.

Historical life developed from the myth, not from religion. Myth, pre-history; religion, over and above history.

They talk of festivities, Carnival, getting together. . . . Good friends of yours, men and women, nice, friendly people. You do not feel even a wish to go, or the least regret. Something else presses.

What a little thing is the life, the pleasure, the work of these girls. So their parents must think. Seen from the outside, they used to seem to you rich and mysterious. They are common household appliances.

[1] A few months earlier, Pavese had been asked to write a series of articles on contemporary Italian literature to launch a new review, *Cultura e realtà*. The first two aroused fierce controversy because some views Pavese expressed in them were considered anti-communistic. (Cf. also the entry for 27th May 1950.) Ed.

You are always talking about: *things before they are known, things after they are known.* . . . The problem is always that—to rationalize, to take cognizance, to make history.

Meanwhile, you have reduced to the imagery of the blood under the fig tree in the vineyard everything that happens and is not yet understood: landscapes, strange coincidences, psychological disturbances, the ups and downs—the cadences—of a life, destinies. (If, for you, there is poetry in these images, it is clear that, by recognizing a doctrine which may *explain* everything, you would become incapable of writing poetry.)

Of course, it is not sufficient to state the unsolved problem—poetry is presenting that problem as it is, making its mystery felt, its "savage" quality. But then, where is the power of *knowledge,* in writing poetry?

18th February

Culture must begin with what is contemporary and documentary, *with what is real,* to soar to the level of the classics, if that be possible. The humanistic error is to begin with the classics. That accustoms us to unreality, to rhetoric, and in the end leads to the cynical disparagement of classical culture, the more so because it has cost us nothing and we have not appreciated its value (as a contemporary presentation of the periods concerned).

26th February

A trip to Tuscany and Emilia. I thought of my essay on poetry and popular culture; thought, above all, of the connection between the countryside and culture, of the natural (botanical and mineral) roots of art. At Florence (Rovezzano) and in Val Pesa, Elsa—Siena—you *felt* why that land has given birth to art. The country expresses the *grace* of Florence and Siena. But when a civilization is no longer linked with the country, what will be the radical sources of its culture?

Are we henceforward to be cut off from the influx of botany, minerals, the seasonal changes of the countryside upon art? It would seem so.

27th February

I saw S. Asciutto again, hard, taciturn, weary. He spoke of his pleasures, his trips into the country and up the mountains after coleoptera, in the rain; he listened absent-mindedly and in silence to my talk about Tuscany, my vivacity, my poses. He never made a comment. The embarrassment I felt would at one time have been disastrous, tragic. What sustains me? The work I have done, the work I am doing.

6th March (Cervinia)

This morning at five or six o'clock. The morning star, huge and quivering on the mountains of snow. Excitement, trepidation, insomnia. C.[1] was sweet and submissive, but none the less detached and firm. All day my heart has been pounding and still has not calmed down. (For three nights I have hardly slept. I talk and talk.) What is called passion, is it not simply this wild beating of the heart, this weakness of the nerves? I am much worse than I was in '34 and '38. Then I was frenzied with desire, but I was not ill.

Yet it all seems to me a passing *wandepunkt*. All of it. But she is a well-known figure, socially and morally. Suppose there were some misunderstanding?

And I? Am I not deluding myself as I used to do, mistaking for human values those simple accessories of distinction, glamour, adventure, the fashionable world? America itself, its sweet, ironic return to my life in terms of human values? Can it be true?

9th March

My heart throbs; I tremble, I cannot stop sighing. Is it possible at my age? What is happening is the same as when I

[1] Constance Dowling. Ed.

was twenty-five. Yet I feel confident and (incredibly) serenely hopeful. She is so good, so calm, so patient. So made for me. After all, it was she who sought me out.

But why did I not dare, on Monday? Was I afraid? . . . It is a terrible step to take.

16th March

It was a terrible step, yet I took it. Her incredible sweetness, her "Darlings," her smile, her long-repeated pleasure at being with me. Nights at Cervinia, nights at Turin. She is a child, an unspoiled child. Yet she is herself—terrifying. From the bottom of my heart, I did not deserve so much.

20th March

"My heart is still with you." A condescending phrase from a superior to an inferior. Why should I be so pleased about it? Obviously, I am receiving favors, not bestowing them. How can one possess without being possessed? Everything depends on that.

From the talk I had this evening (with P.) it seems clear that I am "possessed" *because* I enjoy playing the interesting role of a man who "belongs" to a woman. I ought to be the master and take my pleasure calmly, as though by right. I shall be loved more. Only so shall I be truly loved. But shall I enjoy it more? Whenever I have been the possessor, I have had no pleasure at all. The old story.

Then I must be possessed without showing it. But is it possible to make love with a prudent awareness, a predetermined self-control?

21st March

A hard day. International situations; Italy threatened by covert civil war; rumors of atomic reaction to come in April. Everything seems likely to separate me from her, send her back to America, to blockade Rome, ruin the whole affair.

Did I suffer like this before? Yes, then I suffered from

the fear of death. There is always something to suffer. Resign yourself. Stoicism, this is what counts.

22nd March

Nothing. She has written nothing. She could be dead. I must get used to living as though this were normal.

There are so many things I have not told her. Deep down my terror at the thought of losing her now is not a longing for "possession," but the fear that I shall never more be able to tell her those things. What they may be I do not now know, but they would pour out like a torrent if I were with her. That is creation. Oh God, make me find her again.

23rd March

Love is truly the great manifesto; the urge to *be*, to count for something, and, if death must come, to die valiantly, with acclamation—in short, to remain a memory. Yet my desire to die, to disappear, is still bound up with her: perhaps because she is so magnificently alive that, if my being could blend with hers, my life would have more meaning than before.

25th March

One does not kill oneself for love of *a* woman, but because love—any love—reveals us in our nakedness, our misery, our vulnerability, our nothingness.

26th (morning)

Before leaving for Milan. Nothing. Still nothing. How can I bear it? Now, in the street, by myself, I speak excellent English.

27th (evening)

Nothing. I have a live coal in my breast, embers glowing under the ashes. Oh Constance! Why? Why?

28th March

Good. She has written. I have talked to her long distance. She does not want me at once. Oh well, that is fine. Work.

20th April (After Rome)

Perhaps at this moment she is flying over the Atlantic. For two months. How can I wait so long? And wait for what? Everyone—Lalla, Nat, Doris—tells me it will never do, that we are different, that it will never amount to anything. "What do you want?" I want you, for life. Could that be enough?

26th April, Wednesday

Beyond doubt, there is in her not only herself, but all *my* past life, the unconscious preparation—America, my ascetic restraint, my intolerance of trifling things, my work. She *is* poetry, in the most literal sense. Is it possible that she has not felt it?

Curious, this procession of women—I., L., R., L., and, all unawares, V. and D. They all know or guess that a sacred mystery is taking place within me, and are filled with wonder.

The opinion of all those who know is that she has been very impressed by me, that she thinks more of me than I imagine. Can they all be wrong? They are women.

27th April

And now. Everything is happening at once. Truly, to him that hath shall be given. But he that hath, does not take. The old story.

8th May

The cadence of suffering has begun. Every evening, as dusk settles, my heart constricts until night has come.

10th May

The idea is dawning on me, little by little, that, even if she does come back, it will be as though she were not here.

"I'll never forget you," is what is said to someone one means to leave.

Anyway, how did I act myself towards women who weighed me down, bored me, women I did not want? Exactly like that.

The act—the act—must not be a revenge. It must be a calm, weary renunciation, a closing of accounts, a private, rhythmic deed. The last remark.

12th May

I have written another sketch: *Amore amare—Bitter Love*. It will have the same fate as the last, and even if it did better, what else will it do but take her farther from me?

13th May

Deep, deep, deep down, did I not grab at this amazing love affair, seize upon this undreamed of, fascinating thing, to make myself revert to my old thought—my long-standing temptation, to have an excuse for thinking of it again . . .? Love and Death—*this* is the hereditary pattern.

16th May

Now even the morning is filled with pain.

27th May

My happiness of '48-'49 is paid for in full. Behind that Olympian contentment lay my impotence and my refusal to become involved. Now, in my own way, I have gone down into the abyss: I contemplate my impotence, I feel it in my bones, and I am caught in a political responsibility that is crushing me. There is only one answer: suicide.

Dilemma. Should I act in perfect amity, doing it *all for her own good,* or diabolically explode? A pointless question—already settled by my whole past, by fate: I shall be a diabolical friend, gaining nothing by it—but perhaps I shall have the courage. The courage. Everything will depend on having it at the right moment—when it will do her no harm—but she must know it, she must know it. Can I deny myself that?

Certainly, I know more about her than she does about me.

30th May

All these lamentations are far from stoical.
So what?

22nd June

Tomorrow morning I leave for Rome.[1] How many more times shall I say those words? It is a great stroke of good fortune, no doubt, but how many times will it still bring me pleasure? And then?

This journey looks like being my greatest triumph. Social acclaim, D. will talk to me—all the sweet without the bitter. But then? What then?

Do you know that the two months have passed? And that, any moment, she may return?

14th July

Came back from Rome some time ago. At Rome, apotheoses. But now, this is it. Everything is crashing round me. My last sweetness in life I had from D., not from her.

Stoicism is suicide. People are dying in battle again. If ever there is a peaceful, happy world, what will it think of these things? Perhaps what we think about cannibals, Aztec sacrifices, witchcraft.

> All is the same.
> Time has gone by.
> Some day you came,
> Some day you'll die.
> Someone has died
> Long time ago.

20th July

I cannot finish with style. How she still attracts me.

[1] To receive the Strega Award. Ed.

13th August

It's something very different. It is she, who came from the sea.

14th August

She, too, ends up in the same way. She too. It's all right. By now they are all waves of this sea.

16th August

My dear one, perhaps you are really the best—my real love. But I no longer have time to tell you so, to make you understand—and then, even if I could, there would still be the test—test—failure.

Today I see clearly that from '28 until now I have always lived under this shadow—what some would call a complex. Let them: it is something much simpler than that.

And you are the spring, an elegant, incredibly sweet and lissom spring, soft, fresh, fugitive—earthy and good—"a flower from the loveliest valley of the Po," as someone else would say.

Yet, even you are only a pretext. The real fault, apart from my own, lies with that "agonizing disquietude, with its secret smile."

Why die? I have never been so much alive as now, never so young.

Nothing can be added to the rest, to the past. We always begin afresh.

One nail drives out another. But four nails make a cross.

I have done my part by the world, as best I could. I have worked; I have given poetry to men, I have shared the sorrows of many.

17th August

Suicides are timid murderers. Masochism instead of Sadism.

The pleasure of shaving myself after two months of prison—doing it by myself, in front of a mirror in a hotel room, and outside was the sea.

This is the first time I have drawn up a balance sheet for a year that is not yet over.

In my work, then, I am king. In ten years I have done it all. If I think of the hesitations of former times. . . .

In my life I am more hopeless, more lost than then. What have I accomplished? Nothing. For years I have ignored my shortcomings, lived as though they did not exist. I have been stoical. Was that heroism? No, I made no real effort. And then, at the first onset of this "agonizing disquietude," I have fallen back into the quicksand. Even since March I have struggled. Names do not matter. They are only names that chanced to drift my way; if not those, there would have been others. What remains is that now I know what will be my greatest triumph—and this triumph lacks flesh and blood, life itself.

This is the balance sheet of an unfinished year, that I won't finish.

I have nothing left to wish for on this earth—except the thing that fifteen years of failure bars from me.

Why should it amaze you that other men brush past you, unaware of all this ferment, when you yourself rub shoulders with so many and do not know, do not care, what their anguish may be, their secret cancer?

18th August

The thing most feared in secret always happens.

I write: oh Thou, have mercy. And then?

All it takes is a little courage.

The more the pain grows clear and definite, the more the instinct for life asserts itself and the thought of suicide recedes.

It seemed easy when I thought of it. Weak women have done it. It takes humility, not pride.

All this is sickening.

Not words. An act. I won't write any more.

CPSIA information can be obtained at www.ICGtesting.com
Printed in the USA
BVOW08s1845140316

440304BV00001B/52/P